D0536134

Scratch™ 2.0 Programming for Teens, Second Edition

Jerry Lee Ford, Jr.

Cengage Learning PTR

CENGAGE
Learning®

Professional • Technical • Reference

Australia • Brazil • Japan • Korea • Mexico • Singapore • Spain • United Kingdom • United States

CENGAGE
Learning·
Professional · Technical · Reference

Scratch™ 2.0 Programming for Teens, Second Edition
Jerry Lee Ford, Jr.

Publisher and General Manager, Cengage Learning PTR: Stacy L. Hiquet

Associate Director of Marketing: Sarah Panella

Manager of Editorial Services: Heather Talbot

Senior Marketing Manager: Mark Hughes

Senior Acquisitions Editor: Mitzi Koontz

Project/Copy Editor: Gill Editorial Services

Teen Reviewer: Zach Scott

Interior Layout Tech: MPS Limited

Cover Designer: Mike Tanamachi

Indexer/Proofreader: Kelly Talbot Editing Services

For product information and technology assistance, contact us at **Cengage Learning Customer & Sales Support, 1-800-354-9706**.

For permission to use material from this text or product, submit all requests online at **cengage.com/permissions**.

Further permissions questions can be emailed to **permissionrequest@cengage.com**.

Scratch is a project of the Lifelong Kindergarten Group at the MIT Media Lab. Scratch, the Scratch logo, and the Scratch cat are trademarks of the Massachusetts Institute of Technology. All other trademarks are the property of their respective owners.

All images © Cengage Learning unless otherwise noted.

Cover images: © 2014 Lifelong Kindergarten Group. © 2014 Cengage Learning®.

Library of Congress Control Number: 2013953552

ISBN-13: 978-1-305-07519-1

ISBN-10: 1-305-07519-6

Cengage Learning PTR

20 Channel Center Street

Boston, MA 02210

USA

Cengage Learning is a leading provider of customized learning solutions with office locations around the globe, including Singapore, the United Kingdom, Australia, Mexico, Brazil, and Japan. Locate your local office at: **international. cengage.com/region**.

Cengage Learning products are represented in Canada by Nelson Education, Ltd.

For your lifelong learning solutions, visit **cengageptr.com**.

Visit our corporate website at **cengage.com**.

Printed in the United States of America
1 2 3 4 5 6 7 15 14 13

To my father and my children, Alexander, William, and
Molly, and to my beautiful wife, Mary.

Acknowledgments

There are a number of individuals to whom I owe many thanks for their help and assistance in the development of the second edition of this book. For starters, I need to thank Mitzi Koontz, who served as the book's acquisitions editor. Special thanks also go out to Karen Gill for serving as the book's project editor. In addition, I want to thank Zach Scott for all the valuable input and advice. Finally, thank you to everyone else at Cengage Learning for all their hard work.

About the Author

Jerry Lee Ford, Jr. is an author, educator, and IT professional with over 24 years of experience in information technology, including roles as an automation analyst, technical manager, technical support analyst, automation engineer, and security analyst. He is the author of 37 books and the coauthor of two additional books. His published works include *Getting Started with Game Maker; HTML, XHTML, and CSS for the Absolute Beginner; XNA 3.1 Game Development for Teens; Lego Mindstorms NXT 2.0 for Teens;* and *Microsoft Visual Basic 2008 Express Programming for the Absolute Beginner.* Jerry has a master's degree in business administration from Virginia Commonwealth University in Richmond, Virginia, and has over five years of experience as an adjunct instructor teaching networking courses in information technology.

Contents

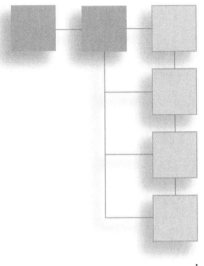

Please download our bonus chapters: **Appendix A, "Finding and Fixing Program Errors"; Appendix B, "Offline Scratch Development"; Appendix C, "Interacting with the Real World"; Appendix D, "What Next?"; and Glossary** from the companion website: **www.cengageptr.com**.

INTRODUCTION

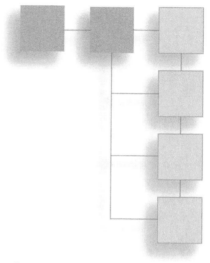

Welcome to *Scratch 2.0 Programming for Teens*! Scratch is a programming language developed by the MIT Media Lab to teach programming to children and other first-time programmers. Scratch was initially released in May 2007. It was recently updated as Scratch 2.0, which was released in May 2013. Scratch 2.0 supports the development of computer games, interactive stories, graphic artwork and computer animation, and all sorts of other multimedia projects.

Scratch 2.0 allows new programmers to create programs by snapping together code blocks. Scratch 2.0 consists of a programming language made up of different code blocks and an easy-to-learn graphical development environment that includes a paint application for creating graphics and built-in sound-editing capabilities. Scratch 2.0 also comes with a huge collection of graphics and sound files, all of which you can use to create your own Scratch 2.0 projects.

As demonstrated in Figure I.1, Scratch 2.0 programs are made up of graphical code blocks, which are snapped together to create scripts. Scratch 2.0 code blocks resemble puzzle pieces in the way they snap together. Scratch 2.0 code blocks can only be snapped together in ways that make sense, preventing new programmers from using them in invalid combinations. In this way, Scratch 2.0 enforces proper programming syntax and ensures that new programmers learn the proper way to assemble and formulate programming logic in their scripts.

Figure I.1
Script code blocks are used as the basis for writing scripts that bring applications to life.
© 2014 Cengage Learning®

Scratch's development was inspired by the method that hip hop DJs use to mix and scratch records to create new and unique music. In Scratch 2.0, new programmers are able to create new application projects that incorporate prebuilt code blocks, graphics, and sound files in all kinds of new combinations. Scratch 2.0 lets programmers modify applications on the fly, allowing changes to be made even while Scratch 2.0 applications are running. The result is an interactive, real-time programming environment that encourages experimentation and learning.

This book's primary goal is to teach you everything you need to know to learn the basics of computer programming with Scratch 2.0. To help accomplish this goal, this book emphasizes learning by doing, which is accomplished through the development of a series of fun and interesting programming projects.

Why Scratch?

Scratch 2.0 is both a programming language and a graphical user environment. It provides everything you need to begin developing computer games, multimedia presentations, interactive stories, graphic artwork, and computer animation. There is nothing to install on your computer; everything is done in your browser window. To get started, all you have to do is open your browser window and type the URL for the Scratch website.

You can use Scratch 2.0 to play digital music and sound effects. Scratch's building block approach to programming sets it apart from other programming languages. This makes Scratch 2.0 easier to learn. Yet Scratch 2.0 provides plenty of programming power, allowing you to build powerful application projects.

If you aspire to one day become a professional programmer, you will find that Scratch 2.0 provides everything you need to build a foundation from which you can make the transition. Scratch 2.0 also packs all the programming power and punch needed to satisfy the programming needs of most computer enthusiasts and hobbyists.

WHAT'S NEW IN SCRATCH 2.0?

As programming languages go, Scratch 2.0 is a relative newcomer. Scratch 1.0 was released in January 2007 but has been updated a number of times since. The previous edition of this book covered Scratch 1.2, which was released in December 2007. In May 2013, Scratch 2.0 was released.

Scratch 2.0 features numerous enhancements and new features not found in previous versions of Scratch. If you own the previous edition of this book or a different book covering an earlier edition of Scratch, you will definitely benefit from reading this book, which highlights and demonstrates the usage and application of the most important of these enhancements.

The most notable new feature of Scratch 2.0 is that you no longer have to download and install Scratch on your computer to use it. All you need is a web browser and a connection to the Internet. Once you're connected to the Scratch website, you'll find the entire Scratch 2.0 programming environment waiting on you, and it is just as fast and reliable as the earlier desktop-based versions of Scratch were. Some of the other new major features of Scratch 2.0 include

- An improved graphical user interface
- Video sensing, which allows Scratch to sense user input (hand and body movement) collected through a computer's video camera
- The ability to store and retrieve cloud data
- The ability to clone or dynamically create copies of sprites during program execution
- An improved Sound Editor
- Support for vector graphics (in addition to bitmap graphics)
- A backpack feature that facilitates the copying of objects from other people's projects into your own projects
- The ability to create custom code blocks and enhance program organization using procedures
- New code blocks that provide lots of new capabilities

There are plenty of other changes in Scratch 2.0 than those previously listed—far too many to introduce and cover here. You'll learn about things like galleries, improved ways of crediting other users when you remix (copy and modify) their projects, and how to follow users by subscribing to their Scratch projects as you make your way through this book.

WHO THIS BOOK IS FOR

Scratch 2.0 Programming for Teens is designed to provide all the instruction that a first-time programmer requires to quickly get up and running. Previous programming experience will certainly be helpful, but it is by no means a requirement of this book. This book makes no assumptions about your computer background other than that you are comfortable working using a web browser to surf the Internet.

This book provides everything you need to get started with Scratch 2.0. Before you know it, you will be creating all kinds of projects, incorporating graphics, sound, and animation. As you learn how to program with Scratch 2.0, you will learn programming principles and techniques that you can later apply to other programming languages. As such, you will be able to apply what you learn about programming with Scratch 2.0 to other programming languages like Microsoft Visual Basic, Java, and C++.

WHAT YOU NEED TO BEGIN

As has been said, starting with Scratch 2.0, you no longer have to download and install Scratch. All you need is a web browser and a connection to the Internet in order to create, edit, and view Scratch 2.0 projects. So the first thing you must have is a relatively recent web browser. Any of the following web browsers is sufficient:

- Firefox 4 or later
- Chrome 7 or later
- Internet Explorer 7 or later

To work with Scratch 2.0, you also need Adobe Flash Player version 10.2 or later. If it is not already installed on your computer, you can download the most current version of Adobe Flash Player from http://get.adobe.com/flashplayer/. Lastly, Scratch 2.0 is designed to work on a computer screen that supports a resolution of 1024×768 or higher.

Tip

If you do not have easy access to the Internet, you can download and install a desktop-based version of Scratch 2.0, as explained in this book's Appendix B, "Offline Scratch Development" (found on the companion website). If your computer and monitor do not support the required screen resolution, you also have the option of downloading and installing an older version of scratch (version 1.4), which supports a resolution of 800×480.

How This Book Is Organized

Scratch 2.0 Programming for Teens is organized into 14 chapters. This book was written with the expectation that you will read it sequentially, from cover to cover. However, if you have some previous programming experience, you may instead want to jump around a bit, focusing on topics that interest you the most.

The first four chapters introduce Scratch 2.0 and its development environment. You also learn about the different components that make up Scratch 2.0 projects and then discover how to create and execute Scratch 2.0 projects.

The next nine chapters are designed to provide instruction on how to work with different types of Scratch 2.0 code blocks. You learn how to use code blocks that move things around, store and retrieve data, and perform math and conditional and repetitive logic. In addition, you learn how to integrate sound and draw lines and shapes.

The last chapter helps bring together everything you have learned. This chapter introduces you to the concept of collision detection and teaches you how to use it as you learn the fundamentals of developing arcade-style computer games.

Companion Website Downloads

You can download the companion website files from www.cengageptr.com/downloads.

On the website, you'll find four appendixes and a glossary. The first appendix provides you with insight and guidance on how to track down and fix programming errors that every programmer makes when developing applications. The second appendix explains how to download and install a desktop-based version of Scratch. This material is for readers who do not have Internet access but still want to learn how to program using Scratch. The third appendix demonstrates how to create Scratch 2.0 projects that interact with a sensor board. The fourth appendix provides a list of websites and reading materials that you will want to explore to continue learning more about Scratch 2.0 and to further your programming knowledge.

Conventions Used in This Book

One of the primary objectives of this book is ease of reading and understanding. To help support this objective, some simple conventions have been used throughout this book to highlight critical information and emphasize specific points. These conventions are briefly described here.

Key terms that you want to understand and remember are highlighted using italic the first time they are instructed. So anytime you see a term in *italic*, take an extra moment to think about it and learn its meaning or purpose.

A `monospace` computer font is used to make things like commands, extensions, and file-names stand out from regular text.

Note

Notes provide additional information about a topic, feature, or idea to help you understand its impact or implications.

Tip

Tips point out programming shortcuts that make you a better and more efficient programmer.

Caution

Cautions identify areas where you are likely to run into problems and provide advice on how to deal with or prevent problems from occurring, making you a better, more efficient, and much happier programmer.

CHAPTER 1

INTRODUCING SCRATCH 2.0

Scratch 2.0 is a programming language developed to help young people between the ages of 8 and 16 learn twenty-first century skills by developing computer programs. The development of Scratch 2.0 and its predecessor versions was inspired by the scratching process that DJs use to create new sounds and music by rubbing old-style vinyl records back and forth on record turntables, creating a new and distinctively different sound out of something that already exists. In similar fashion, Scratch 2.0 application projects mix graphics and sounds so tweens and teens can use them in new and different ways. To get you started with Scratch 2.0 programming, this chapter provides an overview of the language and reviews the steps that you need to follow to get up and running quickly.

The major topics covered in this chapter include

- A review of Scratch 2.0's capabilities and uses
- A review of Scratch 2.0's requirements
- A discussion of the benefits of joining Scratch 2.0's global community
- A demonstration of how to create and execute your first Scratch 2.0 project

GETTING TO KNOW SCRATCH 2.0

With traditional computer and Internet applications, users are limited to working with applications in the way the programmers who developed the applications designed. Scratch 2.0 turns things around by letting users become programmers. Scratch 2.0 is designed to meet the needs of young people between 8 and 16, introducing them to computer technology and improving their learning skills while facilitating creativity and personal expression.

Many people regard computer programming as a mysterious and complex process that requires advanced technical training and education. This is a misperception. Programming languages like BASIC have been around for decades and were developed expressly for teaching first-time programmers how to program. In recent years, a new crop of programming languages have appeared, specifically geared toward helping children and students learn to program. One of the best and newest of these languages is Scratch 2.0.

Scratch 2.0 is a visual programming language made up of a graphic interface that supports application development in which new projects are created by mixing images, sound, and video under the controls of scripts, which specify the application's programming logic. *Scripts* are created by snapping code blocks together, much like Lego blocks are snapped together to create all sorts of unique creations. Each block represents a different command or action that tells the application how to execute. Scratch 2.0 also provides programmers with access to all kinds of media, including graphics and sounds, as well as tools that can be used to create new graphics and sound files.

Scratch 2.0 is an interpreted programming language. This means that application projects are not precompiled (turned into executable code that can be run as a stand-alone application) before their execution. Instead, the code blocks that make up Scratch 2.0 application projects are interpreted and processed each time the application project is executed. Scratch 2.0 is also a dynamic programming language. It allows changes to be made to application projects even while the projects are executing. As such, Scratch 2.0 lets programmers experiment by making application changes on the fly so they can see what type of effect the changes may have on the application's execution.

Imagine—Program—Share!

Scratch 2.0's slogan is *Imagine—Program—Share!* It is designed to encourage creativity by providing you with an easy-to-learn yet powerful programming environment in which you can unleash the power of your imagination. Scratch 2.0 encourages and facilitates the development of application projects using a mixture of media, graphics, sound, and video to create something new.

Scratch 2.0 provides new programmers with everything needed to create and execute application projects. Its programming language is designed to make it as easy as possible for new programmers to jump in and get their feet wet and to receive immediate feedback on their progress. Scratch 2.0 promotes an understanding of programming concepts, including conditional and iterative logic, event programming, the use of variables, mathematics, and the use of graphics and sound effects. By learning to program with Scratch 2.0, new programmers develop an understanding and appreciation of the design process, from idea generation to program development, to testing and debugging and the incorporation of user feedback.

People, especially kids, love to share, as demonstrated through the amazing success of websites like YouTube, which allows people to share home video. Sharing is a fundamental part of the Scratch 2.0 programming experience. Scratch 2.0 application projects are created and executed via the Internet and your web browser. Once you've created them, you can share them with everyone in the Scratch community. This means that other Scratch users can see and execute your Scratch projects. In addition, they can copy and modify your Scratch projects, a process referred to as *remixing*, using them as the basis of learning something new or expressing their own creativity.

Note

Scratch 2.0's website is designed to facilitate a social community where scratch projects are shared with everyone. Projects created on the Scratch website (http://scratch.mit.edu) can be shared by all Scratch community members.

In addition to viewing, executing, and remixing your Scratch projects, other Scratch users can comment on your projects. In this way, Scratch users can interact and share information and ideas with one another from anywhere in the world. By facilitating sharing in this manner on the Scratch 2.0 website, kids are encouraged to share their experiences and learn from one another and gain gratification and confidence from the experience.

Caution

When shared, the contents of Scratch projects are automatically made visible and freely available to the entire Scratch community. Your projects' sound files, graphics, and programming logic are all available for inspection. There is no way to keep the source code hidden.

Scratch Uncovered

Unlike many programming languages, such as Microsoft Visual Basic and C++, Scratch is an open source project. What this means is that all the source code that makes up the Scratch programming language is freely available. In fact, if you want, you can download a copy of the source code for previous versions of Scratch at http://info.scratch.mit.edu/Scratch_Source_Code_Licensed_Code.

Examples of other open source programming languages include Ruby and Perl. However, unlike these programming languages developed by a community of programmers working together collectively, Scratch is developed as a closed development project. All Scratch development is performed by the Lifelong Kindergarten Group at MIT Media lab.

Previous versions of Scratch were developed using another programming language known as Squeak. Squeak is a cross-platform programming language, meaning that you can use it to develop applications on many different computer operating systems. By selecting Squeak as the programming language used to create Scratch, Scratch's development team members ensured that they would be able to create and execute Scratch on different operating systems, including Microsoft Windows and Mac OS X. However, the move from the desktop to the web browser meant rewriting Scratch 2.0 from, well, scratch. Scratch 2.0 was rewritten in Adobe Flash. Since Adobe Flash is supported by most modern web browsers, you can develop Scratch 2.0 applications on most any computing device. An exception to this, as of the writing of the second edition of this book, is the iOS operating system that supports the iPhone and iPad. The iOS operating system does not support Adobe Flash, so you cannot use these devices to work with Scratch.

Scratch 2.0's Building Block Approach to Programming

Scratch 2.0 is different from other programming languages like Visual Basic in that it does not support a text-based approach to programming, as demonstrated here:

```
//Excerpt from a Visual Basic application
If strCurrentAction = "FillCircle" Then
    Dim objCoordinates As Rectangle
        objCoordinates = _
    New Rectangle(Math.Min(objEnd.X, objStart.X), _
    Math.Min(objEnd.Y, objStart.Y), _
    Math.Abs(objEnd.X - objStart.X), _
    Math.Abs(objEnd.Y - objStart.Y))
    Pick_Color_And_Draw("FillCircle", objCoordinates)
End If
```

In text-based programming languages, code statements are formulated by following a complex set of syntax rules. Failure to precisely follow these rules when writing statements leads to syntax errors that prevent applications from running. Scratch 2.0, on the other hand, uses a different approach. Scratch 2.0 application projects are built by selecting and snapping together graphical programming blocks, as demonstrated in Figure 1.1.

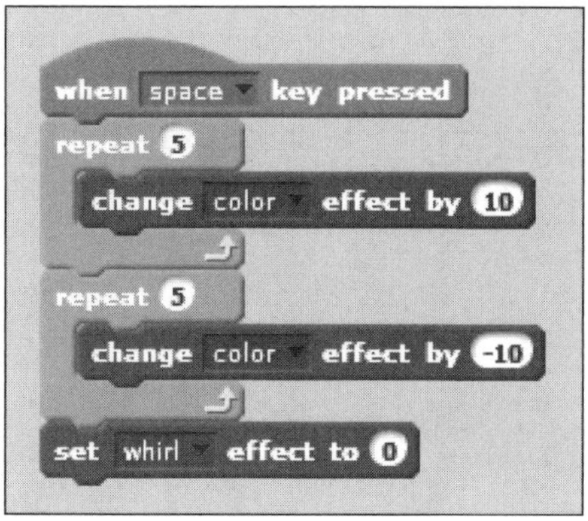

Figure 1.1

An example of how programming logic is outlined in a Scratch 2.0 application project.

© 2014 Cengage Learning®

By using code blocks in place of complex program text statements, Scratch 2.0 significantly simplifies application development while still making use of the same basic programming logic and concepts implemented in other programming languages. As Figure 1.1 demonstrates, each code block represents a different command or action. Blocks fit together like pieces in a puzzle. You can only snap together blocks in ways that make syntactic sense, eliminating syntax errors that proliferate in other programming languages.

Some code blocks are configurable, allowing you to specify things like the number of times an action should execute, text that is to be displayed, or the color to be used when displaying something on the screen. Despite its use of graphical code blocks, Scratch 2.0 supports the same basic set of programming techniques and constructs as do other traditional programming languages. For example, Scratch 2.0 supports variables, conditional and iterative logic, and event-driven programming. Scratch 2.0 also supports the manipulation of graphics and the integration of sound into application projects.

Note

Scratch 2.0 is designed for teaching first-time programmers how to program. To make the learning experience as straightforward and understandable as possible, the developers of Scratch 2.0 have sometimes sacrificed programming power and features in favor of simplicity and ease of learning. The goal of the Scratch 2.0 development team is to promote learning and not to develop a programming language capable of delivering every advanced programming feature required by professional programmers. As a result, Scratch 2.0 lacks some programming features currently supported in advanced programming languages. Instead, Scratch 2.0 focuses on fundamental programming concepts to provide new programmers with a foundation upon which they can later build when and if they decide to move on to other programming languages.

GETTING READY FOR SCRATCH 2.0

The first step in getting ready for Scratch 2.0 project development is to make sure that your web browser is configured to support Scratch development. To make this determination, open your web browser and go to www.scratch.mit.edu. This loads the Scratch 2.0 website, as demonstrated in Figure 1.2.

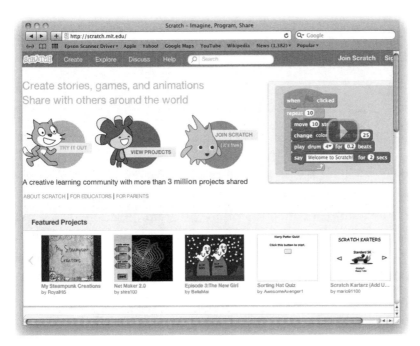

Figure 1.2
The main Scratch 2.0 website as seen on Mac OS X.
© 2014 Lifelong Kindergarten Group

Next, click on one of the Scratch projects displayed in the Featured Projects section to attempt to load and execute that project. If the Scratch project you selected loads as demonstrated in Figure 1.3, click on the green flag icon in the middle of the stage to execute the project.

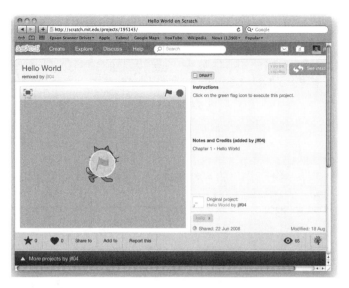

Figure 1.3

The selected Scratch project has been loaded into the browser window.

If the project begins executing, your web browser is configured to support Scratch development. If, on the other hand, the project does not begin executing and you instead see an error message displayed in your web browser, as demonstrated in Figure 1.4, you must download and install Adobe Flash Player so you can configure your web browser to support Scratch 2.0.

Figure 1.4

An error message is displayed if Adobe Flash Player is not installed on your computer.

To download and install Adobe Flash Player on your computer, click on the link or button that is displayed to install it, and follow the instructions that are provided. Once installation is complete, you should be able to refresh your web browser and run the Scratch project, at which point your web browsers should be ready to support Scratch 2.0 project development.

Note

You should be able to develop Scratch 2.0 projects on any Windows, Mac, or Linux computer, as well as on many different types of portable devices such as tablets. Notable exceptions are the iPad and iPod, neither of which supports Adobe Flash Player.

CREATING YOUR FIRST SCRATCH 2.0 APPLICATION

Scratch 2.0 application projects are made up of objects called sprites. A *sprite* is a two-dimensional image drawn on a transparent background. Sprites can be moved around and made to interact with one another. Sprites consist of three primary components, as outlined here:

- **Scripts.** Collections of code blocks that outline the programming logic controlling the operation of sprites.

- **Costumes.** Images that are used to display the sprite on an area of the Scratch 2.0 Project Editor referred to as the *stage*. Sprites can consist of any number of costumes.

- **Sounds.** Sound effects that are played during application execution when certain events occur or as background audio.

You can change a sprite's appearance by assigning it different costumes. To move a sprite and control its behavior, you snap together code blocks to create scripts. Sprites can have any number of scripts associated with them. Scripts can be run by double-clicking the code blocks that they're made of, in which case each block in the script is executed in top-down order. You can also set things up so that scripts automatically run when various events occur. For example, you can configure script execution to occur when a sprite is clicked or when it interacts with other sprites.

Sprites are displayed and interact with one another on a *stage*. As such, sprites are often referred to as *actors*. Scratch 2.0's stage is located in the upper-right corner of its graphical interface.

Note

You can select sprites from a predefined collection of graphics supplied with Scratch 2.0. You can also copy and paste them from your hard drive or the Internet, or you can create them using Scratch 2.0's built-in Paint Editor or capture them via a web camera connected to your computer.

Creating a New Scratch 2.0 Project

Now that you are familiar with the basic components of sprites, let's spend a few minutes learning how to create your first Scratch 2.0 application project. All new Scratch 2.0 projects automatically contain a single sprite, representing an image of a kitten. By default, the sprite, named Sprite1, does not have scripts but does have two costumes and two sounds associated with it. Using this sprite, let's create a Scratch 2.0 application project that makes the kitten meow and say "Hello World!" when clicked.

The first step in creating a new Scratch 2.0 project is to open your web browser and type http://scratch.mit.edu in the URL field. This displays the Scratch 2.0 main web page as shown in Figure 1.5.

Click on Create
to start a new project

Figure 1.5

The main Scratch 2.0 web page as shown using Internet Explorer.

© 2014 Lifelong Kindergarten Group

To create a new project, click on the Create button located in the upper-left corner of the screen, just to the right of the SCRATCH button. In response, the Scratch Project Editor is displayed, as shown in Figure 1.6.

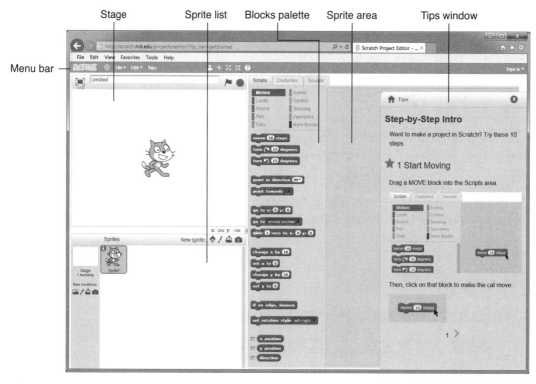

Figure 1.6
Creating a new Scratch 2.0 application project.
© 2014 Lifelong Kindergarten Group

As Figure 1.6 shows, the Scratch 2.0 Project Editor is organized into a number of separate components. For starters, there is a menu bar that runs across the top, providing easy access to common user commands. Beneath it, on the upper-left side of the Project Editor, is the stage.

The stage displays the default costume belonging to Sprite1. Just beneath the stage is the sprite list, which displays a list of all the sprites that make up the application project. In the center of the Project Editor is the blocks palette, which contains code blocks, organized into 10 different categories. You will use selected code blocks to create a script that makes the kitten talk. To the left of the blocks palette is the sprite area. To the right of the blocks palette is the scripts area. Code blocks can be dragged and dropped from the blocks palette onto the scripts area to develop the program code that makes Scratch projects run.

Shown in Figure 1.6 is the Scratch 2.0 Tips window, which provides easy access to help information about Scratch 2.0. In the upper-right corner of the Tips window is a Close button that, when clicked, slides the Tip windows out of view, leaving only the left edge of the windows visible on the right side of the Project Editor. You can redisplay the Tips windows at any time by clicking on their edge.

Note

Chapter 2, "Getting Comfortable with the Scratch 2.0 Development Environment," provides a detailed overview of all the components that make up the Scratch 2.0 IDE.

Changing Sprite Attributes

The application project that you are creating is designed to work with the default sprite. Rather than use the sprite's default name of Sprite1, let's assign it a more descriptive name. To do so, click on the lowercase letter *i* icon located in the upper-left corner of the image of the script displayed in the sprites area, as shown in Figure 1.7.

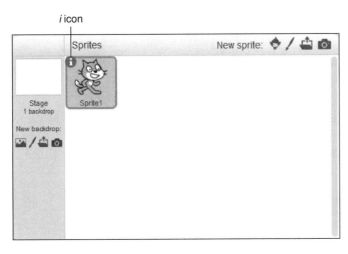

Figure 1.7
Sprite information is accessible by clicking on a sprite's *i* icon.
© 2014 Lifelong Kindergarten Group

In response, the sprite list changes, as shown in Figure 1.8, displaying the sprite's name and a number of other pieces of information.

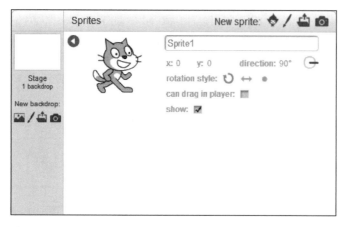

Figure 1.8
Viewing and modifying sprite properties.
© 2014 Lifelong Kindergarten Group

To modify the sprite's assigned name, overtype its default name of Sprite1 with the word Cat, and then click on the arrow icon located in the upper-left corner of the sprite area to restore the sprites list's normal display. The name change you just made is now reflected in the sprite list.

Adding Code Blocks

Now that you have changed the name of the sprite, it is time to add the code blocks required to make the cat meow and say "Hello World!". Let's begin by clicking on the Sound category located at the top of the blocks palette. This displays a collection of code blocks that control the playback of sound effects. Locate the code block labeled play sound and drag and drop it onto the sprite area, as shown in Figure 1.9.

Figure 1.9
Using a sound block to make the kitten meow.

By default, this code block is automatically set up to play an audio file that makes a meow sound. Next, click on the Looks category located on the blocks palette. This displays a collection of code blocks that control the appearance of a sprite. Locate the code block labeled say Hello! for 2 secs, and drag and drop it onto the sprite area, as shown in Figure 1.10.

Figure 1.10
Using a looks block to make the kitten say something.
© 2014 Lifelong Kindergarten Group

By default, this code block displays a text string inside a graphical bubble caption. This code block has two editable fields: a text field and a numeric field. Since the kitten is supposed to display the message "Hello World!" when clicked, replace the text "Hello!" with "Hello World!"

As previously stated, you can run a script at any time by double-clicking on it. To test this, double-click on one of the two code blocks that you have added. Then watch the kitten on the stage, and you'll hear it meow and display its text message. Rather than having to double-click on the script to make the kitten do its thing, let's set things up so that the kitten automatically meows and talks whenever you click on it. You accomplish this by clicking on the Event category located at the top of the code block area and then dragging and dropping the control block labeled when this sprite clicked on top of the two buttons you have already added to the sprite's script, as demonstrated in Figure 1.11.

Figure 1.11
Using a control block to control script execution.
© 2014 Lifelong Kindergarten Group

The `when this sprite clicked` block automatically snaps in place as you move it toward the top of the script. With this block now in place, click on the script file and see what happens. As demonstrated in Figure 1.12, the kitten responds by meowing and talking (displaying "Hello World!" in a text caption bubble).

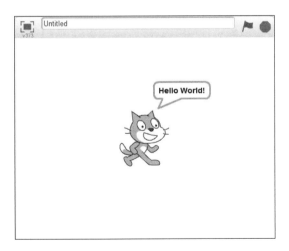

Figure 1.12
Executing your new Scratch project.
© 2014 Lifelong Kindergarten Group

Saving Your Work

Okay, now that you have your new Scratch 2.0 application project working, it is time to save your work. If you have already registered with the Scratch 2.0 website and you logged on to the Scratch 2.0 website using your username and password, your new project has already been saved automatically. If you try to create a new project without first logging in to the website, you lose the project unless you log in. To log in, click on the Sign In button located in the upper-right corner of the web page. In response, the Sign In window is displayed, as shown in Figure 1.13.

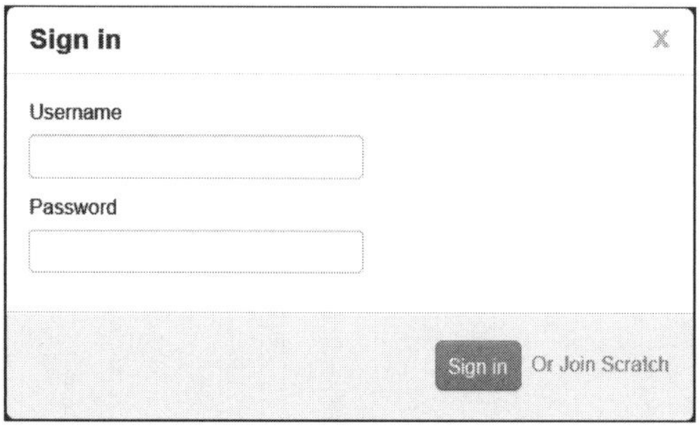

Figure 1.13
Logging into the Scratch 2.0 website.
© 2014 Lifelong Kindergarten Group

Type in your username and password. You are then logged into the Scratch 2.0 website, and the Login button is replaced by your username. Clicking on your username displays a drop-down list that provides easy access to your Scratch Profile page, My Stuff page, Account settings, and the Sign out command. Once you are logged in, your project is saved automatically. You can assign a name to your project by typing the name in the text field located just above the stage.

Tip

You can return later and view and modify your project by logging in, clicking on your username, and then selecting the My Stuff link from the drop-down menu that is displayed. You can also create one or more studios where you can organize the Scratch projects you are going to create.

That's it. At this point, you have gone through all the steps necessary to create, test, modify, execute, and then save a new Scratch 2.0 application project. Now that wasn't too tough, was it? Now, before wrapping up this chapter, let's spend a few minutes learning about Scratch 2.0's global community of users and how you can tap in to learn more about Scratch 2.0.

JOINING SCRATCH 2.0'S GLOBAL COMMUNITY

Scratch 2.0 is supported by a global community of students, teachers, schools, parents, and computer enthusiasts and hobbyists. Scratch 2.0 is available in many languages, including English, Spanish, German, French, Italian, Hungarian, Hebrew, Polish, Dutch, Romanian, and Russian. The Scratch 2.0 website, located at http://scratch.mit.edu helps bring together people from around the world and facilitates the development of the Scratch 2.0 community.

The Scratch 2.0 website provides access to all kinds of resources that help Scratch programmers learn more about the language. It provides access to online documentation and training videos. It also offers access to tons of articles and documentation on how to work with Scratch 2.0 code blocks.

Sharing Your Application Projects

The Scratch 2.0 website promotes project sharing by enabling any project created on the Scratch 2.0 website to be shared and made fully accessible to everyone who visits. Not only can these projects be viewed, but anyone who chooses to can take any project and modify it, a process referred to as *remixing*, and then save it as his own project. The only requirement is that credit must be appropriately given to authors for their work.

Note

As you learn more about Scratch and become a participating member of the Scratch communication, you will join the ranks of other Scratchers. Scratcher is a term used to describe Scratch programmers.

The Scratch 2.0 website truly put its slogan of "Imagine—Program—Share!" into action. Its design is centered on facilitating and encouraging Scratch 2.0 programmers to show off their work and to learn from the work of others. As Figure 1.14 shows, the Scratch 2.0 website actively promotes Scratch 2.0 applications on the Project tab located on the website's Explore page (http://scratch.mit.edu/explore/?date=this_month), which means that you can expect to see any Scratch 2.0 projects that you upload posted there as well.

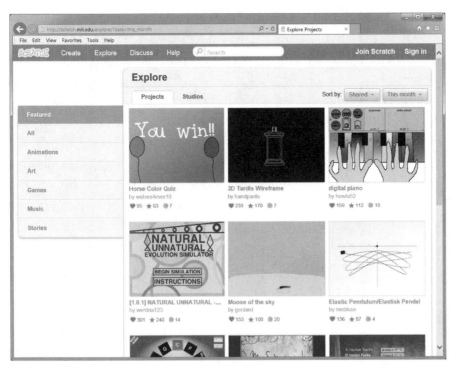

Figure 1.14

The Scratch 2.0 website facilitates sharing by promoting Scratch 2.0 projects and making them available to everyone.

© 2014 Lifelong Kindergarten Group

Note

You can click on any project that you see to open, view, and interact with it. If you wish, you can scroll down to the bottom of any project's page and post comments, sharing your thoughts about the project. Sharing, after all, is at the heart of what Scratch is all about.

The Scratch 2.0 website lets members organize and share their Scratch 2.0 projects in studios. You can post your Scratch 2.0 projects in different studios or create a studio of your own. As Figure 1.15 demonstrates, the Scratch 2.0 website actively promotes member studios.

Figure 1.15

You can create your own studio and use it to promote your programming skills.

© 2014 Lifelong Kindergarten Group

Note

Studios used to be called galleries in previous versions of Scratch. You may still find them occasionally referred to this way in some Scratch documentation or in user postings in various Scratch forums.

If you decide to create your own studio, you can customize it by assigning it a name and a description and by determining whether you want to let anyone else upload Scratch 2.0 projects into it.

Registering with the Scratch 2.0 Website

Although anyone can access the Scratch 2.0 website and create new Scratch projects, you must register with the Scratch 2.0 website if you want to be able to save, share, and work on projects another day. This means signing up for a free account, which you can do by clicking on the Join Scratch button located in the right corner at the top of every page on the Scratch 2.0 website. Clicking on this button launches the Join Scratch wizard, as shown in Figure 1.16.

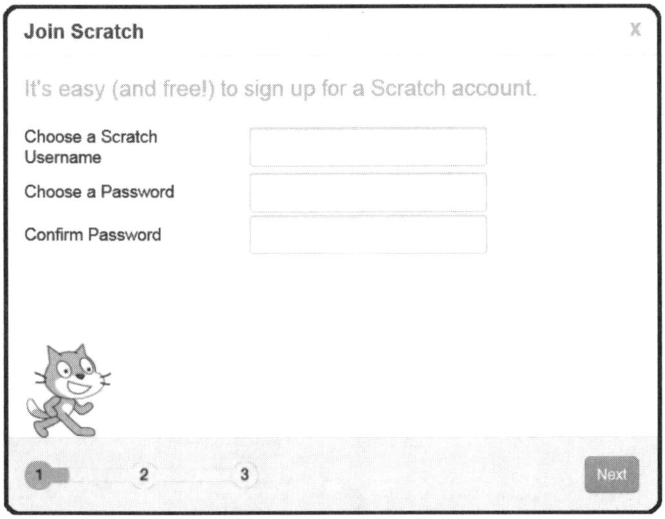

Figure 1.16
Registering for a free account on the Scratch 2.0 website.
© 2014 Lifelong Kindergarten Group

From here, you can type in your proposed username and an initial password and then click on the Next button. If you supply a username that someone else has not already taken, the window shown in Figure 1.17 is displayed.

Figure 1.17
The Scratch 2.0 website collects a few basic pieces of information about you during the registration process.
© 2014 Lifelong Kindergarten Group

From here, you must specify your birth month and year, gender, country, and email address and then click on the Next button. This displays the windows shown in Figure 1.18, thanking you for joining the Scratch community.

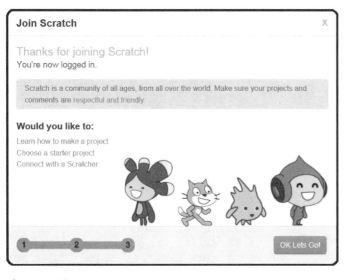

Figure 1.18
Completion of the registration process.
© 2014 Lifelong Kindergarten Group

You are now registered with the Scratch 2.0 website. Your username should now be displayed in the upper-right corner of the web page. The Scratch 2.0 website gives its members the ability to comment on any Scratch 2.0 application on the website. The website also provides access to a collection of forums designed to host conversation between students, teachers, and Scratch 2.0 enthusiasts from all over the world.

Changing Your Scratcher Status

When you first register with the Scratch 2.0 website, you are assigned New Scratcher status. This is easily evidenced by displaying your profile page, as shown in Figure 1.19.

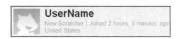

Figure 1.19
New Scratchers are assigned New Scratcher status.
© 2014 Lifelong Kindergarten Group

As a new Scratcher, you have a few restrictions. You cannot access cloud data. You cannot post links to non-Scratch sites. You must wait at least 30 seconds between posting comments. To change your status from New Scratcher to Scratcher and remove these restrictions, all you have to do is be active on the Scratch 2.0 website. Develop or remix some projects, participate in the forums, post some comments about other Scratchers' projects, and in no time you will find a link displayed on your profile page that says "Become a Scratcher." Click on it to be promoted to full Scratcher status.

Figure 1.20

After being active on the Scratch 2.0 website for a while, you can earn full Scratcher status.

© 2014 Lifelong Kindergarten Group

Keeping in Touch

In addition to facilitating project sharing and allowing comments to be posted about projects, the Scratch 2.0 website hosts a number of online forums at http://scratch.mit.edu/discuss, as shown in Figure 1.21.

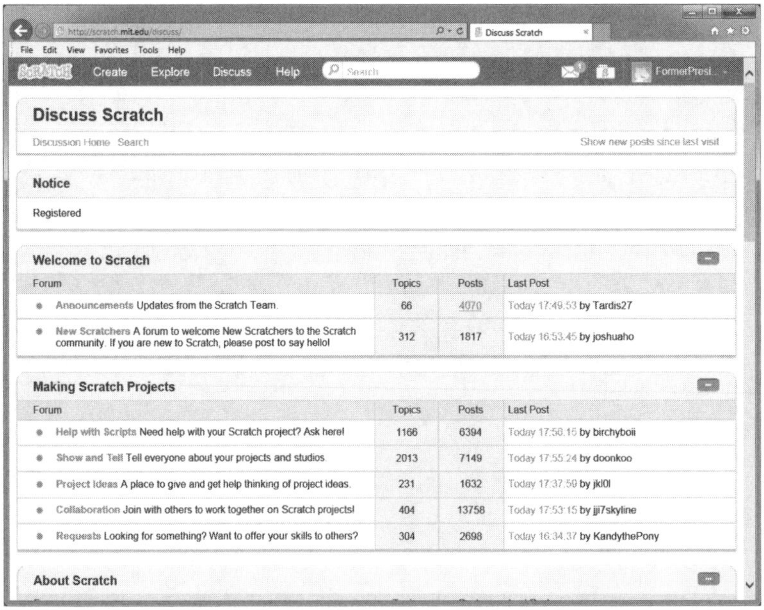

Figure 1.21

Members of the Scratch 2.0 community can communicate freely and discuss ideas using the forums hosted on the Scratch 2.0 website.

© 2014 Lifelong Kindergarten Group

As Figure 1.21 shows, forums have been set up to facilitate the following range of topics.

- Announcements
- New Scratchers
- Help with Scripts
- Show and Tell
- Project Ideas
- Collaboration
- Requests
- Bugs and Glitches
- Questions About Scratch
- Suggestions
- Advanced Topics
- Connecting to the Physical World

These forums let you learn directly from other Scratch 2.0 programmers. By reading the discussions that are posted, you can learn new programming techniques and find out about problems encountered by other programmers and their solutions. Most important of all, you can post questions and get answers.

CHAPTER 2

GETTING COMFORTABLE WITH THE SCRATCH 2.0 DEVELOPMENT ENVIRONMENT

To become an effective Scratch 2.0 programmer, you need to become intimately familiar with its Project Editor. In this chapter, you will learn about the stage on which applications execute and the sprite list that Scratch 2.0 uses to display and organize sprites used in your applications. You will learn how to work with editors that create scripts, costumes, and sound effects. You will also learn all about Scratch 2.0's paint program, which you can use to create your own custom graphics files. By the time you have completed this chapter, you will have a solid understanding of all the features and capabilities of the Scratch 2.0 Project Editor and will be ready to begin using it to create your own Scratch 2.0 application projects.

An overview of the major topics covered in this chapter includes

- How to work with menu and toolbar buttons
- How to add, remove, and modify the sprites that make up your Scratch 2.0 applications
- An explanation of the coordinates system used to control placement of sprites on the stage
- How to edit and modify scripts, costumes, and sounds
- How to create new sprites using Scratch 2.0's built-in Paint Editor

GETTING COMFORTABLE WITH THE SCRATCH 2.0 PROJECT EDITOR

Scratch 2.0 is a graphical programming language. Scratch 2.0 projects are made up of different types of media, including graphics and sound, and use scripts made up of different code blocks. Scratch 2.0 projects are created using its Project Editor available via the Scratch 2.0 website. As shown in Figure 2.1, Scratch 2.0's Project Editor is composed of numerous components.

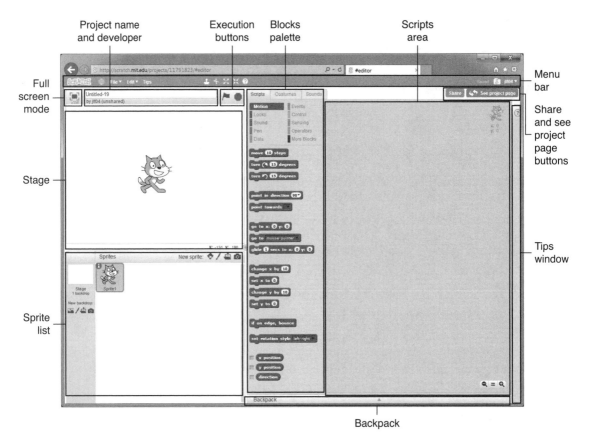

Figure 2.1

The Scratch 2.0 Project Editor facilitates the development and execution of Scratch 2.0 applications.

© 2014 Lifelong Kindergarten Group

Together, all the components identified in Figure 2.1 provide a robust and powerful, yet intuitive and fun, work environment, providing everything needed to develop Script applications. The rest of this chapter offers a detailed overview of each of the major components that make up the Scratch 2.0 Project Editor.

Getting Familiar with Menu Bar Commands

Like most graphic applications, Scratch 2.0 has a menu bar made up of a collection of buttons located at the top of the Project Editor, as shown in Figure 2.2.

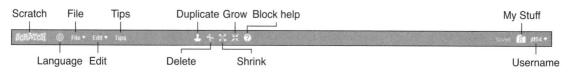

Figure 2.2
The menu bar provides easy access to commands that you can use to create and save Scratch 2.0 projects.
© 2014 Lifelong Kindergarten Group

These buttons provide access to commands that allow you to create and save Scratch 2.0 projects, download them to and upload them from your computer, access Scratch 2.0 documentation, and copy, delete, access, and manage your Scratch 2.0 profile and projects. The following list provides an explanation of the buttons that make up the menu bar.

- **Scratch.** Displays the main Scratch 2.0 website page.

- **Language.** Displays a selectable list of languages that Scratch 2.0 supports.

- **File.** Provides access to a drop-down list of commands used to create a new Scratch project, save the current project, save a copy of the current project, go to your MyStuff page, download and upload your project to and from your computer, and revert the current project to its last saved state.

- **Edit.** Provides access to a drop-down list of commands used to undelete a project, shrink and restore the size of the stage, and enable/disable turbo mode. (When enabled, turbo mode speeds up script execution, which can be important for certain types of Scratch 2.0 projects, like complicated games).

- **Tips.** Displays the Tips window, which slides out from the right side of the Scripts area, displaying links to help and block documentation.

- **Duplicate.** Creates an identical copy of an existing project resource, such as a sprite or script.

- **Delete.** Deletes the selected project resource, such as a sprite or script.

- **Grow.** Increases the size of a sprite.

- **Shrink.** Decreases the size of a sprite.

- **Block Help.** Displays help documentation for the selected code block.

- **My Stuff.** Displays your My Stuff page, providing quick access to your Scratch projects and studios.
- **Username.** Displays your registered username and, when clicked, provides access to your profile links, My Stuff page, Account settings, and the Sign Out command.

Note

Scratch projects downloaded to your computer are saved using an `.sb2` file extension.

Most of the commands in the previous list are self-explanatory. However, the Language menu merits additional explanation. When clicked, the Language menu displays a list of languages from which you can select. Depending on the language selected, a complete translation may be available. In other cases, only scripts and code blacks may be translated.

Tip

You can display a tooltip for the button controls shown on the Scratch 2.0 Project Editor by moving the mouse pointer over the button.

Running Scratch 2.0 Applications on the Stage

The stage is the area on the Scratch 2.0 Project Editor, located on the upper-left side, as shown in Figure 2.3, where your Scratch 2.0 applications execute. The stage provides a place for the application sprites to interact with one another and the user.

Figure 2.3
The stage provides the canvas upon which sprites are displayed and interact with one another.
© 2014 Lifelong Kindergarten Group

The stage is 480 units wide and 360 units high. The stage is mapped out into a logical grid using a coordinate system made up of an X-axis and a Y-axis, as demonstrated in Figure 2.4.

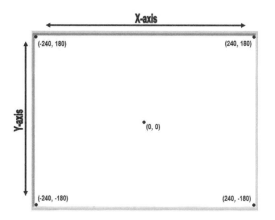

Figure 2.4
Sprites are placed on the screen and moved around using a system of coordinates.
© 2014 Lifelong Kindergarten Group

As you can see, the X-axis runs from coordinates 240 to –240, and the Y-axis runs from coordinates 180 to –180. The middle of the stage has a coordinate location of (0, 0). Scratch 2.0 keeps you informed of the pointer's location whenever it is moved over the stage by displaying its (X, Y) coordinate position in the mouse x: and mouse y: fields just beneath the bottom-right side of the stage.

The stage can be assigned one or more backdrops, allowing you to change its appearance during application execution. By default, all Scratch 2.0 applications are assigned a blank backdrop. You can add new backdrops by clicking on one of the five icons located just under the stage thumbnail, located on the left side of the sprite list. These icons, listed next, allow you to select or create a new backdrop to your project.

- **Choose Backdrop from Library.** Displays a list of backdrop images supplied with Scratch 2.0 from which you can select and add backdrops to your projects.

- **Paint New Backdrop.** Replaces the scripts area with Scratch 2.0 built-in Paint Editor, which you can then use to draw and save your own backdrop.

- **Upload Backdrop from File.** Displays the Select File(s) to Upload by scratch.mit.edu dialog, allowing you to upload a graphic image and use it in your project.

■ **New Backdrop from Camera.** Displays a Camera window, which you can use to capture a picture to be used as a backdrop if you have a video camera connected to your computer.

You can also add, edit, and remove backdrops to your Scratch 2.0 projects by clicking on the Backdrops tab located at the top center of the Scratch 2.0 Project Editor. Here you see the same four buttons for adding/creating backdrops, a list of all backdrops currently added to your project, and Scratch 2.0's built-in Paint Editor, which you can use to edit your backdrop(s).

Running Applications in Full-Screen Mode

As you saw in Chapter 1, "Introducing Scratch," when you create the Hello World project, Scratch 2.0 runs your applications on the stage within the Project Editor by default. However, if you click on the View Full Screen icon, located in the upper-left corner of the stage, you can run your Scratch 2.0 application project in a full-screen browser view. To see how this works, open the Hello World project that you created in Chapter 1. Next, click on the View Full Screen icon to switch to full-screen mode. Once you're in full-screen mode, single-click on the sprite representing the kitten and watch as your application executes, as demonstrated in Figure 2.5.

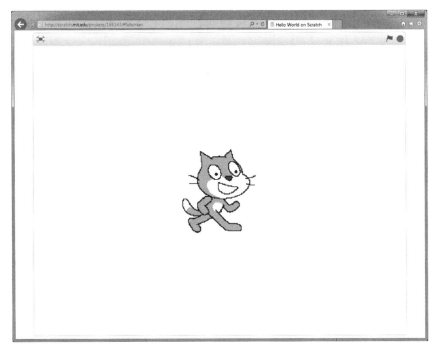

Figure 2.5
Running a Scratch 2.0 application project in full-screen mode.
© 2014 Lifelong Kindergarten Group

You can exit full-screen mode at any time by either clicking on the Regular Screen icon located in the upper-left side of the stage (when in full-screen mode) or pressing the Escape key.

Note

Scratch 2.0 supports three screen sizes: regular, full screen, and featured. Featured screen mode is a slightly reduced screen size that you see when viewing and interacting with Scratch 2.0 projects marked as featured programs from within Profile pages.

Controlling Application Execution

Whether running your application from the Project Editor's stage, in featured mode, or in full-screen mode, you can automatically start any scripts that begin with the green flag control block by clicking on the green Flag button located in the upper-right corner of the Project Editor, as shown in Figure 2.6. By clicking on the red Stop button located right next to the green Flag button, you can stop the execution of your Scratch 2.0 applications any time.

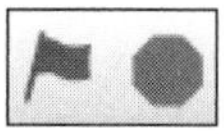

Figure 2.6
The green Flag and red Stop buttons provide control over script execution.
© 2014 Lifelong Kindergarten Group

Working with the Sprite List

Scratch 2.0 applications are made up of sprites that interact with one another as they move around the stage. Every sprite in a Scratch 2.0 application is displayed as a thumbnail in the sprite list area, located on the lower-left portion of the Scratch 2.0 Project Editor, as shown in Figure 2.7. Although it has no impact on a Scratch 2.0 application, you can reorganize the order in which sprites are displayed in the sprite list by dragging and dropping thumbnails to any location that makes sense to you.

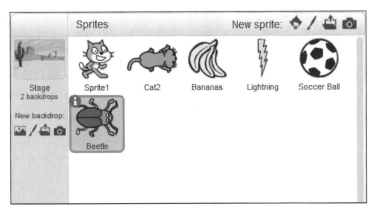

Figure 2.7
The sprite list displays a thumbnail for each sprite in an application.
© 2014 Lifelong Kindergarten Group

Working with Sprites

In addition to a thumbnail, Scratch 2.0 displays the name of each sprite. To work with a sprite and edit its scripts, costumes, and sound effects, just click on its thumbnail. The currently selected sprite is then highlighted by a blue outline. Once it's selected, you can click on the Scripts, Costumes, and Sounds tabs located at the top center of the Project Editor to edit a sprite's scripts, costumes, and sound effects.

If you right-click on a sprite's thumbnail in the sprite list, the following list of menu options is displayed.

- **Duplicate.** Makes a copy of the sprite.
- **Delete.** Removes a sprite from the project.
- **Save to a Local File.** Saves a copy of the sprite to a local file on your computer.
- **Hide.** Leaves the sprite in an invisible state on the stage.

Tip

> By right-clicking on a sprite located on the stage, you can also duplicate, delete, and save a copy of the sprite to a local file on your computer, but you cannot hide a sprite this way. The sprite is saved as a file with a `.sprite2` file extension on your computer.

The sprite list also displays a thumbnail representing the application project's stage. When the stage's thumbnail is selected, you can add scripts to the stage, modify the stage's backdrop by assigning it one or more graphics files, and add sounds to the stage. If you left-click on the small *i* icon located in the upper-left corner or a sprite in the sprite list, you can view and configure its properties.

Examining Sprite Details

Figure 2.8 shows the properties for a sprite named `Sprite1`. You can change a sprite's name by typing over it. The sprite's current coordinates and direction are displayed just to the right of the sprite's image.

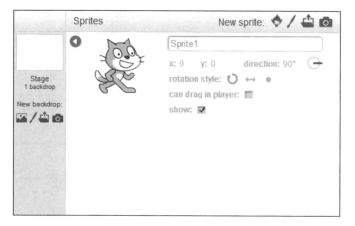

Figure 2.8

Changing a sprite's name and viewing detailed information about it.

© 2014 Lifelong Kindergarten Group

Take note that just to the right of the sprite's coordinates and direction properties is a circle with a blue line emanating from its center. It shows the sprite's currently assigned direction. By default, the sprite's default direction is set to 90 degrees. You can change the sprite's direction by dragging the outside edge of this line to a new direction.

Just beneath the sprite's coordinates and direction are three small graphics images that can be used to specify the sprite's rotation style. These three options are mutually exclusive, meaning that you can select only one. Table 2.1 identifies the rotational style represented by each of these options.

Table 2.1   Sprite Rotational Options

Button	Name	Description
↺	Can Rotate	Rotates the sprite's costume by up to 360 degrees when the sprite's direction is changed.
↔	Only face left-right	Toggles the direction that the sprite's costume faces from left to right and vice versa.
●	Don't rotate	Maintains the sprite costume's current direction.

© 2014 Lifelong Kindergarten Group

Tip

To get a feel for the effect that Scratch 2.0's rotational options have on a sprite, click on each of them and observe the rotational movement of the sprite in the Current Sprite Info section.

Beneath the rotation style options is a check box that can set or clear the ability to drag the sprite when the project is executing in Featured mode or when run from the Scratch 2.0 website. The last of the sprite settings is the Show setting. It is selected by default, allowing the script to be seen on the stage. Clearing this option makes the sprite invisible on the stage.

Generating New Sprites

Scratch 2.0 makes it easy for you to work with sprites by providing four different options for adding them to your applications. You access these options through the New Sprite icon located in the top-right corner of the sprites list, as shown in Figure 2.9.

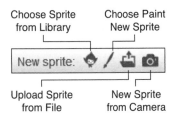

Figure 2.9

The New Sprite buttons provide access to tools for adding and creating new sprites.

© 2014 Lifelong Kindergarten Group

When clicked, the Choose Sprite from Library icon displays the Sprite Library window shown in Figure 2.10, providing access to different collections of graphics files that you can add to your Scratch 2.0 applications as sprites. To select and add a sprite, click on one of the available collection links shown on the left side of the Sprite Library window, click on the sprite you want to add to your project, and then click on the OK button located in the bottom-right corner of the window. The sprite that you selected then appears in the center of the stage, and a thumbnail representing the sprite is added to the sprite list.

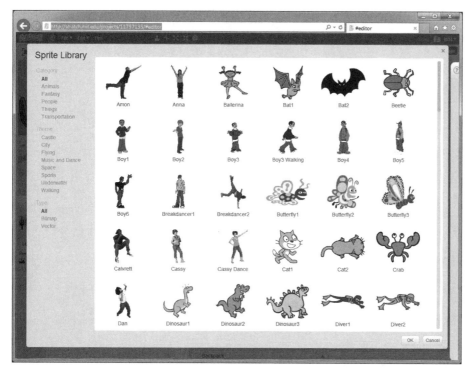

Figure 2.10

Scratch 2.0 provides easy access to a wide selection of ready-made sprites.

When clicked, the Paint New Sprite icon starts Scratch 2.0's Paint Editor program. This program provides everything you need to draw new sprites on a transparent background. You learn the ins and outs of how to work with the Paint Editor program a little later in this chapter.

When clicked, the Upload Sprite from File icon displays the Select File(s) to Upload by scratch.mit.edu dialog, allowing you to upload a graphic image and use it in your project. Lastly, the New Sprite from Camera icon displays a Camera window, which you can use to capture a picture to be used as a sprite (if you have a video camera connected to your computer).

Tracking Mouse Pointer Location

As you learn how to develop your own Scratch 2.0 applications, you need to keep track of the initial placement and subsequent movement of sprites on the stage. Scratch 2.0 assists you in this task by keeping track of mouse-pointer movement whenever you move the pointer across the stage (see Figure 2.11). You can use this information, which is automatically displayed at the top-right corner of the sprite list, to identify the coordinate data that you need to incorporate into your application code as you develop the programming logic that drives your Scratch 2.0 projects.

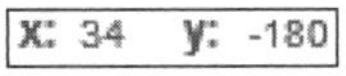

X: 34   y: -180

Figure 2.11
The Scratch 2.0 Project Editor makes it easy to track the mouse pointer's location when it moves around the stage.
© 2014 Lifelong Kindergarten Group

Note

Coordinate data is displayed for the currently selected sprite in the upper-right corner of the scripts area.

Switching Between Code Block Groups

Like applications created by any programming language, Scratch 2.0 applications execute program code made up of collections of code blocks that manipulate sprites and interact with the user. Scratch 2.0's program code is organized into scripts belonging to sprites on the stage. You can assign every sprite in an application one or more scripts. In addition, the stage can execute its own scripts.

As you have already seen, the first step in creating a script is to select the sprite (or the stage) to which the script will belong. You do this by clicking on the appropriate thumbnail in the sprites list. You can then add code blocks by dragging the blocks from the blocks palette and dropping them into the scripts area when the Script tab is selected. The blocks palette is organized into two sections. The top section contains 10 button controls, each of which represents a different category of code block. Each of these control categories is color-coded. The currently selected category is easily identified because it is filled in with its assigned color. The left-hand edge of the nonselected buttons shows the color of the code blocks belonging to its category. The bottom portion of the blocks palette shows all the programming blocks belonging to the currently selected category of code block. For example, Figure 2.12 shows how the blocks palette looks when the Motion category has been selected.

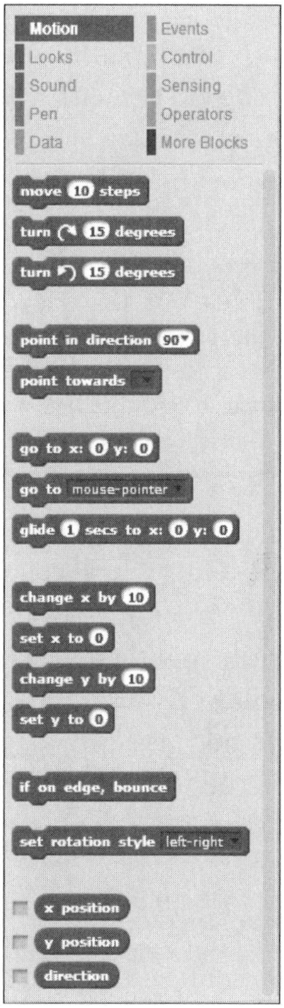

Figure 2.12

Each category of code blocks is designed to accomplish a related set of tasks.

Tip

You can click on the Block Help menu button, turning the mouse's pointer into a circular question mark character. You can then click on any programming block displayed on the blocks palette to display information about the block and how to work with it in the Tips window. The Tips window automatically slides out into the Project Editor from the right side of the scripts area.

Getting Comfortable with the Scripts Area

The last major part of the Scratch 2.0 Project Editor that you need to become familiar with is the scripts area. The scripts area is controlled by three tabs, which allow you to add scripts, costumes, and sounds to sprites.

Editing Scripts

As you have already seen, Scratch 2.0 scripts are created by dragging code blocks from the blocks palette onto the scripts area (when the Scripts tab has been selected). Of course, you must add the code blocks in a manner that makes logical sense, which is what Chapters 5 through 13 are designed to teach you.

Tip

As you add new scripts and modify existing ones, it is easy to leave the scripts area a mess. One way of dealing with this situation is to spend a few minutes dragging and dropping scripts so that they line up and are evenly spaced. However, a much faster and easier option is to right-click on a free area within the scripts area and then click on the `cleanup` command located in the pop-up menu that is displayed. In response, Scratch 2.0 realigns all your scripts for you.

Adding Costumes

A sprite can have one or more costumes, allowing it to change its appearance as an application executes. Sprite costumes are managed by selecting a sprite and then clicking on the Costumes tab located at the top center of the program editor. A sprite must have at least one costume. For example, Figure 2.13 shows a sprite that has two costumes. Each costume is assigned a unique name and number (displayed just under the costume's image).

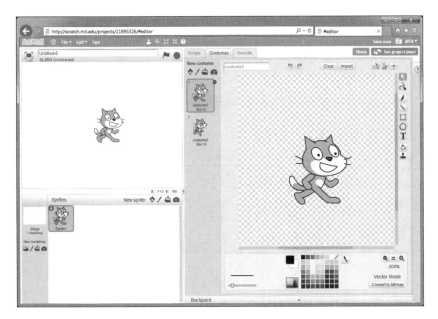

Figure 2.13
Adding and editing sprite costumes.
© 2014 Lifelong Kindergarten Group

By default, Scratch 2.0 only displays a sprite's first costume. You can drag and drop costumes to change their position in the list. When moved, the number assigned to the costume is automatically changed as well.

Scratch 2.0 gives you four different ways of adding new costumes to sprites. Each of these options is represented by a small icon located just above the costume images located at the top center of the program editor. Table 2.2 explains the function initiated by each of these options.

Table 2.2   Options for Adding Costumes to Sprites

Button	Name	Description
	Choose Costume from Library	Allows you to incorporate a graphics image from one of Scratch 2.0's image collections
	Paint New Costume	Allows you to paint a new bitmap or vector graphics image using Scratch's built-in Paint Editor
	Upload Costume from File	Allows you to retrieve a graphics image from a file on your computer
	New Costume from Camera	Allows you to retrieve a graphics image from a video camera attached to your computer

© 2014 Lifelong Kindergarten Group

Note

Scratch 2.0 can work with different types of bitmap-supported graphics files, including GIF, JPG, BMP, and PNG files. Scratch 2.0 can also work with animated GIF files. An *animated GIF* file is a graphic made up of two or more frames, each of which is displayed as an automated sequence when the GIF file is displayed. When editing vector graphics, Scratch works with SVG files.

Once you've added a costume, you can modify it by selecting it. This displays the costume in the Paint Editor's canvas area. You can also add a new costume to a sprite by Shift-clicking on an existing costume and selecting Duplicate from the list of menu options that appears. Alternatively, you can click on the Duplicate button, which changes the mouse pointer to look like the Duplicate button, and then click on Costume, which has already been added to your project. Once the copy of the costume has been added, you can select it to display it in the Paint Editor's canvas area, allowing you to modify it using the Paint Editor.

You can delete a costume from a sprite by Shift-clicking on it and then selecting Delete from the menu that appears. Alternatively, you can delete a costume by clicking on the Delete button, which changes the mouse pointer to look like the Delete button, and then clicking on the costume that you want to remove. You can also delete a costume by clicking on the small X button that is displayed on the top-right side of the costume when it has been selected. You can export it as a stand-alone costume by Shift-clicking on it and selecting Save to Local File from the pop-up menu that appears.

Tip

If you accidentally delete the costume from your project, you can restore it by clicking on the Edit menu and then clicking on the Undelete menu item.

Note

The stage can be assigned a graphic to be used as a backdrop upon which the application's sprites are displayed. In fact, the stage can be assigned a series of backdrops, allowing an application to change backdrops during application execution. To view, edit, and make a copy of a backdrop, select the stage thumbnail located on the left side of the sprites list. When you do this, the Costumes tab in the scripts area changes to the Backdrops tab, allowing you to modify and work with application backdrops. From here, you can also create new backdrops using the Paint Editor, discussed later in this chapter, allowing you to create any backdrop you want. Alternatively, you can add additional backdrops to your projects by clicking on any of the following icons, located at the top of the list of backdrop thumbnails: Choose Costume from Library, Paint New Costume, Upload Costume from File, New Costume from Camera.

Adding Sound Effects

Just as sprites can have different costumes, they can have one or more sounds assigned to them (or to the stage), which can be played during application execution, either as background music or as sound effects during program execution. Scratch 2.0 can play back MP3 files as well as most WAV, AU, and AIF audio files. To view the sound files associated with a sprite or backdrop, click on the stage thumbnail or the desired sprite in the sprites list and then click on the Sounds tab in the scripts area. A list of the sound files belonging to the selected sprite or the stage is displayed, as demonstrated in Figure 2.14.

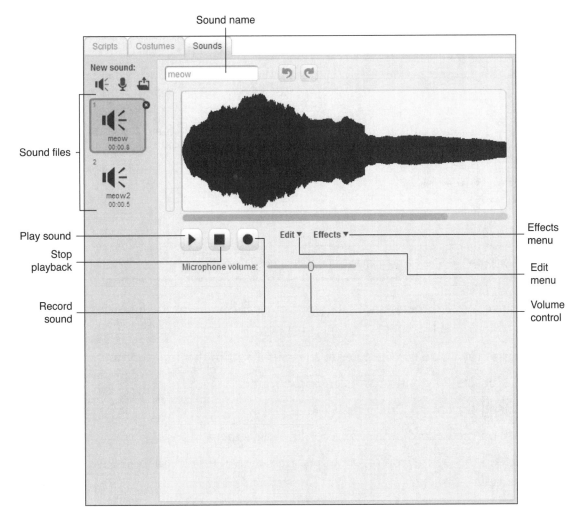

Figure 2.14
Displaying the sounds associated with a sprite.
© 2014 Lifelong Kindergarten Group

By default, every sprite and the stage comes with a single sound file already associated with it. This is the pop sound, which when played makes a brief popping sound, like that of a bubble bursting. Scratch 2.0 provides three different ways of adding additional sounds to your sprites and the stage. These options are briefly described in Table 2.3.

Table 2.3 Options for Acquiring Sound Files

Button	Name	Description
🔈	Choose Sound from Library	Allows you to incorporate a graphics image from one of Scratch 2.0's image collections
🎤	Record New Sound	Creates and adds a new empty sound to the project, allowing you to then click on the Record button and create your own sound
⬆	Upload Sound from File	Allows you to retrieve a sound from an audio file located on your computer

© 2014 Lifelong Kindergarten Group

Note

Your computer must have a microphone for you to record your own sounds.

Once you've selected the Sounds tab, you can perform any of the following actions on any sound files that belong to a sprite or backdrop.

- Change the name used to refer to the sound within the application.
- Click on the Play button to listen to the sound.
- Click on the Stop button to halt sound playback.
- Click on the Record button to record a replacement sound.
- Click on the Delete icon on the upper-right side of the sound to remove it from the application project.
- Use the slider control to increase or decrease the microphone volume.

As demonstrated in Figure 2.15, sound files are graphically represented in the Sound Editor. You can edit and modify sounds by clicking on a portion of the sound file, dragging the mouse pointer across the sound file, and then releasing the mouse button. The result is a selected portion of the sound file, as demonstrated in Figure 2.15.

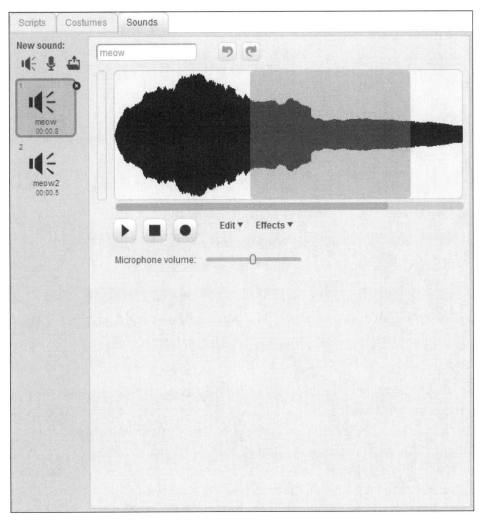

Figure 2.15
Displaying the sounds associated with a sprite.
© 2014 Lifelong Kindergarten Group

Now that you have a portion of the sound selected, you can click on the Sound Editor's Edit menu and execute any of the following commands to modify the sound.

- **Undo.** Undoes the previous action.
- **Redo.** Reapplies the previous action.
- **Cut.** Removes the selected portion of the sound file.
- **Copy.** Copies the selected portion of the sound file.

- **Paste.** Pastes a previously copied portion of a sound file to a specified location within the current sound file.

- **Delete.** Deletes the selected portion of the sound file.

- **Select All.** Selects the entire contents of the sound file.

In addition to the basic edit functions outlined in the previous list, the Sound Editor allows you to apply a number of advanced specialized effects on a sound file. You implement the special effects via the following commands located on the Effects menu.

- **Fade In.** Used to fade in a selected portion of a sound file.

- **Fade Out.** Used to fade out a selected portion of a sound file.

- **Louder.** Used to increase the loudness of a selected portion of a sound file.

- **Softer.** Used to increase the softness of a selected portion of a sound file.

- **Silence.** Used to replace the specified portion of a sound file with silence.

- **Reverse.** Used to flip or reverse the selected portion of a sound file.

Backpack

The backpack allows Scratchers to quickly and easily move resources like sprites, scripts, backdrops, sounds, and costumes between projects. The backpack is located on the bottom-right side of the Project Editor. When not in use, the backpack is kept tucked away at the bottom of the Project Editor, with only the upper edge of its window's title bar visible. To access the backpack and see its contents, click on the small triangle icon located in the middle of the window. In response, the backpack slides upward from the bottom of the Project Editor and displays its contents, as demonstrated in Figure 2.16.

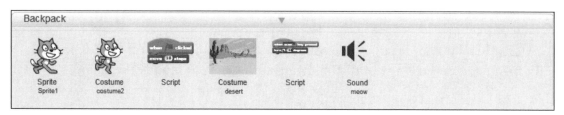

Figure 2.16
Use the backpack to collect and move project resources into and out of your projects.

To add a project resource, such as a script, to your backpack, simply click on the resource, drag it onto your backpack, and drop it. You can drag and drop project resources from your or anyone else's Scratch 2.0 project into your backpack. So, if you come across a Scratch 2.0 project that, for example, has a sound file that you want to use in a project of your own, you can click on the See Inside project button to display the project's contents in the Project Editor, click on the Sounds tab, locate the sound file, and then drag and drop it onto your backpack. To add the sound file to your Scratch 2.0 project, all you have to do is open your project in the Project Editor, display the contents of your backpack, and then drag and drop the sound file onto your project's stage on one of its sprites.

Note

Whenever you view a Scratch 2.0 project in regular screen mode, you notice a See Inside button displayed in the upper-right corner of the screen. If you click on this button, Scratch opens the project in the Project Editor, allowing you to see how it is made. If you want, you can then click on the orange Remix button, which appears in the upper-left corner of the project page. A copy of the project is then created, which you can then tinker with and modify to your heart's content. When you are done, click on the blue See Project Page button, and you see any instructions as well as notes and credits that the project's original developer provided. In addition, you see the original name of the project and the username of its developer, thus providing due credit to the project's original developer. Both the project name and the username are displayed as links to the original project and to the developer's Profile page.

Tip

You can click on the blue Follow button when visiting any Scratch 2.0 developer's Profile page to receive updates on that Scratcher's projects. The updates automatically appear in the What's Happening section of the main Scratch 2.0 page (http://scratch.mit.edu) anytime you view it.

ADDING PROJECT INSTRUCTIONS, NOTES, AND CREDITS

Another important feature of Scratch 2.0 is the ability to add and update project instructions for working with your projects, in addition to project notes about the development of your projects and credits for other Scratchers for any content or program code you may have remixed into your projects.

Scratch 2.0 allows you to add project instructions, notes, and credits by clicking on the See Project Page button located at the upper-right corner of the Project Editor. This displays a web page similar to the one shown in Figure 2.17.

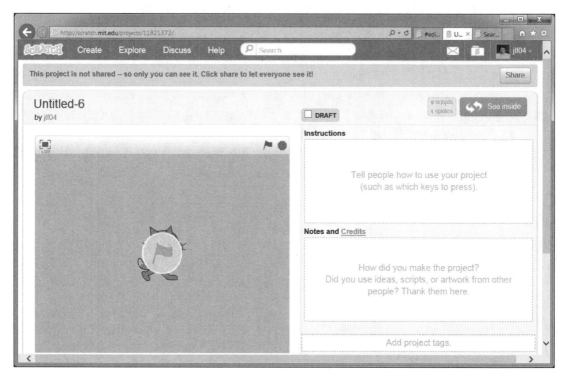

Figure 2.17

Viewing and updating a Scratch 2.0 project's instructions, notes, and credits.

© 2014 Lifelong Kindergarten Group

From this page, you can change the name assigned to your Scratch 2.0 project. You can also click on the Share button located in the upper-right corner of the page to make your project viewable by other scratchers. In addition, this page lets you provide instructions for interacting with your project. Just type them into the Instructions field, which operates like a simple Notepad program. Similarly, you can enter text into the Notes and Credits field.

Tip

Use the Instructions field to tell other Scratchers how to interact with your projects. For example, explain what buttons they should press, what rules they have to follow, and so on. Use the Notes and Credits field to help document your Scratch 2.0 project, leaving behind information that explains the application's purpose and why you designed it the way you did. You should also use the Notes and Credits field to acknowledge and give credit to any Scratchers whose work you may have borrowed or been inspired by. The text saved in these two fields is displayed on the same web page as your project when displayed in regular mode and will therefore be readily available to other Scratchers.

Lastly, to make it easier for other Scratchers to find your project, you can add project tags to the text field located at the bottom-right corner of the page. When you click on this field, a list of predefined tags is displayed. You can add one or more of these tags by clicking on it. Double-clicking on clear space in the text field redisplays the list of pre-defined tags, allowing you to click on another one. Alternatively, you can create your own tags by typing in a keyword that is descriptive of your project. The Scratch 2.0 website search engine uses these tags to identify programs of interest to Scratchers who use the website's search capability to find projects they are interested in.

CREATING NEW SPRITES USING SCRATCH'S PAINT EDITOR

In addition to using the sprites supplied with Scratch and graphics that you acquire from the Internet, you can always create your own using Scratch 2.0's built-in Paint Editor. The Paint Editor operates in either of two modes: bitmap or vector. Bitmap graphics are saved as a collection of pixels that, when drawn, lay out a graphic. Vector graphics, on the other hand, are stored as a collection of rules that tell a vector editor how to construct a graphic.

The Paint Editor is switchable between modes. Both modes have advantages and disadvantages. Vector graphics are more difficult to paint than bitmap graphics but result in smoother images when graphics are resized. It is usually easier for people new to graphic development to learn how to work in bitmap mode. Vector graphics look smoother than bitmap graphics because the edges of vector graphics gradually turn transparent. In contrast, bitmap images look pixilated when their size is changed. In bitmap mode, everything that is drawn on the editor canvas is treated as a single image or object. In vector mode, each object that is drawn is treated as a separate independent object.

The current mode in which the Paint Editor is operating is displayed in the lower-left corner of the Paint Editor. Beneath it is a button that, when clicked, switches the Paint Editor's mode. When you're switching from vector to bitmap mode, anything painted on the drawing canvas is converted into a single bitmap image. As such, it becomes subject to pixilation when resized. When switched from bitmap to vector mode, the bitmap image is converted to a single object that remains separate and distinct from any other objects that you may paint.

Although it does not have all the bells and whistles that applications like Corel PaintShop Pro and Adobe Photoshop do, Scratch's built-in Paint Editor, shown in Figure 2.18, provides you with everything you need to draw or modify graphics for use as sprites and backdrops.

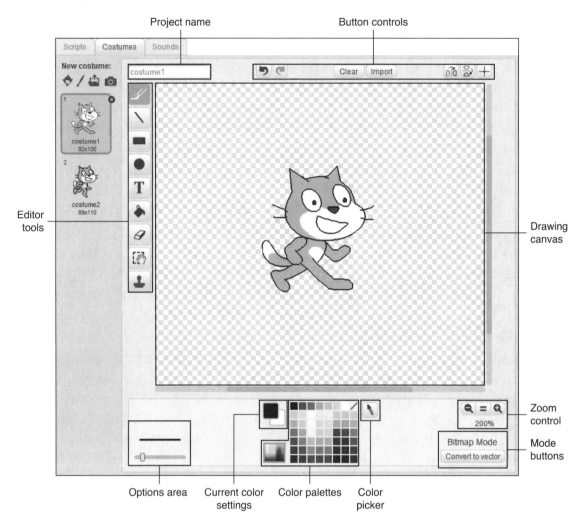

Figure 2.18
Painter editor's bitmap mode within Scratch 2.0 provides everything you need to create and edit sprites, costumes, and backdrops.
© 2014 Lifelong Kindergarten Group

Figure 2.18 shows how the Paint Editor appears when operating in bitmap mode. When run in vector mode, as demonstrated in Figure 2.19, the Paint Editor looks very much the same as it does in bitmap mode, except that the editor tools are different and have been moved from the left to the right side of the Paint Editor.

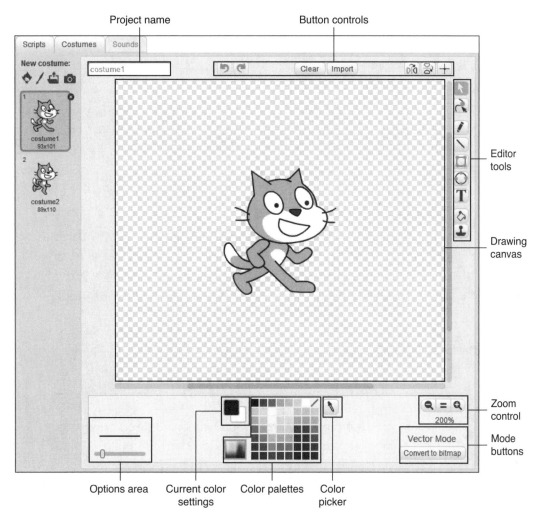

Figure 2.19

Painter editor's vector mode within Scratch 2.0 provides everything you need to create and edit sprites, costumes, and backdrops.

© 2014 Lifelong Kindergarten Group

Many of the basic features and functionality of the Paint Editor are the same regardless of which mode it is operated in. These features are reviewed in the sections that follow. Except where noted, Paint Editor features are available in both bitmap and vector modes.

Examining the Drawing Canvas

You can use the Paint Editor program to create or modify new sprites, costumes, and backdrops. Most of the space on the Paint Editor's window is dedicated to a drawing canvas. To draw on the canvas, you select different drawing commands from the Editor Tools area and then use the mouse to draw on the canvas. You can work with different colors and apply a range of special effects.

If the size of the graphic being worked on exceeds the available area, scrollbars are enabled on the right side and the bottom of the drawing canvas, allowing you to scroll and view all parts of the graphic. You can also use the Zoom In and Zoom Out buttons located at the bottom of the window to temporarily increase or decrease the magnification of the drawing canvas.

Working with Editor Tools

When you're creating or editing a graphic image on the drawing canvas, the buttons located in the editor tools area of the Paint Editor's toolbar provide access to essential features and functionality. Table 2.4 shows an overview of the functionality provided by the buttons that are available when the Paint Editor is operated in bitmap mode.

Table 2.4   Bitmap Paint Tools

Button	Name	Description
	Brush	Allows you to draw freehand on the drawing canvas using the current foreground color and brush size.
	Line	Allows you to draw straight lines using the current foreground color.
	Rectangle	Allows you to draw filled-in or outlined rectangle shapes using the current foreground color.
	Ellipse	Allows you to draw filled-in or outlined ellipses using the current foreground color.
	Text	Allows you to include text as part of a drawing using different font types.
	Fill with color	Allows you to fill in enclosed areas with either a gradient or a solid color, depending on the selected option specified in the Options area.

	Erase	Allows you to erase selected portions of the drawing canvas using the current eraser size. Erased portions of the drawing canvas are returned to a transparent state.
	Select	Allows you to select a rectangular portion of the drawing canvas and move it to a different part of the drawing canvas (cut and paste).
	Select and duplicate	Allows you to select a rectangular portion of the drawing canvas and copy it to different parts of the drawing canvas (copy and paste).

© 2014 Lifelong Kindergarten Group

Table 2.5 shows an overview of the functionality provided by each of the buttons that are available when the Paint Editor is operated in vector mode.

Table 2.5   Vector Paint Tools

Button	Name	Description
	Select	Allows you to select a rectangular portion of the drawing canvas and copy it to different parts of the drawing canvas (copy and paste).
	Reshape	Used to bend or change the shape of a vector object's spline by dragging its points and moving them around.
	Pencil	Allows you to draw freehand on the drawing canvas using the current foreground color and brush size.
	Line	Allows you to draw straight lines using the current foreground color.
	Rectangle	Allows you to draw filled-in or outlined rectangle shapes using the current foreground color.
	Ellipse	Allows you to draw filled-in or outlined ellipses using the current foreground color.
	Text	Allows you to include text as part of a drawing using different font types.

Table 2.5   Vector Paint Tools (*Continued*)

Button	Name	Description
	Color a Shape	Allows you to fill in enclosed areas with either a gradient or a solid color, depending on the selected option specified in the Options area.
	Duplicate	Allows you to select a vector object and create a duplicate of it.
	Forward a Layer	Moves a vector object up one layer.
	Back a Layer	Moves a vector object back one layer.
	Group	Groups multiple vector objects into a single object.
	Ungroup	Breaks up a group of vector objects back into a series of individual objects.

Regardless of the mode the Paint Editor is operated in, most of the buttons in the editor tools area accept configuration options that further refine the functionality provided by the button controls. When one of these buttons is selected, its configuration options are displayed in the bottom-left position of the Paint Editor. For example, Figure 2.20 shows the four configuration options that are provided when the Fill button has been selected. These options set the fill style that is applied and include the application of a solid color and the use of a horizontal gradient, vertical gradient, or radial gradient.

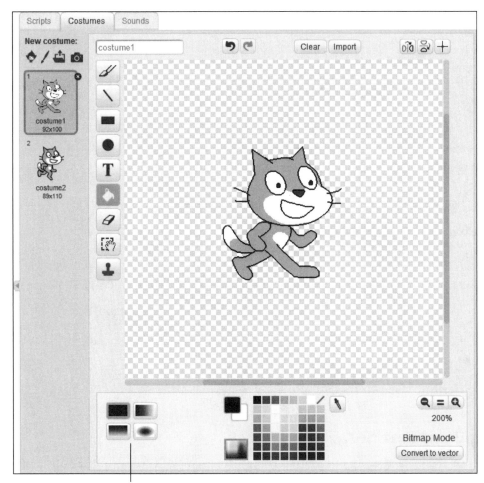

Fill with color configuration options

Figure 2.20
The content of the options area changes based on the selected toolbar button.
© 2014 Lifelong Kindergarten Group

Note

A *gradient* is a color created by blending the foreground and background colors.

Working with Button Controls

As shown in Figure 2.21, Scratch 2.0's Paint Editor program includes a number of button controls that can initiate an assortment of different actions.

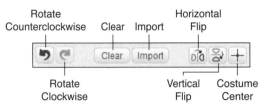

Figure 2.21
The Paint Editor provides access to key functionality through various button controls.
© 2014 Lifelong Kindergarten Group

The following list identifies each of these buttons and explains its purpose.

- **Rotate Counterclockwise.** Rotates the drawing canvas counterclockwise.
- **Rotate Clockwise.** Rotates the drawing canvas clockwise.
- **Clear.** Clears any graphics currently displayed on the drawing canvas.
- **Import.** Opens an image from a graphics file stored on your computer.
- **Horizontal Flip.** Flips the drawing canvas horizontally.
- **Vertical Flip.** Flips the drawing canvas vertically.
- **Costume Center.** Used to specify a sprite's rotation center.

Specifying Color Settings

The Paint Editor lets you specify current color settings for both foreground and background drawing using the current Color Settings control located just under the drawing canvas. To set the current foreground color, click on the top square and then select a color from one of the color palettes that is displayed beneath the control. Likewise, you can set the current background color by selecting the bottom square and then selecting a color from one of the color palettes.

Configuring a Sprite's Rotation Center

One final but important Paint Editor feature that you definitely need to know how to use is the Set Rotation Center button located in the upper-right corner of the Paint Editor. When clicked, this button displays a set of crosshairs on the Paint Editor's drawing canvas, as demonstrated in Figure 2.22. You can then use drag and drop to move the crosshair over the portion of the sprite that you want to set up as the sprite's rotational center when the sprite is rotated on the stage.

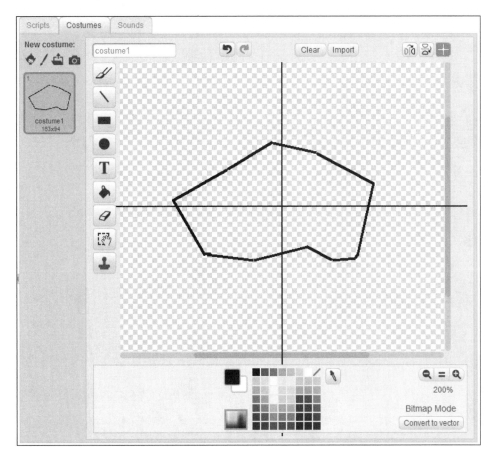

Figure 2.22

Crosshairs make it easy to set a sprite's rotational center.

© 2014 Lifelong Kindergarten Group

The sprite shown in Figure 2.22 is that of a rock that might be used in a space shooter game like *Asteroids*. In this type of game, the asteroid moves around the screen, threatening to destroy the player's ship by colliding with it. To provide a realistic look and feel, you might want to tell Scratch 2.0 to rotate the rock as it moves around the screen. By setting up the rock's rotation point as the center of the sprite, it appears to rotate or spin around its center. On the other hand, by setting its rotation point to be one of the edges of the rock, you can make it rotate in a more wobbly manner.

Chapter 3

A Review of the Basic Components of Scratch Projects

As you have already seen, Scratch application projects are composed of backdrops and sprites. Sprites interact and move about the stage under the programmatic control of scripts made up of code blocks. This chapter explains the different types of code blocks and how they work together to create scripts. It also reviews the 10 categories into which all of Scratch 2.0's 148-plus code blocks are grouped. Although this chapter does not offer an in-depth review of each code block, it provides a series of tables that you can bookmark and use as a quick reference when developing new Scratch applications.

An overview of the major topics covered in this chapter includes

- A detailed explanation of the six different types of Scratch blocks
- A demonstration of how to work with and configure monitors
- A review of all 148 code blocks that make up Scratch scripts
- An explanation of how to display help information for individual code blocks

Working with Blocks and Stacks

To bring the backdrops and sprites that make up Scratch applications to life, you must create scripts. Scripts are created by dragging and dropping code blocks from the blocks palette to the scripts area and snapping them together, creating stacks. You can run scripts by double-clicking on one of the code blocks. You can also configure scripts to automatically execute when predefined events occur.

You can drag a code block around the scripts area. As demonstrated in Figure 3.1, when you drag a block near other blocks, a white indicator bar appears to designate locations where a valid connection can be made. You can snap code blocks to the top and bottom of stacks or insert them into the middle of the stack. In some cases, you can insert code inside other code blocks.

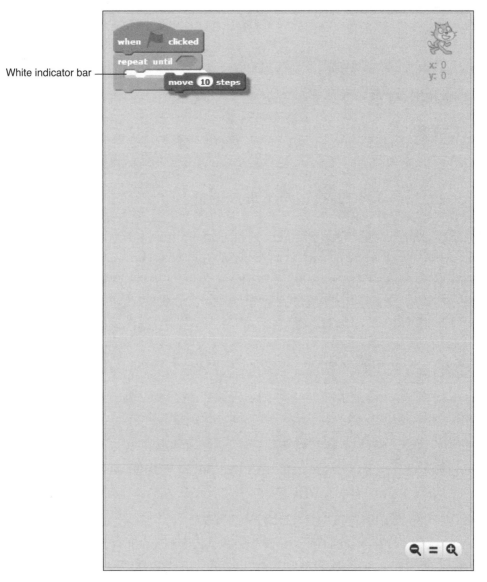

White indicator bar

Figure 3.1
Use the visual indicator to determine valid connection points.

You can move code stacks by clicking on their uppermost blocks and dragging them to a new location. If you drag a block from the middle of a stack, all the code blocks underneath it are dragged out as well.

Tip

You can copy a stack of code blocks from one sprite to another by dragging and dropping the stack onto the thumbnail of a sprite located in the sprite list.

Arguments

Many code blocks accept input known as *arguments*. For example, there are move blocks that accept and process argument data, instructing them how far to move or rotate a sprite, and there are looks blocks that can change the size of a sprite based on a numeric argument. Scratch 2.0 code blocks support six different types of arguments. A sampling of these code blocks is shown in Figure 3.2.

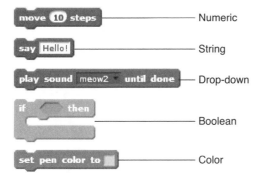

Figure 3.2

Examples of code blocks that process different types of argument data.

© 2014 Lifelong Kindergarten Group

Code blocks that present/contain an oval or a hexagon shape can receive argument data from other code blocks. You can, therefore, drag and drop oval-shaped blocks onto code blocks that present/contain an oval or rectangular input field. Similarly, you can drag and drop hexagon-shaped blocks onto code blocks that present/contain a hexagon. Figure 3.3 shows an example of how this works.

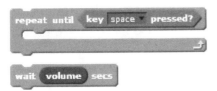

Figure 3.3

Examples of passing data to code blocks to be processed as arguments.

© 2014 Lifelong Kindergarten Group

The first example in Figure 3.3 shows a control block with a sensing block inside. The second example in Figure 3.3 shows another control block, this time with a sound block inside. In both cases, the value of the embedded code block is passed as an argument to the code block that contains them.

Default Values

As you may have already noticed, many Scratch 2.0 code blocks display a default value. Every code block that processes argument data has an assigned default value, even those that do not display that value. Figure 3.4 shows an example of several code blocks that accept and process arguments and shows these code blocks' default values.

Figure 3.4

Every Scratch 2.0 code block has a default value.

© 2014 Lifelong Kindergarten Group

You can change code block default values if necessary, although in many cases there is no need to do so.

Note

Code blocks that present/process Boolean arguments do not display a default value. These blocks have a default value of `false`.

Six Basic Types of Scratch Blocks

Scratch applications are made up of sprites that interact with one another and the user. Sprites are controlled and animated by scripts. Sprites can have any number of scripts, each of which is designed to perform a specific task or action. Scripts are made up of one or more Scratch code blocks. In total, there are 148 different Scratch 2.0 blocks, each of which is designed to fulfill a specific purpose. These blocks can be broadly classified into six categories, as outlined here:

- Stack blocks
- Hat blocks
- Reporter blocks
- Boolean blocks
- C blocks
- Cap blocks

Working with Stack Blocks

The majority of code blocks that Scratch provides are stack blocks. *Stack blocks* are code blocks with a notch at the top and a bump at the bottom. The notches and bumps serve as visual indicators that identify how the blocks can be snapped together to create programming logic. Figure 3.5 shows an example of a typical stack block.

Figure 3.5
An example of a code block that is used to halt the playback of an audio file.
© 2014 Lifelong Kindergarten Group

The notch on the top indicates that the code block can be attached to the underside of another code block. The bump at the bottom of the code block allows other code blocks to attach to its underside.

Some stack blocks include an input area inside them that allows you to specify a value by typing in a number. For example, the stack block shown in Figure 3.6 lets you assign the color to be used when drawing by inserting a color-associated numeric value.

Editable text field

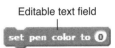

Figure 3.6
You use this code block to specify the color to be used when drawing.
© 2014 Lifelong Kindergarten Group

To modify the value assigned to a block like the one shown in Figure 3.6, click on the white area within the code block and type in a new value. Some code blocks let you configure them by selecting a value from a pull-down list, as demonstrated in Figure 3.7.

Figure 3.7
This code block has a pull-down menu that you can use to configure how it operates.
© 2014 Lifelong Kindergarten Group

Working with Hat Blocks

A *hat block* is a code block with a rounded or curved top and a bump at the bottom, visually indicating that it can be snapped on top of other stack blocks. Hat blocks provide the ability to create event-driven scripts. An *event-driven* script is one that automatically executes when a specified event occurs. An example of an event that can automatically trigger script execution is when the user clicks on the green Flag button. When this event occurs, any scripts that begin with the hat block shown in Figure 3.8 are automatically executed.

Figure 3.8
This hat block automatically runs a script when the user clicks on the green flag.
© 2014 Lifelong Kindergarten Group

Script execution can also be triggered when the user clicks on a sprite. You can set this up by adding the code block shown in Figure 3.9 to the beginning of the script.

Figure 3.9
This hat block runs a script whenever the user clicks on the sprite to which this script belongs.
© 2014 Lifelong Kindergarten Group

Note

Every sprite in an application can potentially have its own scripts. You can automate the execution of any or all of the scripts using hat blocks. In addition to sprites, the stage can have scripts.

Working with Reporter Blocks

A third type of Scratch code block is a reporter block. A *reporter block* is a code block that has rounded sides and is specifically designed as a mechanism for providing input for other code blocks to process. For example, the code block shown in Figure 3.10 is a typical reporter block.

Figure 3.10
This code block retrieves a numeric value indicating a sprite's volume.
© 2014 Lifelong Kindergarten Group

As you can see, this reporter block has rounded sides. As such, it can only fit into code blocks like the one shown in Figure 3.11.

`set volume to 100 %`

Figure 3.11
You can provide input to this code block by either keying it in or by using a reporter block.
© 2014 Lifelong Kindergarten Group

Working with Boolean Blocks

As demonstrated in Figure 3.12, a Boolean block has angled sides. This particular code block returns a value of `true` if the user has pressed the spacebar or `false` if the spacebar has not been pressed. Because it has angled sides, a Boolean block can only be embedded inside code blocks that contain an input area whose sides are also angled.

`key space ▼ pressed?`

Figure 3.12
Angled code blocks pass Boolean data to other code blocks for processing.
© 2014 Lifelong Kindergarten Group

Note

Boolean is a term used to identify data that has one of two values: either `true` or `false`.

To take advantage of a Boolean block like the one shown in Figure 3.12, you need to embed the Boolean block into another code block that has been designed to work with it. For example, Figure 3.13 shows one such code block.

`wait until`

Figure 3.13
This code block pauses script execution until a specified event is true.
© 2014 Lifelong Kindergarten Group

Figure 3.14 demonstrates how a Boolean block looks after being embedded within another code block.

Figure 3.14
This particular combination of code blocks pauses script execution until the user presses the spacebar.
© 2014 Lifelong Kindergarten Group

C Blocks

C blocks are shaped like and named after the letter *C*. C blocks are used to set up a loop of blocks within scripts that repeatedly execute for as long as a tested condition evaluates as `true`. Scratch 2.0 has five different C blocks, all of which are control blocks. Figure 3.15 shows an example of one of the C blocks. This block repeatedly executes any code blocks that you choose to embed inside it until a tested condition evaluates as `true`.

Note

You will learn about the application of repetitive and conditional programming logic in Chapter 9, "Controlling Script Execution."

Figure 3.15
This code block repeatedly executes other stack blocks that have been embedded within it.
© 2014 Lifelong Kindergarten Group

Cap Blocks

Cap blocks halt the execution of scripts. Cap blocks have a notch on top and a flat bottom, which signifies the end of a script. As such, you cannot attach other blocks to the bottom of a cap block. Figure 3.16 shows an example of a cap block.

Figure 3.16
This code block has been configured to stop the execution of all scripts in the project.
© 2014 Lifelong Kindergarten Group

KEEPING AN EYE OUT WITH MONITORS

You have probably noticed that Scratch displays a small check box just to the left of certain code blocks in the blocks palette, as demonstrated in Figure 3.17.

Figure 3.17

An example of a code block capable of displaying a monitor on the stage.

© 2014 Lifelong Kindergarten Group

The presence of a check box indicates that the code block is capable of displaying a monitor on the stage. You click on the check box to display the monitor on the stage and clear the check box to hide it. A monitor displays the value of a variable, list, or Boolean on the stage. To display the monitor, just click on the check box to select it. When you do so, a gray monitor automatically appears on the stage, as demonstrated in Figure 3.18. The color shown behind the value reported in the display mirrors the color of the monitor's associated block.

> Sprite1 volume   `100`

Figure 3.18

An example of the default monitor for the volume block.

© 2014 Lifelong Kindergarten Group

By default, monitors are displaying in normal readout mode. However, you can modify the way the monitors look by Shift-clicking the R key and clicking on the monitor and then selecting Large Readout from the pop-up menu that appears. As a result, the appearance of the monitor will change, displaying its value in a larger font, as demonstrated in Figure 3.19.

`100`

Figure 3.19

Monitors can be configured to display a large readout.

© 2014 Lifelong Kindergarten Group

Tip

You can also toggle between monitor formats by double-clicking on the monitor.

Numeric variable-based monitors support a third format, which includes a slider display option, as demonstrated in Figure 3.20. Unlike values displayed in normal readout and large readout, you can manually change the value assigned to a value using the slider view of a monitor by dragging the slider to the left or right.

Figure 3.20

Variable monitors also support a display format that includes a slider.

© 2014 Lifelong Kindergarten Group

You can also specify a minimum and maximum range for a slider by Shift-clicking the R key and selecting Set Slider Min and Max from the list of options that appears. This opens the Slider Range window, as shown in Figure 3.21.

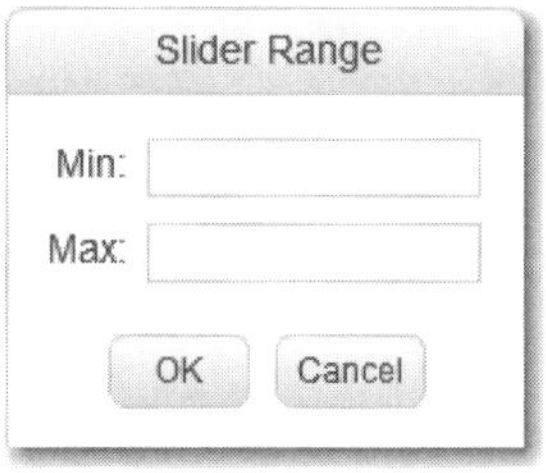

Figure 3.21

Specifying a minimum and maximum range for a monitor configured to display as a slider.

© 2014 Lifelong Kindergarten Group

List-based monitors are also supported. They allow you to display the contents of a list, as demonstrated in Figure 3.22.

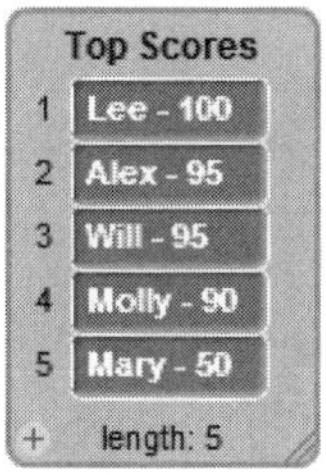

Figure 3.22

You can use list monitors to display the contents of lists.

© 2014 Lifelong Kindergarten Group

You can populate list-based monitors with data programmatically or key data into them directly by clicking on an open row in the list and typing in a value. You can also resize list-based monitors by right-clicking on the small handle located on the lower-right side of the monitor and dragging into or out from the monitor. You can manually add new rows to a list by clicking on the plus icon located on the lower-left side of the monitor. If a list has more rows than can be displayed within the monitor, a scrollbar is displayed, allowing you to scroll up and down the list.

You will learn about variables and lists and their use in Chapter 7, "Storing and Retrieving Data."

TEN CATEGORIES OF SCRATCH BLOCKS

Scratch provides access to many different code blocks. These code blocks are organized into 10 categories and are made available on the blocks palette. Each of these categories of code blocks is described in the following list.

- **Motion.** Code blocks that control sprite placement, direction, rotation, and movement.
- **Looks.** Code blocks that affect sprite and backdrop appearance and can display text.
- **Sound.** Code blocks that control the playback and volume of musical notes and audio files.
- **Pen.** Code blocks that you can use to draw using different colors and pen sizes.
- **Data.** Code blocks that you can use to store data used by applications when they execute.
- **Events.** Code blocks that trigger script execution.
- **Control.** Code blocks that repeatedly execute programming logic using loops or perform conditional logic.
- **Sensing.** Code blocks that you can use to determine the location of the mouse pointer and its distance from other sprites and to determine whether a sprite is touching another sprite.
- **Operators.** Code blocks that perform logical comparisons, rounding, and other arithmetic operations.
- **More Blocks.** Custom code blocks that programmers can create as well as specialized code blocks that facilitate the use of Scratch 2.0 to programmatically interact with a PicoBoard and the LEGO WeDo Robotics kit.

You can view the code blocks belonging to a given category by clicking on one of the 10 labeled button categories at the top of the blocks palette. Note that each category of code block is color coded, making it easy to distinguish between code blocks from different categories.

Each of these categories of code blocks is reviewed in the sections that follow. This review covers Scratch's entire collection of code blocks, indicating which ones support monitors and providing a brief description of each code block's usage.

Moving Objects Around the Drawing Canvas

Motion blocks, colored blue, control a sprite's placement on the stage. There are motion blocks that let you set the direction a sprite moves, and there are blocks that move sprites. There are also motion blocks that report on a sprite's location and direction. Table 3.1 outlines all the code blocks that fit into this category.

Table 3.1   Scratch Motion Blocks

Block	Monitor	Description
move 10 steps	No	Moves a sprite forward or backwards a specified number of steps.
turn ↻ 15 degrees	No	Rotates a sprite a specified number of degrees in a clockwise direction.
turn ↺ 15 degrees	No	Rotates a sprite a specified number of degrees in a counterclockwise direction.
point in direction 90▾	No	Points a sprite toward a specified direction (0 = up, 90 = right, −90 = left, 180 = down).
point towards	No	Points a sprite toward either the mouse pointer or a specified sprite.
go to x: 0 y: 0	No	Moves a sprite to a specified set of coordinates on the stage.
go to mouse-pointer	No	Moves a sprite to either the location of the mouse pointer or another sprite.
glide 1 secs to x: 0 y: 0	No	Moves a sprite to the specified coordinate position over a specified number of seconds.
change x by 10	No	Changes the position of a sprite on the X-axis by a specified number of pixels.

Table 3.1   Scratch Motion Blocks (*Continued*)

Block	Monitor	Description
set x to 0	No	Changes a sprite's location on the X-axis to a specified value.
change y by 10	No	Changes the position of a sprite on the Y-axis by a specified number of pixels.
set y to 0	No	Changes a sprite's location on the Y-axis to a specified value.
if on edge, bounce	No	Changes a sprite's direction when it makes contact with one of the edges of the stage.
set rotation style left-right	No	Sets a sprite's rotation style to left-right to rotate it horizontally, all around to flip it vertically, or don't rotate to make it face one direction.
x position	Yes	Retrieves a value representing a sprite's coordinate on the X-axis (between –240 and 240).
y position	Yes	Retrieves a value representing a sprite's coordinate on the Y-axis (between –180 and 180).
direction	Yes	Retrieves a value representing a sprite's current direction (0 = up, 90 = right, –90 = left, 180 = down).

You will learn more about motion blocks in Chapter 5, "Moving Things Around."

Changing Object Appearance

Looks blocks modify sprite and backdrop appearance and display text within pop-up bubbles. Looks blocks are colored purple. There are looks blocks that let you modify sprite costumes and colors. There are also blocks that let you modify a sprite's size and control whether a sprite is visible on the stage. Table 3.2 outlines all of the code blocks that fit into this category.

Table 3.2   Scratch Looks Blocks

Block	Monitor	Description
`say Hello! for 2 secs`	No	Displays a text message in a speech bubble for a specified number of seconds.
`say Hello!`	No	Displays a text message in a speech bubble or removes the display of a speech bubble when no text is specified.
`think Hmm... for 2 secs`	No	Displays a text message in a thought bubble for a specified number of seconds.
`think Hmm...`	No	Displays a text message in a thought bubble or removes the display of a thought bubble when no text is specified.
`show`	No	Tells Scratch to display a sprite.
`hide`	No	Suppresses the display of a sprite on the stage, preventing it from interacting with other sprites.
`switch costume to costume2`	No	Changes a sprite's costume, modifying its appearance.
`next costume`	No	Changes a sprite's costume to the next costume in the sprite's costume list, jumping back to the beginning of the list when the end of the list is reached.
`switch backdrop to backdrop1`	No	Alters the stage's appearance by assigning it a different backdrop.
`switch backdrop to backdrop1 and wait`	No	Waits until all hat blocks have executed and then alters the stage's appearance by assigning it a different backdrop.
`next backdrop`	No	Changes the stage's backdrop to the next backdrop in the backdrop list.
`change color effect by 25`	No	Modifies a sprite's appearance by applying and modifying a special effect (color, fisheye, whirl, pixelate, mosaic, brightness, or ghost) by a specified numeric value.

Table 3.2 Scratch Looks Blocks (*Continued*)

Block	Monitor	Description
set color effect to 0	No	Applies a special effect (color, fisheye, whirl, pixelate, mosaic, brightness, or ghost) to a sprite by a specified numeric value.
clear graphic effects	No	Restores a sprite to its normal appearance, removing any special effects that may have been applied.
change size by 10	No	Modifies the size of a sprite by a specified numeric amount.
set size to 100 %	No	Sets a sprite's size to a percentage of its original size.
go to front	No	Places a sprite on top of other sprites, placing it on the top layer and ensuring its display.
go back 1 layers	No	Moves a sprite back a specified number of layers, allowing other sprites to be displayed on top of it.
costume #	Yes	Retrieves a numeric value representing a sprite's current costume number.
backdrop #	Yes	Retrieves a numeric value representing the stage's current backdrop number.
backdrop name	Yes	Retrieves the name of the stage's current backdrop from the backdrop list.
size	Yes	Retrieves a percentage value representing a sprite's current size when compared to its original size.

© 2014 Lifelong Kindergarten Group

You will learn more about looks blocks in Chapter 10, "Changing the Way Sprites Look and Behave."

Making Some Noise

Sound blocks, colored pink, play music and add sound effects to your Scratch application projects. There are sound blocks that let you play sounds and drum beats, select different types of instruments, control playback volume, and modify tempo. Table 3.3 outlines all the code blocks that fit into this category.

Table 3.3   Scratch Sound Blocks

Block	Monitor	Description
play sound meow	No	Plays the specified sound file while allowing the script file in which it is inserted to keep executing.
play sound meow until done	No	Plays the specified sound file, pausing script execution until the sound file has finished playing.
stop all sounds	No	Halts the playback of any sound files currently being played.
play drum 1 for 0.25 beats	No	Plays a drum sound selected from the block's pull-down menu a specified number of seconds.
rest for 0.25 beats	No	Pauses sound playback for a specified number of beats.
play note 60 for 0.5 beats	No	Plays a musical note selected from the block's pull-down menu a specified number of beats.
set instrument to 1	No	Specifies the instrument to be used when playing musical notes.
change volume by -10	No	Changes a sprite's volume by a specified value.
set volume to 100 %	No	Sets a sprite's sound volume to a specified percentage level.
volume	Yes	Retrieves a numeric value representing a sprite's sound volume.
change tempo by 20	No	Alters a sprite's tempo by a specified number of beats per minute.
set tempo to 60 bpm	No	Assigns the number of beats per minute to be used as a sprite's tempo.
tempo	Yes	Retrieves a numeric value representing a sprite's tempo.

© 2014 Lifelong Kindergarten Group

You will learn more about sound blocks in Chapter 11, "Spicing Things Up with Sounds."

Drawing Lines and Shapes

Pen blocks, colored mint green, draw any combination of shapes and lines using a virtual pen. There are pen blocks that let you enable and disable drawing, set color and pen size, and apply shading. Table 3.4 outlines all the code blocks that fit into this category.

Table 3.4   Scratch Pen Blocks

Block	Monitor	Description
clear	No	Erases or clears away anything drawn by the pen or stamped from the stage.
stamp	No	Draws or stamps the image of a sprite onto the stage.
pen down	No	Places the pen in a down position, allowing drawing operations to occur as the pen is moved around the stage.
pen up	No	Disables drawing operations by lifting the pen.
set pen color to ■	No	Specifies the color to be used when drawing.
change pen color by 10	No	Changes the color used when drawing by a specified amount.
set pen color to 0	No	Specifies the color to be used when drawing based on a numeric range in which 0 is red (at the low end of the spectrum) and 100 equals blue (at the high end of the spectrum).
change pen shade by 10	No	Modifies the shading used when drawing by a specified amount.
set pen shade to 50	No	Specifies the shade to be used when drawing based on a numeric range in which 0 is the darkest possible shading and 100 represents the maximum possible amount of light.
change pen size by 1	No	Modifies the thickness of the pen based on a numeric increment.
set pen size to 1	No	Specifies the thickness or width of the pen used when drawing.

© 2014 Lifelong Kindergarten Group

You will learn more about pen blocks in Chapter 12, "Drawing Lines and Shapes."

Storing and Retrieving Data

Data blocks come in two subcategories: those that deal with variables and those used to create and manage lists. *Variables blocks* store and retrieve string and numeric values. You need to use variables to store data as your application execute. For example, if you create a game that challenges the player to try to guess a randomly generated number, you need to use a variable to store and refer back to this number.

Scratch 2.0 supports a new type of variable known as a *cloud variable*, which stores variables on Scratch servers in the Internet cloud, allowing you to save and retrieve data that can be accessed by all actively executing copies of the Scratch 2.0 project. This facilitates the creation of projects that do things like maintain a list of player high scores.

You can use variables in conjunction with conditional programming logic to control the execution of other code blocks. You can also use variables to control the repeated execution of code blocks embedded within code block loops. Variables blocks are colored orange. You can create and name custom variable blocks and assign them a starting value. You can also modify their values during script execution. Other code blocks can retrieve variable values and use them as input. The top five items in Table 3.5 outline all the code blocks that Scratch 2.0 provides for working with variables.

List blocks store and retrieve lists of associated data. List blocks are colored dark orange. A list is made up of one or more items, which work like variables except that when there is lots of data being stored, it is easier to work with lists to store and manage the data as a group rather than try to manage data collections as individual items.

Tip

Lists are sometimes referred to as single-dimensional arrays in other programming languages.

The bottom 10 items in Table 3.5 outline all the code blocks that Scratch 2.0 provides for working with lists.

Table 3.5 Scratch Variable Blocks and List Blocks

Block	Monitor	Description
☑ High Score	Yes	Retrieves the value assigned to a variable.
set High Score ▾ to 0	No	Assigns a value to a numeric variable.
change High Score ▾ by 1	No	Modifies the value assigned to a numeric value stored in a variable by the specified amount.
show variable High Score ▾	No	Displays a variable's stage monitor.
hide variable High Score ▾	No	Hides a variable's stage monitor.
☑ Top Scores	Yes	Retrieves a list's contents.
add thing to Top Scores ▾	No	Adds an item to the end of a list.
delete 1▾ of Top Scores ▾	No	Removes an item from a list.
insert thing at 1▾ of Top Scores ▾	No	Adds an item to a list at the specified location.
replace item 1▾ of Top Scores ▾ with thing	No	Replaces an item in a list based on the item's position within the list.
item 1▾ of Top Scores ▾	No	Retrieves an item based on its specified position within a list.
length of Top Scores ▾	No	Returns a value indicating how many items are stored in a list.
Top Scores ▾ contains thing	No	A condition that can be used to determine if a specified value is stored in a list.
show list Top Scores ▾	No	Displays a list monitor on the stage.
hide list Top Scores ▾	No	Hides a list monitor, preventing its display on the stage.

© 2014 Lifelong Kindergarten Group

You learn more about data blocks and how to work with variables and lists blocks in Chapter 7, "Storing and Retrieving Data."

Event-Driven Programming

Event blocks, which are brown, initiate the execution of scripts and send messages to other sprites, allowing sprites to synchronize their execution. Scratch 2.0 provides eight different event blocks. Event blocks that initiate script execution are hat blocks, whereas the blocks that send messages are stack blocks. Table 3.6 outlines all the code blocks that fit into this category.

Table 3.6   Scratch Control Blocks

Block	Monitor	Description
when [green flag] clicked	No	Executes the script to which it has been attached whenever the green Flag button is pressed.
when space key pressed	No	Executes the script to which it has been attached whenever a specified keyboard key is pressed.
when this sprite clicked	No	Executes the script to which it has been attached whenever the user clicks on the sprite to which the script belongs.
when backdrop switches to backdrop1	No	Executes the script to which it has been attached whenever a specified backdrop is switched to on the stage.
when loudness > 10	No	Executes the script to which it has been attached when the first specified value exceeds the second specified value.
when I receive message1	No	Executes the scripts to which it has been attached when a specified broadcast message is received.
broadcast message1	No	Sends a broadcast message to all sprites without pausing script execution.
broadcast message1 and wait	No	Sends a broadcast message to all sprites to trigger a predefined action and then pauses script execution, waiting until all sprites have completed their assigned action before allowing the script in which the block resides to continue executing.

You learn more about events blocks in Chapter 9, "Controlling Script Execution."

Implementing Looping and Conditional Logic

Control blocks, colored gold, are used to stop script execution, pause script execution, and conditionally execute other code blocks based on whether a tested condition evaluates as true. There are also control blocks that let you set up loops to repeatedly execute collections of embedded code blocks.

Scratch 2.0 provides several new code blocks that support the creation and management of clones. A *clone* is a temporary copy of a sprite that can be used to add instances of sprites to Scratch projects when they execute. Table 3.7 outlines all the code blocks that fit into this category.

Table 3.7   Scratch Control Blocks

Block	Monitor	Description
wait 1 secs	No	Pauses script execution for a specified number of seconds, after which the script resumes its execution.
repeat 10	No	Repeats the execution of all the code blocks embedded inside it a specified number of times.
forever	No	Repeatedly executes all the code blocks embedded inside it.
if then	No	Executes all the code blocks embedded within the control if the specified condition evaluates as true.
if then else	No	Executes the code blocks embedded in the top half of the control (between the If and Else) if the specified condition evaluates as true and executes all the code blocks embedded in the bottom half of the control (after Else) if the condition evaluates as false.
wait until	No	Pauses script execution until a specified condition becomes true.
repeat until	No	Repeats all the code blocks embedded inside it until a tested condition evaluates as true.

	No	Halts all script execution within all sprites, a specified script, or other scripts in a sprite.
`stop all ▼`		
`when I start as a clone`	No	Triggers script execution for a clone if one is created.
`create clone of myself ▼`	No	Creates a temporary duplication of a specified sprite.
`delete this clone`	No	Deletes the current clone.

You learn more about control blocks in Chapter 9, "Controlling Script Execution."

Sensing Sprite Location and Environmental Input

Sensing blocks, colored sky blue, determine the location of the mouse pointer, its distance from other sprites, and whether a sprite is touching another sprite. Table 3.8 outlines all the code blocks that fit into this category.

Table 3.8   Scratch Sensing Blocks

Block	Monitor	Description
`touching ▼ ?`	No	Retrieves a Boolean value of true or false depending on whether the sprite is touching a specified sprite, edge, or mouse pointer as selected from the block's pull-down menu.
`touching color ■ ?`	No	Retrieves a Boolean value of true or false depending on whether the sprite is touching a specified color.
`color ■ is touching ■ ?`	No	Retrieves a Boolean value of true or false depending on whether the first specified color inside the sprite is touching the second specified color on the backdrop or on another sprite.
`distance to ▼`	No	Retrieves a numeric value representing a sprite's distance from another sprite or from the mouse pointer.

Table 3.8   Scratch Sensing Blocks (*Continued*)

Block	Monitor	Description
ask What's your name? and wait	No	Displays a question in a speech bubble and displays an entry field prompting the user to enter keyboard input that is captured and stored in a variable named answer.
answer	Yes	Retrieves the value stored in a variable named answer, which is supplied by the last use of the ask and wait block.
key space pressed?	No	Retrieves a Boolean value of true or false depending on whether a specified key is pressed.
mouse down?	No	Retrieves a Boolean value of true or false depending on whether a mouse button is pressed.
mouse x	No	Retrieves the location of the mouse pointer on the X-axis.
mouse y	No	Retrieves the location of the mouse pointer on the Y-axis.
loudness	Yes	Retrieves a numeric value, from 1 to 100, representing the volume of the computer's microphone.
video motion on this sprite	Yes	Senses motion or direction in video supplied via a webcam.
turn video on	No	Turns video on and off.
set video transparency to 50 %	No	Specifies the amount of transparency of a video as a percentage value.
timer	Yes	Retrieves a numeric value representing the number of seconds that the timer has run.
reset timer	No	Resets the timer back to its default value of zero.
x position of Sprite1	No	Retrieves the property value (x position, y position, direction, customer #, and size of volume) for the backdrop of a specified sprite.

Block		Monitor	Description
`current minute ▾`		Yes	Retrieves the current year, month, date, day of week, hour, minute, or second.
`days since 2000`		No	Retrieves the number of days since 2000.
`username`		No	Retrieves the name of the person viewing the Scratch project.

You learn more about sensing blocks in Chapter 6, "Sensing Sprite Position and Controlling Environment Settings."

Working with Operators

Operator blocks perform arithmetic operations, generate random numbers, and compare numeric values to determine their relationship to one another. Operator blocks are green. There are operator blocks that can be used to round numeric values and to execute a host of mathematical functions, like determining the absolute value or the square root of a number. Table 3.9 outlines all the code blocks that fit into this category.

Table 3.9   Scratch Operator Blocks

Block	Monitor	Description
`○ + ○`	No	Adds two numbers and generates a result.
`○ - ○`	No	Subtracts one number from another and returns the result.
`○ * ○`	No	Multiplies two numbers and generates a result.
`○ / ○`	No	Divides one number into another and returns the result.
`pick random ① to ⑩`	No	Generates a random number within the specified range.
`▮ < ▮`	No	Returns a Boolean value of `true` or `false` depending on whether one number is less than another.

Table 3.9   Scratch Operator Blocks (*Continued*)

Block	Monitor	Description
	No	Returns a Boolean value of true or false depending on whether one number is equal to another.
	No	Returns a Boolean value of true or false depending on whether one number is greater than another.
	No	Returns a Boolean value of true or false depending on whether two separately evaluated conditions are both true.
	No	Returns a Boolean value of true or false depending on whether either of two separately evaluated conditions is true.
	No	Reverses the Boolean value from true to false or false to true.
	No	Concatenates or places two strings right next to one another.
	No	Retrieves a letter from a string based on its specified position within the string.
	No	Returns the numeric length of a string.
	No	Retrieves the remainder portion of a division operation between two numbers.
	No	Returns the nearest integer value for a specified number.
	No	Returns the result of the selected function (abs, sqrt, sin, cos, tan, asin, acos, atan, Ln, log, E^, and 10^) when applied to the specified number.

You learn more about operator blocks in Chapter 8, "Doing a Little Math."

Custom and Specialized Blocks

A new category of code blocks in Scratch 2.0 is more blocks. More blocks facilitate the creation of custom user-defined code blocks, which function as custom procedures within Scratch 2.0 projects. Procedures based on more blocks can receive and process data passed to them as arguments and reduce the size and complexity of scripts in Scratch 2.0 projects by allowing commonly performed programming logic to be grouped in a procedure that can be called on to execute whenever necessary.

There are two subcategories of more code blocks available in Scratch 2.0: one that facilitates the development of projects that interact with Scratch sensor boards, and another that lets you develop program code that works with the LEGO WeDo Robotics Kit. By default, neither of these subcategories is displayed. To make them visible, you must Shift-click on the Scratch 2.0 program editor's Edit menu. When you do, a number of hidden menu items is displayed, as shown in Figure 3.23.

Figure 3.23
Viewing hidden menu items.
© 2014 Lifelong Kindergarten Group

To enable the display of either the Sensor board blocks or LEGO WeDo blocks, all you have to do is click on the appropriate menu items to enable their display on the more blocks list.

Note

A *Scratch Board*, also known as a *PicoBoard*, is a special piece of hardware that you can purchase from www.sparkfun.com and attach to your computer. Once it's attached, you can use the sensor board to collect and process environment- and user-provided input. You learn how to programmatically interact with and control Scratch Boards in Appendix C, "Interacting with the Real World," on the companion website.

The LEGO WeDo Robotics kit (www.legoeducation.us/eng/categories/products/elementary/lego-education -wedo) is a construction set for young people that helps them learn the basic principles of robotic development. Using this kit, you can create robots and other sorts of creations equipped with a motor and sensors and then bring them to life by programming them with Scratch 2.0.

Table 3.10 outlines all the code blocks that fit into the more blocks category.

Table 3.10   Scratch More Blocks

Block	Monitor	Description
Restart_Game	No	A custom block or procedure created by clicking on the Make a Block button located on the more blocks palette, generating a dialog where the block is named and any arguments defined. The result is a define block with the procedure inside.
define Restart_Game	No	A hat block used to define a custom block.
sensor button pressed ?	Yes	Retrieves a Boolean value of true or false depending on whether a specified sensor is being pressed on a sensor board attached to the computer.
when button pressed	No	A specialized code block used to start the execution of a script when a specified event occurs on a sensor board attached to the computer.
slider sensor value	Yes	Retrieves the value being reported by one of the sensors on a Scratch sensor board.
turn motor on for ❶ secs	No	A specialized code block used to interact with a LEGO WeDo robotic kit and turn its motor for a specified number of seconds.
turn motor on	No	A specialized code block used to interact with a LEGO WeDo robotic kit and turn on its motor.

turn motor off	No	A specialized code block used to interact with a LEGO WeDo robotic kit and turn off its motor.
set motor power (100)	No	A specialized code block used to interact with a LEGO WeDo robotic kit and set its motor power.
set motor direction this way	No	A specialized code block used to interact with a LEGO WeDo robotic kit and set its motor direction.
when distance < (20)	No	A specialized code block used to interact with a LEGO WeDo robotic kit and start the execution of a script when distance is less than a specified value.
when tilt = (1)	No	A specialized code block used to interact with a LEGO WeDo robotic kit and start the execution of a script when the tilt equals a specified value.
distance	Yes	A specialized code block used to interact with a LEGO WeDo robotic kit and retrieve a value reporting the distance sensor value.
tilt	Yes	A specialized code block used to interact with a LEGO WeDo robotic kit and retrieve the tilt of a robot.

© 2014 Lifelong Kindergarten Group

You learn more about more blocks in Chapter 13, "Improving Code Organization."

GETTING HELP WITH CODE BLOCKS

In addition to bookmarking and referring back to the tables provided in this chapter to find out what a given code block does, you can view help information for any Scratch 2.0 code block by clicking on the Question Mark icon located on the Program Editor menu bar. Doing so turns the mouse pointer into a circular question mark, allowing you to then click on the code block that you want to learn about, as demonstrated in Figure 3.24.

Figure 3.24
Accessing help for a given Scratch 2.0 code block.
© 2014 Lifelong Kindergarten Group

Once you have clicked on the code block you wish to know more about, the program editor opens the Tips window, displaying an explanation of the purpose of the code block as well as an example of its usage as demonstrated in Figure 3.25.

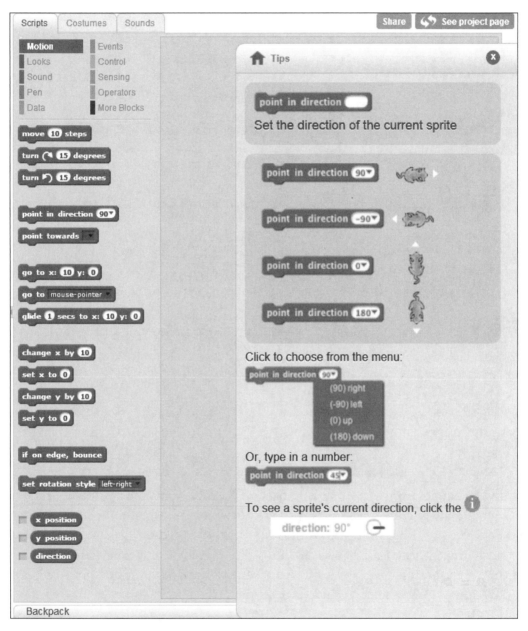

Figure 3.25
Viewing help for a Scratch 2.0 code block that has been added to the scripts area.
© 2014 Lifelong Kindergarten Group

CHAPTER 4

MR. WIGGLY'S DANCE— A QUICK SCRATCH PROJECT

So far, you have been presented with an overview of Scratch and its capabilities and learned how to work with its Project Editor. You have also been given an overview of all the code blocks that make up the Scratch programming language and learned the basic steps involved in creating Scratch applications. Now that you are more familiar with Scratch and its key components, let's put this new knowledge to use by creating a new Scratch application project, examining in detail the steps involved in creating and executing Scratch applications.

The topics covered in this chapter include

- A review of the programming concepts that Scratch can teach you
- A detailed overview of how to build Scratch applications

PROGRAMMING WITH SCRATCH

As a beginner's programming language, Scratch teaches you a number of critical programming concepts that you will be able to later rely on should you decide to make the jump to other more traditional and industrial-strength programming languages like Microsoft Visual Basic, C++, and JavaScript. The programming concepts that you can learn from Scratch include

- **Sequential processing.** This involves the processing of application code blocks, in the order that they are laid about, starting at the beginning of a script and continuing to the end.

- **Conditional programming logic.** This involves the conditional execution of code blocks based on data collected during application execution.

- **Use of variables and lists.** This involves the storage, retrieval, and modification of data during application execution.

- **Iterative processing.** This involves the repeated execution of code blocks to process large amounts of information or to control the repeated execution of code blocks required to direct the execution of a game or application.

- **Boolean logic.** This involves the application of programming logic that executes based on the analysis of `true`/`false` data provided by Scratch during program execution.

- **Interface design.** This involves the development of user-friendly and intuitive application stage layout, making it easy for users to interact with applications.

- **Program synchronization.** This involves the passage and receipt of messages between application scripts for coordinating the execution of different parts of an application.

- **Procedural programming.** This involves the organization of commonly used pieces of program code into callable units allowing for reduced program size and better program organization.

- **Event handling.** This involves the initiation of script execution based on the occurrence of predefined events, such as the pressing of keyboard keys, the pressing of the green Flag button, or the receipt of a synchronization message.

- **Application and game development.** This involves the creation of different types of computer application projects.

- **Sprite programming.** This involves the use of sprites as the basis for developing graphical programs.

- **Application troubleshooting.** This involves the identification, location, and elimination of programming errors, or bugs, that prevent applications from executing as they are supposed to.

You will learn more about each of these programming concepts as you make your way through the remainder of this book.

Note

As powerful and fun as Scratch is, there are some programming concepts that it does not teach. These concepts include the ability to process file input and output and the ability to support advanced object-oriented programming techniques. However, as a first-time programmer, these concepts can be challenging to learn and, by omitting them, the developers of Scratch have produced a streamlined yet powerful learning environment, which will prepare you to later make the jump to programming languages that support these advanced programming concepts.

CREATING THE MR. WIGGLY'S DANCE APPLICATION

The rest of this chapter is dedicated to leading you through the development of the Mr. Wiggly's Dance application. In this Scratch application, a comical cartoonish character named Mr. Wiggly dances around the stage to music, as demonstrated in Figure 4.1.

Figure 4.1

Mr. Wiggly practices his dance moves, dancing back and forth across the stage.

© 2014 Lifelong Kindergarten Group

Because Mr. Wiggly is bashful, his skin changes color as he dances, as demonstrated in Figure 4.2. Although not immediately obvious when viewed in black and white, if you compare the color of Mr. Wiggly in Figures 4.1 and 4.2, you will notice that he has definitely begun to blush, betraying his discomfort at dancing in front of an audience.

Figure 4.2
The bashful Mr. Wiggly's skin color changes as he dances.
© 2014 Lifelong Kindergarten Group

At the end of each dance, Mr. Wiggly pauses for a moment to reflect on how things are going before deciding to keep on dancing, as demonstrated in Figure 4.3.

Figure 4.3
Mr. Wiggly pauses at the end of each dance only to decide to keep dancing.
© 2014 Lifelong Kindergarten Group

You can create the Mr. Wiggly's Dance application project by following a series of steps, as outlined here:

1. Create a new Scratch application project.

2. Add a stage backdrop.

3. Add and remove sprites to and from the project.

4. Import a music file into the application.

5. Script audio playback.

6. Add the programming logic required to make Mr. Wiggly dance.

7. Test the execution of your new project.

Since this book has yet to provide a detailed explanation of how to work with all the Scratch code blocks used in this application project, brief explanations are provided. You learn the ins and out of programming with code blocks in Chapters 5 through 13. As you make your way through each of the steps in this project, try to keep your focus on the overall process being followed, and do not get caught up in the specifics. Later, once you have finished reviewing Chapters 5 through 13, you can always return and review this project again and clear up any questions you may have.

Step 1: Creating a New Scratch Project

The first step in creating a Scratch project is to start Scratch by loading the Scratch 2.0 website into your web browser (http://scratch.mit.edu) and then clicking on the Create button. When Scratch is loaded, the program editor automatically creates a new project. If, on the other hand, Scratch has already been started and you have been working with it for a while, you can create and start a new Scratch application project by clicking on the File button located on the Scratch menu bar and then clicking on New. In response, a new project is opened in the Project Editor, as shown in Figure 4.4.

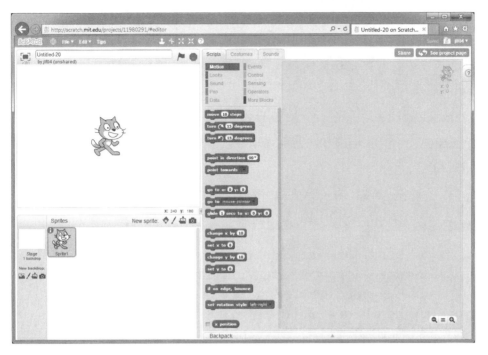

Figure 4.4

New Scratch application projects come supplied with a single sprite.

© 2014 Lifelong Kindergarten Group

New Scratch projects come equipped with a single sprite with two costumes representing a cat. You can choose to incorporate this sprite into your application or remove it.

Step 2: Adding a Backdrop to the Stage

With your new Scratch application project now created, it is time to get to work. Let's begin by adding a suitable backdrop to the stage to help set the mood of the application. Backdrops are associated with the stage, so to add a backdrop to your application, you must click on the blank stage thumbnail located in the sprite list. Once selected, the stage thumbnail is highlighted with a blue outline, as shown in Figure 4.5.

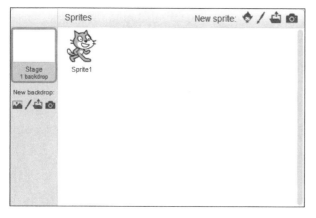

Figure 4.5
Selected thumbnails in the sprite list are highlighted with a blue outline.
© 2014 Lifelong Kindergarten Group

Once you have selected the stage thumbnail, you can modify its backdrop by clicking on the Backdrops tab located at the top of the scripts area. When you do so, the currently assigned stage backdrop is displayed, as shown in Figure 4.6.

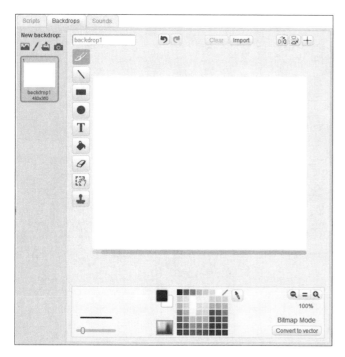

Figure 4.6
The Backdrop tab lets you create, import, edit, and rename backdrops.
© 2014 Lifelong Kindergarten Group

To replace the currently assigned blank backdrop with something more interesting, click on the Choose Backdrop from Library icon. This opens the Backdrop window. Once the window is opened, click on the link for Indoors, located on the left side of the window, select the chalkboard thumbnail, as shown in Figure 4.7, and click on the OK button.

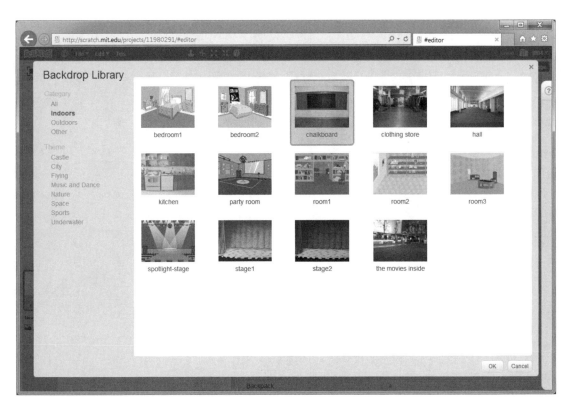

Figure 4.7
Importing a new backdrop into your Scratch application project.
© 2014 Lifelong Kindergarten Group

Once imported, the new backdrop is added to the application's current list of backdrop files, as shown in Figure 4.8. As you can see, the thumbnail is automatically assigned a name and a number.

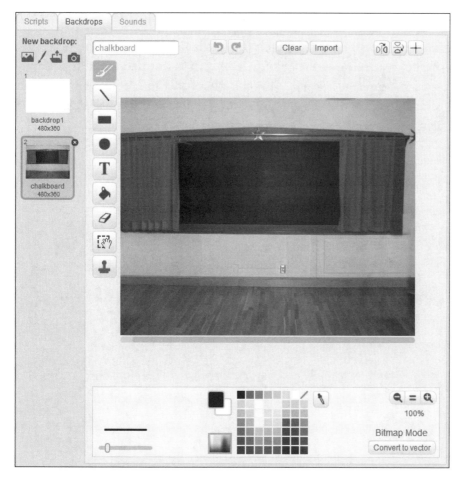

Figure 4.8
Scratch applications can have any number of backdrops and can switch between them during execution.
© 2014 Lifelong Kindergarten Group

Since this application requires only one backdrop, you can remove the default blank backdrop, named `backdrop1`, from your project by selecting its thumbnail and then clicking on the small Delete icon, which is on the upper-left side of the thumbnail.

Tip

Removing backdrops, costumes, and sound files no longer needed by your Scratch applications reduces their size. There is a 50MB project size limit at this site. Graphic and audio files tend to be relatively large, so removing any that you do not need can have a significant impact on the size of your applications.

Step 3: Adding and Removing Sprites

The next step in the development of this Scratch project is to add a sprite representing Mr. Wiggly to the project and remove the cat sprite, which is not needed in this application. To add the sprite representing Mr. Wiggly, click on the Choose Sprite from Library icon, as shown in Figure 4.9. This icon is the far left icon that makes up the collection of new sprite icons, located at the top-right corner of the sprite list.

Figure 4.9

Click on the Choose Sprite from Library icon to access a collection of ready-made sprites.

© 2014 Lifelong Kindergarten Group

Scratch provides ready access to all kinds of sprites, organized into the following five categories:

- Animals
- Fantasy
- People
- Things
- Transportation

The sprite that you want to use to represent Mr. Wiggly is located in the Animals category. Open the Animals collection and then scroll down until you locate the Monkey2 sprite, as shown in Figure 4.10.

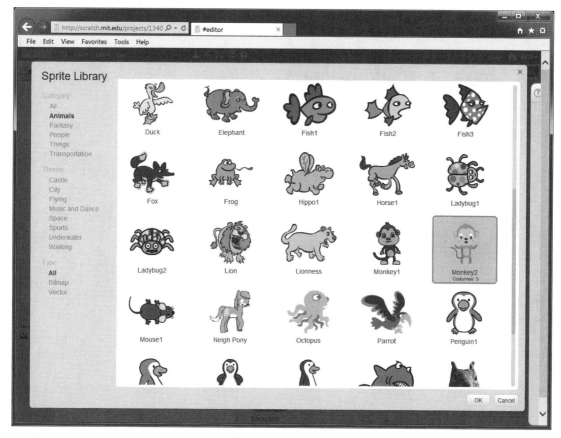

Figure 4.10

Selecting the sprite that will be used to represent Mr. Wiggly.

Select the Monkey2 sprite by clicking on it, and then click on the OK button. The Sprite Library window closes, and the new sprite is added to the middle of the stage, as shown in Figure 4.11.

Figure 4.11
A thumbnail representing the sprite is added to the sprite list.
© 2014 Lifelong Kindergarten Group

When contrasted against the stage's backdrop, Mr. Wiggly's default placement in the middle of the stage makes it look like he is floating on air. To put things into proper perspective, drag and drop Mr. Wiggly about one inch lower down the stage, so that it looks like he is standing on the floor.

Since the Mr. Wiggly's Dance application does not need the default cat sprite, go ahead and remove this sprite from the application project by selecting the Delete button on the Scratch toolbar and then clicking on the thumbnail for the cat located in the sprite list.

Tip

You can also remove the cat sprite from the application by Shift-clicking on its thumbnail in the sprite list and then selecting Delete from the pop-up menu that is displayed.

Step 4: Adding Mr. Wiggly's Music

Now that you have taken care of the sprites that the application needs, it is time to import the sound file. To do this, click on the thumbnail representing the stage in the sprite list, and then click on the Sounds tab in the scripts area. In response, Scratch displays all the sound files belonging to the stage. By default, the stage and every sprite in a Scratch application is assigned a sound file named pop, as shown in Figure 4.12.

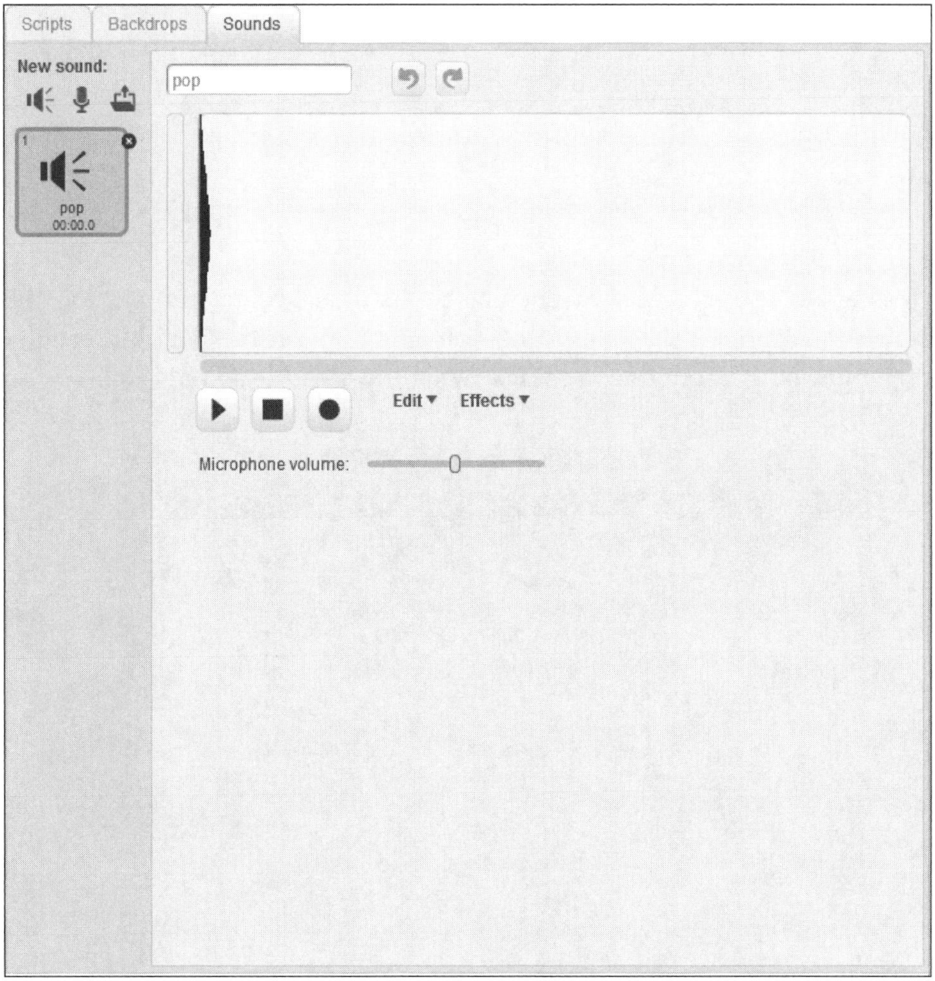

Figure 4.12

The stage and all sprites supplied by Scratch come equipped with the same sound file.

© 2014 Lifelong Kindergarten Group

Scratch provides ready access to all kinds of prerecorded audio files. The name of the sound file that Mr. Wiggly will dance to is eggs. To add this file to the sprite, click on the Choose Sound from Library icon located at the upper-left side of the Sound Editor. In response, Scratch displays the Sound Library window. This window contains eight categories of sounds by default, listed next, and is where Scratch stores its audio files.

- Animal
- Effects
- Electronic
- Human
- Instruments
- Music Loops
- Percussion
- Vocals

Drill down into the Music Loops folder by clicking on its link. Locate and click on the eggs file, as shown in Figure 4.13. If you want, you can click on the Play button displayed just to the right of the Sound icon to hear what the eggs file sounds like.

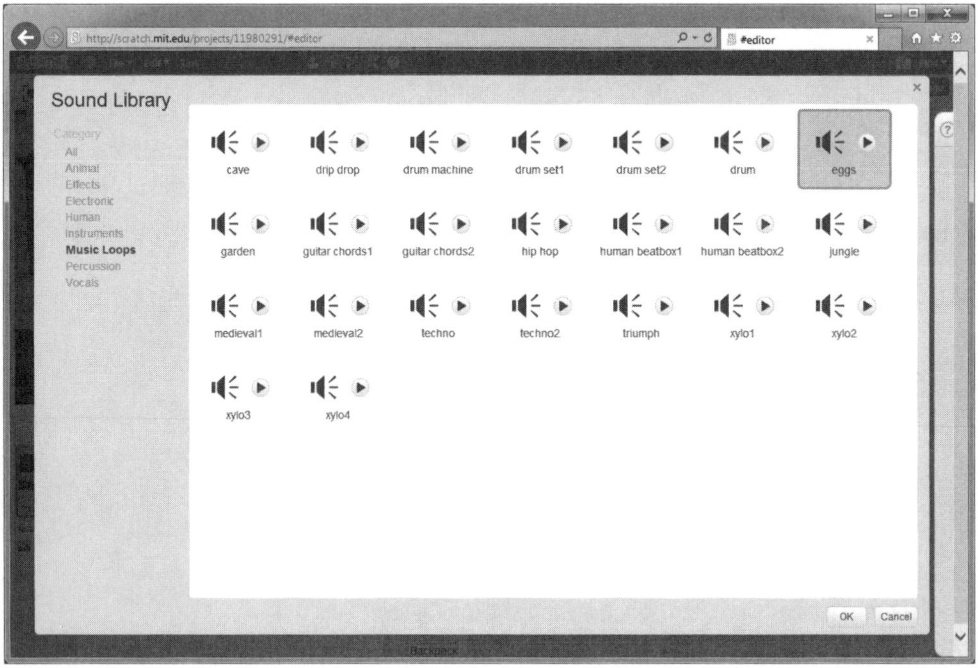

Figure 4.13

Importing a sound file into a Scratch application project.

© 2014 Lifelong Kindergarten Group

Click on the OK button to import the sound file into your application project, as shown in Figure 4.14. Note that for each sound file, a number of pieces of information are displayed. You can see the name of the file and the length of time that it takes to play the file. You can also see a graphical depiction for the currently selected sound. Note that the eggs sound file takes 15.2 seconds to play. You need to remember this information a little later when programming the playback of this sound file.

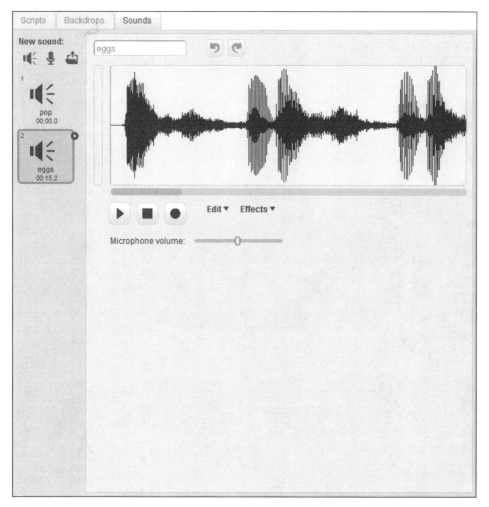

Figure 4.14

You can add any number of sound files to a sprite.

© 2014 Lifelong Kindergarten Group

This application does not need the default pop sound file; therefore, you can delete it by selecting and then clicking on the small Delete icon located at the upper-right side of the Sound thumbnail.

Step 5: Playing the Dance Music

It is time to begin putting together the program code logic required to make your new application work. In total, you need to create two scripts for this project: one for the stage and another for the sprite representing Mr. Wiggly. The script belonging to the stage will be made up of code blocks that are responsible for playing the application's background music. The script belonging to the sprite will contain the programming logic required to make Mr. Wiggly dance.

Begin by clicking on the Scripts tab located at the center-top of the program editor. Next, select the stage's thumbnail in the sprite list. This allows you to begin developing the state's script. To do so, click on the Events category in the blocks palette and then drag and drop an instance of the `when green flag clicked` block onto the scripts area, as demonstrated in Figure 4.15. This hat code block automatically executes the script to which it is attached whenever the green Flag button is clicked.

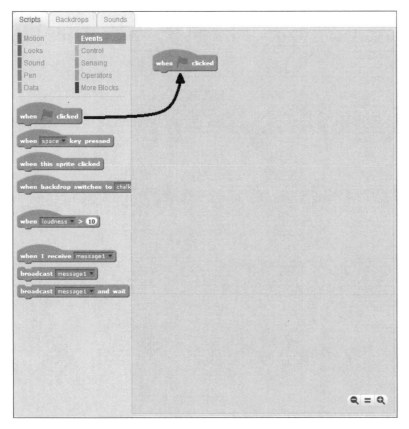

Figure 4.15

This block is used to automatically execute the script whenever the green Flag button is clicked.

Since the application's background music is supposed to be played over and over again for as long as the application runs, you need to set up a loop that repeatedly plays the sound file. To set this up, click on the Control category in the blocks palette and drag and drop an instance of the forever code block to the scripts area, attaching it to the bottom of the when green flag clicked block, as shown here.

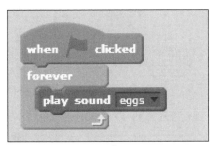

© 2014 Cengage Learning®

Now that you have the loop set up, click on the Sound category in the blocks palette and then drag and drop an instance of the play sound code block onto the scripts area, embedding it inside the forever code block. Notice that the play sound code block has already been configured to play the eggs sound, which makes sense given that it is the only sound that is currently assigned to the stage. At this point, the script that you are developing should look like the example shown here.

Note

Scratch automatically populates the play sound code block with a list of all the sound files that you added previously to the stage, making it easy for you to access them when working with sound code blocks.

© 2014 Cengage Learning®

At this point, you only need to add one last code block to the script to finish it. To do so, click on the Control category in the blocks palette and then drag and drop an instance of the `wait secs` code block over the scripts area, inserting it inside the `forever` code block, immediately following the `play sound` block. Next, overtype the `wait secs` block's default value of 1 with a new value of 15.2, as shown here.

© 2014 Cengage Learning®

The `wait secs` block is needed to pause the loop for 15.2 seconds, allowing for the complete playback of the sound file, before the loop repeats and begins playing it again.

Note

Now that this script has been written, you can test it by double-clicking on it. In response, Scratch repeatedly plays back the sound file. Once you are convinced that everything is working correctly, click on the red Stop Everything button to halt the script's execution so that you can move on to the next step in the development of this application.

Note

In addition to playing an audio file using the combination of the `play sound` and `wait sec` code blocks shown in the previous figure, you can use the code block shown here, which does the same thing as these two code blocks.

© 2014 Cengage Learning®

Step 6: Making Mr. Wiggly Dance

Now that you have finished work on the stage's script, it is time to write the script that makes Mr. Wiggly dance. To do so, click on the thumbnail of the sprite representing Mr. Wiggly (in the sprite area). In response, Scratch should clear out the script's area so that you can begin script development for this sprite.

The first step in the development is to click on the Events category in the blocks palette and then drag and drop an instance of the when green flag clicked block onto the scripts area, as demonstrated here.

© 2014 Cengage Learning®

This hat code block automatically executes the script to which it is attached whenever the green Flag button is clicked.

In this application, Mr. Wiggly is supposed to dance over and over again without stopping (until the user stops running the application). To set this up, drag and drop an instance of the forever code block onto the scripts area and attach it to the bottom of the when green flag clicked block, as shown here.

© 2014 Cengage Learning®

Next, it is time to add a pair of code statements to move Mr. Wiggly 25 steps to the right and then pause for 2 seconds. This is accomplished by dragging and dropping the move steps and wait secs blocks to the scripts area, embedding them inside the forever code block, as shown here.

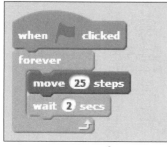

© 2014 Cengage Learning®

Note that, by default, the move steps block is set to 10. You need to replace this with a value of 25. You should also change the default value of 1 in the wait secs block to 2. Next, you need to add a series of move steps and wait secs code blocks, which, when executed, move Mr. Wiggly 25 steps to the right followed by 4 moves to the left at 25 steps each and then another 2 moves back toward the right. This is accomplished by adding and configuring 7 sets of a code block, as shown here.

© 2014 Cengage Learning®

To complete the development of this script, you need to add two looks blocks, as shown here.

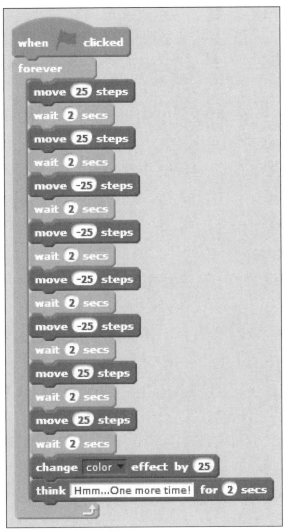

The change effect by code block modifies Mr. Wiggly's color each time the loop finishes its execution, simulating the feeling of embarrassment that Mr. Wiggly experiences when he dances. Lastly, the think for secs code block displays a text message in a pop-up bubble that shows Mr. Wiggly thinking about and then deciding to keep dancing.

Step 7: Testing the Execution of Your New Project

At this point, your copy of the Mr. Wiggly's Dance application should be complete. Click on the text field located at the top-left side of the Project Editor and type Mr. Wiggly's Dance as the name of your new project.

The previous edition of this book would have instructed you at this point to save your work. However, since Scratch 2.0 now runs in your web browser instead of as a standalone application on your desktop, you do not have to worry about saving your project. Scratch 2.0 takes care of that automatically for you.

Go ahead and run your new project and see how it works. Since both of the application's scripts are configured to execute whenever the green Flag button is pressed, all you have to do is click on that button and sit back and watch as the bashful Mr. Wiggly dances about the stage for your amusement.

CHAPTER 5

MOVING THINGS AROUND

This chapter is the first of nine chapters designed to teach you how to work with all the code blocks that make up the Scratch programming language. This chapter's focus is on demonstrating how to work with motion code blocks. Using these code blocks, you can create Scratch applications that can move sprites around the stage, rotate sprites, point them in different directions, change sprite location, detect collisions with the edge of the stage, and report on a sprite's direction and coordinates. This chapter also introduces you to Scratch cards as a means for learning how to perform different types of tasks. You also learn how to create a new virtual fish tank application.

The major topics covered in this chapter include

- Moving and rotating sprites
- Changing sprite direction and location
- Changing sprite location and detecting collisions with the edge of the stage
- Retrieving and reporting information about a sprite's coordinates and direction

WORKING WITH MOTION CODE BLOCKS

To move sprites around the stage when your Scratch applications execute, you need to learn how to work with motion code blocks. As previously stated, motion blocks control sprite placement, direction, rotation, and movement. In total, Scratch provides access to 17 different motion blocks, which you can work with by clicking on the Motion category located at the top of the blocks palette and then dragging and dropping motion blocks onto the scripts area, where you can configure them and use them in creating scripts.

If you look closely at the various motion blocks, you notice that Scratch organizes them into six subgroupings, each of which is separated by a blank space in the blocks palette. These subgroupings include

- Motion blocks that move and rotate sprites
- Motion blocks that point sprites in different directions or toward different objects
- Motion blocks that change a sprite's location and control whether a sprite jumps to its new location or glides to it
- Motion blocks that change a sprite location by setting or modifying the value of its X-axis and Y-axis coordinates
- Motion blocks that control a sprite's movement when it touches the edges of the stage and that set its rotation style
- Motion blocks that report on a sprite's position and direction

Examples of how to work with the motion code blocks in each of these subgroups are provided throughout the rest of this chapter.

MOVING AND ROTATING SPRITES

Scratch 2.0 provides access to three motion blocks that move sprites and rotate them on their axis. These code blocks are shown in Figure 5.1.

Figure 5.1
These control blocks are designed to give you control over the relative movement and rotation of sprites.
© 2014 Lifelong Kindergarten Group

The first of these blocks allows you to specify the number of steps that a sprite should be moved on the stage (in whatever direction the sprite is currently pointing). By default, the code block specifies a value of 10. However, you can change this value to suit your needs. You can even enter a negative value to move the sprite in the opposite direction to what it is pointing.

In addition, you can drag and drop any numeric based reporter block you want into this code block's entry field when specifying a value. The next two code blocks provide the ability to rotate a sprite on its axis, clockwise and counterclockwise, as indicated by the direction of the arrow displayed on the blocks.

The following sample script demonstrates how to use the first two blocks to move a sprite around the stage in a clockwise manner.

© 2014 Cengage Learning®

This script executes whenever the green Flag button is clicked. Once this event has occurred, four pairs of motion code blocks are executed at one-second intervals. This application uses the default cat sprite that is supplied as part of every new Scratch project. To create and test your own copy of the application, create a new Scratch application, click on the thumbnail of the cat sprite, and drag it to the upper-left corner of the stage. Next, click on the Costumes tab, and then click on the image of the cat in the middle of the drawing canvas. An enclosing square appears around the costume. Click on the right corner of the box, hold down the left mouse button, and drag the mouse upward, shrinking the size of the costume by 50 percent before letting go of the mouse button. The size of the sprite on the stage changes accordingly. Make sure that the sprite's rotational center remains in the middle of its graphics image by clicking on the Set Costume Center button and then clicking on the center position within the costume in the drawing canvas.

The first motion block in the script moves the sprite 400 steps. Since the cat, by default, is pointed 90 degrees to the left, this moves the sprite from the upper-left corner of the stage to the upper-right corner of the stage. The second motion block in the script rotates the sprite 90 degrees to the right. The next pair of motion blocks moves the sprite down to the bottom-right corner of the stage and rotates it by another 90 degrees. The third pair of motion blocks moves the sprite to the bottom-left corner of the stage and rotates it again. Finally, the last pair of motion blocks moves it back to the upper-left corner of the stage and rotates it by another 90 degrees, putting the sprite back in its starting position.

Note

All the sprites that Scratch supplies have a predefined rotation axis. You can change the rotation axis for these sprites and set the rotation point for new sprites that you create or import into Scratch by editing the sprite using Scratch's Paint Editor program and then specifying a new rotation axis using the program's Set costume center control.

A sprite's rotation is also affected by the selection of one of the three rotation icons, visible when viewing sprite properties. To view these properties, select the sprite in the sprite list and then click on the blue *i* icon that is displayed in the sprite thumbnail's upper-left corner. Once displayed, you can see and change the sprite's rotation setting. You will see that, by default, the cat sprite is configured to rotate as needed up to 360 degree when the sprite's direction is changed. As a result, when the script changes the sprite's rotation by 90 degrees, the image of the cat rotates as well.

Figure 5.2 demonstrates the movements of the cat sprite as it moves from corner to corner, clockwise around the screen.

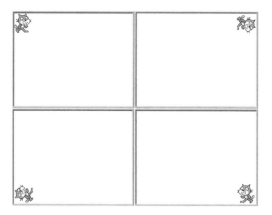

Figure 5.2
The cat's direction is changed by 90 degrees immediately after each move, readying it for its next move.
© 2014 Lifelong Kindergarten Group

If you want, you can modify the script to move the sprite around the stage in a counterclockwise direction by modifying it, as demonstrated here.

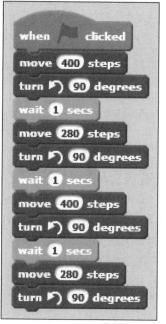

© 2014 Cengage Learning®

Before testing the execution of the project, drag the sprite down from the upper-left corner of the stage down to the lower-left side of the stage. Then click on the green Flag icon and watch as the cat moves in the opposite pattern around the stage.

SETTING SPRITE DIRECTION

Scratch provides access to two motion blocks that can point a sprite in a specified direction or point a sprite toward the mouse pointer or a specified sprite. These code blocks are shown in Figure 5.3.

Figure 5.3
You can use these code blocks to point a sprite toward a specified direction or object.
© 2014 Lifelong Kindergarten Group

The first of these blocks allows you to point a sprite in a particular direction as specified by the assignment of a numeric value representing the number of degrees that the sprite should be turned. You can select a value of 0 = up, 90 = right, -90 = left, 180 = down from the block's drop-down list, or you can type in an integer value in the range of 0 to 360. For example, the following script demonstrates how to rotate a sprite 360 degrees, 90 degrees at a time, at one-second intervals.

```
when        clicked
point in direction  90▾
wait  1  secs
point in direction  180▾
wait  1  secs
point in direction  270▾
wait  1  secs
point in direction  360▾
wait  1  secs
point in direction  90▾
wait  1  secs
```

© 2014 Cengage Learning®

This example uses the default cat sprite. Figure 5.4 shows an example of the four directions that the sprite turns when the script is executed. Note that for this example to work, the sprite must be set to rotate 360 degrees.

Figure 5.4
An example of the four possible directions that the point in direction code block can point a sprite.
© 2014 Lifelong Kindergarten Group

The second motion block shown in Figure 5.3 lets you point a sprite toward either the mouse pointer or another sprite, as demonstrated in the following script.

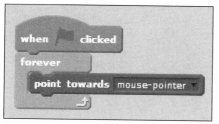

In this example, the sprite is continuously repositioned so that it points toward the mouse pointer. Therefore, whenever the mouse pointer is moved around the stage, the image of the cat follows, as demonstrated in Figure 5.5.

Figure 5.5

The cat rotates as necessary to continue facing the mouse pointer.

Note

For the sprite shown in Figure 5.5 to continuously reposition itself, the motion block must be embedded within a control block that sets up a loop. It must repeatedly execute the motion block, allowing it to react every time the mouse pointer is moved.

REPOSITIONING A SPRITE

Scratch provides access to three motion blocks that move a sprite to a specified coordinate location on the stage, move a sprite to the location currently occupied by the mouse pointer or another sprite, or move a sprite to a specified coordinate position over a specified number of seconds. These code blocks are shown in Figure 5.6.

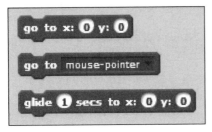

Figure 5.6
You can use these code blocks to move a sprite to a specific location.
© 2014 Lifelong Kindergarten Group

The first of these three motion blocks allows you to reposition a sprite to any location on the stage by specifying X-axis and Y-axis coordinates for the sprite. For example, the following script demonstrates how to reposition a sprite in the middle of the stage, pointing it in a 90-degree direction. The ability to do this might come in handy in an arcade-style game where the player's spaceship collides with another object and is destroyed and a new instance of the ship needs to be placed in the center of the play area to start a new round of play.

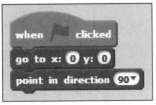

© 2014 Cengage Learning®

The following script demonstrates how to move a sprite to the location on the stage currently occupied by the mouse pointer.

© 2014 Cengage Learning®

Figure 5.7 shows an example of the output that is generated when this script is run. If you look closely, you see that in each of the three examples, the cat sprite remains positioned directly under the mouse pointer no matter where it is moved on the stage.

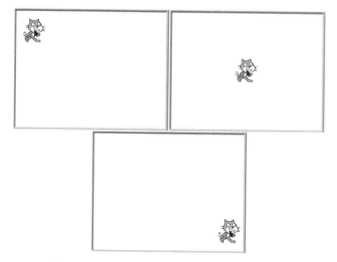

Figure 5.7

As this figure demonstrates, the sprite automatically moves around the stage following the mouse pointer.

© 2014 Lifelong Kindergarten Group

This next script demonstrates how to reposition a sprite to a specific location on the stage. Instead of simply making the sprite appear at a specified location, as demonstrated in the last two examples, this script repositions the sprite by moving or gliding to its new position in a smooth motion.

```
when [flag] clicked
forever
    glide 1 secs to x: -200 y: 140
    wait 2 secs
    glide 1 secs to x: 200 y: -140
```

© 2014 Cengage Learning®

CHANGING SPRITE COORDINATES

Scratch provides four motion blocks that modify the location of a sprite on the stage by either assigning it new coordinates or changing the sprite's coordinates by incrementing or decrementing their values. These code blocks are shown in Figure 5.8.

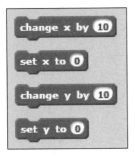

Figure 5.8
These code blocks provide the ability to modify a sprite's location by changing its coordinates.
© 2014 Lifelong Kindergarten Group

The following script demonstrates how to move a sprite across the stage in a series of eight steps. When first started, the script moves the sprite to the left side of the stage and then, using a loop, the sprite is moved by incrementing the value assigned to the X-axis coordinate by 50 and its Y-axis coordinate by –10 each time the loop repeats itself. As a result, the sprite is repeatedly repositioned and thus moved across the stage (in a descending angle over a period of eight seconds).

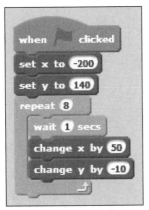

© 2014 Cengage Learning®

BOUNCING SPRITES AROUND THE STAGE AND CONTROLLING ROTATION STYLE

As a sprite is moved around the stage, it may eventually come into contact with one of the edges of the stage. Using the motion block shown next, you can instruct Scratch to bounce the sprite off the edge of the stage.

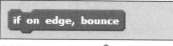

The following script demonstrates how to use this code block to bounce a sprite around the stage.

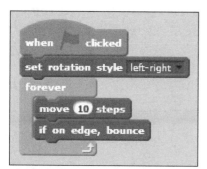

This script reverses the direction that a sprite is traveling whenever it collides with the edge of the stage. If you were to add this script to the cat sprite in a new application, the cat would move across the stage from side to side until you halted the application's execution.

As sprites move around the stage, you may find that you want to take control over how the sprite rotates when it bounces off the edge of the stage. Using the motion block shown next, you can instruct Scratch to rotate the sprite left-right, to rotate all around to flip the sprite vertically, or don't rotate.

The following example demonstrates how to limit a sprite's rotation to left and right as it makes contact with the edge of the stage.

KEEPING TRACK OF SPRITE COORDINATES AND DIRECTION

Scratch provides three motion (reporter) blocks that can be used to retrieve and display information regarding the value of the sprite's X- and Y-coordinates as well as the sprite's direction. These code blocks are shown in Figure 5.9.

Figure 5.9
These code blocks provide the ability to retrieve and display a sprite's coordinates and direction.
© 2014 Lifelong Kindergarten Group

Note

Scratch's stage coordinate system allows for a coordinate range of −240 to 240 on its X-axis and a coordinate range of 180 to −180 on its Y-axis.

To set up an example that demonstrates how to work with these reporter blocks, create a new Scratch application and add the following script to the default cat sprite.

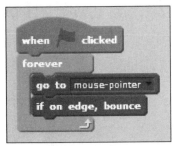

© 2014 Cengage Learning®

When executed, this script moves the cat sprite around the stage to wherever the mouse pointer is located, bouncing it off the edge of the stage when necessary. After adding the script, select each of the reporter blocks by clicking on the check box just to the left of each block in the blocks palette. Once you have done this, three monitors should be visible on the stage, as demonstrated in Figure 5.10.

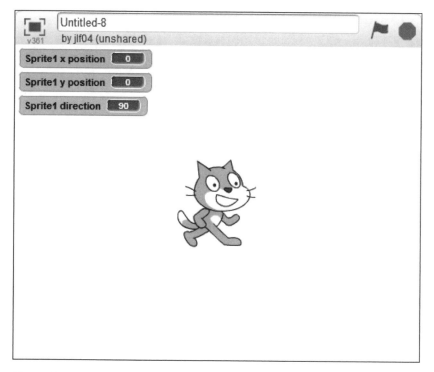

Figure 5.10
Displaying a sprite's coordinates and direction.
© 2014 Lifelong Kindergarten Group

Once you have set up the application's monitors, run the application, move the mouse pointer around the stage, and keep an eye on the values that the monitors report.

TAKING ADVANTAGE OF SCRATCH CARDS

One resource available to Scratch programmers is Scratch cards. *Scratch cards* are PDF files that you can print, cut out, glue together, and then use as a quick reference for performing certain tasks. You can download Scratch cards for free at http://scratch .mit.edu/help/cards/, as shown in Figure 5.11.

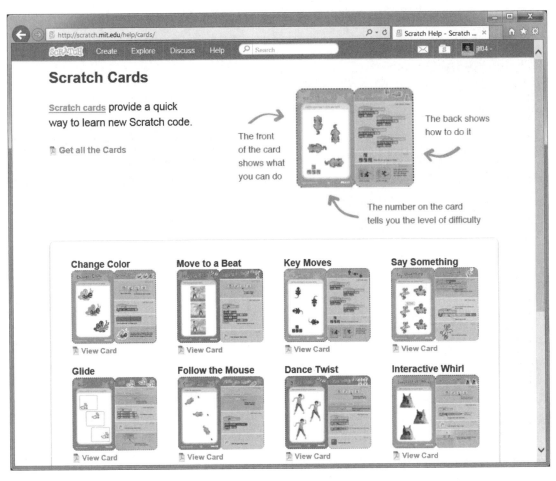

Figure 5.11
Scratch cards serve as quick reference for performing specific types of tasks.
© 2014 Lifelong Kindergarten Group

The front of each Scratch card identifies the type of task that the card is designed to show you how to perform, and the back of the card provides detailed instruction on how to perform the task. As of the writing of the second edition of this book, a dozen Scratch cards were available. The PDF files for each of these Scratch cards is descriptively named to identify the task that the card teaches you to perform. The list of available Scratch cards includes

- Change Color
- Move to a Beat
- Key Moves
- Say Something

- Glide
- Follow the Mouse
- Dance Twist
- Interactive Whirl
- Animate It
- Moving Animation
- Surprise Button
- Keep Score

Figure 5.12 shows what the PDF file for the Key Moves Scratch card looks like. As you can see, the left side of the Scratch card demonstrates the movement of the sprite, and the right side of the card provides an example of the code blocks needed to move the sprite in each of the four demonstrated directions. In addition, each Scratch card includes an extra tip that helps you further enhance the task being performed.

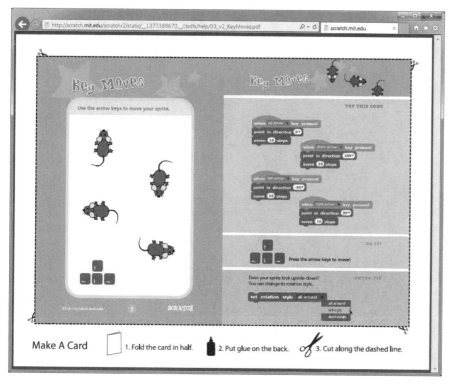

Figure 5.12

The Key Moves Scratch card demonstrates how to move a sprite around the stage using the keyboard arrow keys.

Note

There are five Scratch cards that provide information specific to moving sprites around the stage. These Scratch cards are briefly described here:

- **Key Moves.** Demonstrates how to move a sprite around the stage using keyboard keys.
- **Move to a Beat.** Demonstrates how to create an animated dance sequence that moves to a drum beat.
- **Moving Animation.** Demonstrates how to animate the movements of a sprite using an alternative series of costumes.
- **Glide.** Demonstrates how to move a sprite around the stage from one point to another in a smooth motion.
- **Follow the Mouse.** Demonstrates how to script the movement of a sprite so that it follows the movement of the mouse pointer on the stage.

CREATING THE VIRTUAL SCRATCH FISH TANK

The rest of this chapter is dedicated to leading you through the development of a virtual fish tank application. In this Scratch application, five sprites, representing a range of underwater creatures, busily swim around the fish tank, represented by a suitable backdrop, as demonstrated in Figure 5.13.

Figure 5.13
An example of the virtual fish tank application in action.
© 2014 Lifelong Kindergarten Group

This application will be created by following a series of steps, as outlined here:

1. Create a new Scratch application project.
2. Add a stage backdrop.
3. Add and remove sprites to and from the project.
4. Add a sound file into the application.
5. Add the programming logic required to play a backdrop sound effect.
6. Add the programming logic required to animate fish tank activity.
7. Save and execute your work.

Step 1: Creating a New Scratch Project

The first step in creating this Scratch project is to load the Scratch Project Editor in your browser and then click on Create to start a new Scratch application project. Alternatively, if you already have Scratch up and running, you can create a new project by clicking on the File menu and then selecting New.

Step 2: Adding a Backdrop to the Stage

Once you have a new application project ready to go, you can begin by adding a suitable backdrop to the stage that gives the virtual fish tank an appropriate look and feel. To set this up, click on the blank thumbnail representing the stage in the sprite list, and then click on the Choose Backdrop from Library icon located just under the stage thumbnail. Next, scroll down until you find the underwater3 backdrop. Select it, and then click on the OK button. Once the new backdrop has been added, go ahead and remove the blank stage backdrop from the application.

Step 3: Adding and Removing Sprites

The next step in the development of the virtual fish tank application is to add sprites to the application representing different marine life. Before doing this, remove the cat sprite from the application, since it is not needed. To do so, Shift-click on its thumbnail in the sprites list and select Delete from the pop-up menu that appears.

In total, you need to add five new sprites. To add the first sprite, click on the Choose Sprite from Library icon located at the top-left side of the sprite area. This opens the sprite Library window. Select the Animals category, scroll down and select the starfish sprite, and then click on the OK button. Next, click on the sprite's thumbnail in the sprites area, and then change the name assigned to the sprite to violet.

Using the same set of steps described earlier, add the following list of sprites to the application project, renaming each sprite as indicated in Table 5.1.

Table 5.1   Additional Sprites Used in the Fish Tank Project

Sprite Filename	Sprite Application Name
fish1	Purple
fish2	Yellow
fish3	Spotted
octopus	Squid

© 2014 Cengage Learning®

Once you have added all five sprites, move the sprites to random locations on the stage. Next, change the direction that each sprite moves by selecting each sprite one at a time and then clicking on the *i* icon, accessing sprite properties. From here, you can change the sprite's direction by repositioning the direction of the blue line displayed on the small circle, representing the sprite's direction. You should also set each sprite's rotation style to left-right.

Tip

To make the virtual fish tank more interesting, set up the fish and the octopus so that each moves in a different direction and angle.

Finally, if you have not already done so, remove the default sprite from the project. After all, there is no place for a kitten in a fish tank.

Step 4: Adding a Suitable Audio File to the Stage

Now that the application's backdrop and sprites have been added, it is time to add an audio file that, when played, gives the virtual fish tank a realistic feeling. Specifically, we'll add an audio file that makes bubble sounds when played. To accomplish this task, click on the thumbnail representing the stage in the sprite list, and then click on the Sounds tab in the scripts area. Next, click on the Choose Sound from Library icon to display sounds supplied with Scratch 2.0. Locate and double-click on the bubbles sound to add it to the stage.

Step 5: Playing the Audio File

Now it is time to add the programming logic needed to make your new application run. In total, you need to add six scripts to the project: one for the stage and one for each of the application's five sprites.

The script to be added to the stage is responsible for playing the background sound effect that makes the virtual fish tank sound like a real fish tank. To create it, click on the stage thumbnail located in the sprites area, and then select the Scripts tab located at the top of the scripts area. Next, add and configure the following code blocks exactly as shown here:

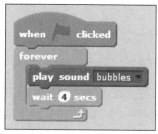

© 2014 Cengage Learning®

This script consists of a hat block that executes whenever the green Flag button is pressed. When this occurs, a loop is set up that repeatedly executes two blocks. The first code block is a sound block that plays the audio file you previously added to the stage. The second code block pauses script execution for four seconds to give Scratch time to finish playing the audio file, before allowing the loop to repeat and play it again.

Step 6: Animating the Swimming of the Fish

With the programming logic required to provide the application's background sound effect now in place, it is time to write the scripts to animate the movement of the fish and octopus. To set this up, you need to add a small script to each of the sprites, which provides the programming logic required to control the movement of the sprites as they move (or swim) around the fish tank.

Scripting the Movement of the Star Fish

Let's begin by automating the movement of the sprite named violet. Do so by clicking on the sprite's thumbnail and then creating the following script for it.

© 2014 Cengage Learning®

As you can see, this script is set up to begin executing the moment the user clicks on the green Flag button. It contains a control block that sets up a loop that repeats the execution of two embedded motion blocks. The first motion block moves the sprite in its current direction every time the loop repeats. The second motion block tells Scratch to bounce the sprite off the edge of the stage when reached. As a result, the sprite appears to swim around the fish tank from side to side and, depending on whether you have adjusted its direction as instructed at the end of Step 3, it moves up and down as well.

Scripting the Movement of the Purple Fish

Next, let's create a script that controls the movement of the purple fish. Rather than build this script from scratch, let's take a shortcut. With the script for the violet sprite (the starfish) currently displayed on the scripts area, drag and drop the script onto the thumbnail representing the purple sprite in the sprites list. This adds an exact copy of the script to the purple sprite, which you can then view and modify by clicking on the purple sprite's thumbnail.

To make things interesting, modify the number of steps that the purple sprite is moved from 1 to 2, as shown here.

© 2014 Cengage Learning®

Other than moving the purple fish at a little faster pace than the starfish, the programming logic that controls both sprites is identical. In fact, the programming for all the remaining fish and the octopus is identical, except for variances in the number of steps the sprites are moved.

Scripting the Movement of the Yellow Fish

Using drag and drop, add a copy of the purple sprite's script to the yellow sprite, and then modify it as shown here.

© 2014 Cengage Learning®

As you can see, the yellow sprite has been configured to move at the same pace as the violet sprite.

Scripting the Movement of the Spotted Fish

Once again, using drag and drop, add a copy of the yellow sprite's script to the spotted sprite, and then modify it as shown here.

© 2014 Cengage Learning®

This time the sprite has been configured so that it moves two steps at a time.

Scripting the Movement of the Octopus

Last but not least, drag and drop the script for the spotted sprite onto the sprite representing the octopus, and then modify it as shown here.

© 2014 Cengage Learning®

As you can see, this sprite has been configured to move slower than any of the other sprites, at just a half step at a time.

Step 7: Executing Your New Scratch Application

At this point, your copy of the virtual fish tank application should be complete and should look like the example shown in Figure 5.14.

Figure 5.14
The completed application consists of a backdrop, five sprites, and six scripts.
© 2014 Lifelong Kindergarten Group

If you have not done so yet, click on the text field located at the top of the stage and specify a name for your new Scratch project. You might also want to click on the See Project Page button so you can specify instructions and notes for your new project. When you're done, go ahead and run your new project. Since all the scripts in the application are configured to execute when the green Flag button is pressed, all you have to do is click on the green Flag button and then sit back and relax as you watch and listen to your virtual fish tank.

CHAPTER 6

SENSING SPRITE POSITION AND CONTROLLING ENVIRONMENTAL SETTINGS

To create many interactive computer applications, you need the ability to detect when certain things are happening. For example, in a car racing game, it would be important to be able to detect when two cars (sprites) bump into one another, and in a game that uses predefined keystrokes as input for controlling certain game functions, you need to be able to detect when those keys have been pressed. Scratch 2.0 provides the ability to detect or sense when things happen using sensing blocks. This chapter demonstrates how to work with various sensing blocks and guides you through the creation of a new Scratch 2.0 application: the Family Scrapbook.

The major topics covered in this chapter include learning how to

- Detect mouse pointer location and mouse button status
- Detect when keyboard keys are pressed
- Determine when a sprite collides with other objects on the stage
- Keep track of a sprite's distance from other objects and retrieve different sprite properties
- Work with a timer and detect the loudness of microphone input
- Prompt for and collect user input
- Collect and process video input
- Retrieve information about the current time and user's name

WORKING WITH SENSING CODE BLOCKS

An important capability needed by a graphical programming language that works with sprites is the ability to determine when certain things happen. For example, sprite-based applications typically need to know when sprites collide with one another or when the user presses certain keystrokes. This type of functionality is provided in Scratch 2.0 by sensing blocks.

Sensing blocks also determine the location of the mouse pointer and a sprite's distance from other sprites. Sensing blocks are colored sky blue. In total, Scratch 2.0 provides access to 20 different sensing blocks, which you can work with by clicking on the Sensing category located at the top of the blocks palette.

Scratch 2.0 organizes sensing blocks into eight subgroupings, each of which is separated by a blank space in the blocks palette. These subgroupings include

- Sensing blocks that determine whether a sprite has made contact with the mouse pointer, another sprite, or the edge of the stage; whether a sprite or color is touching another color; or what the sprite's distance is from the mouse pointer or another sprite

- Sensing blocks that prompt the user for input and which retrieve user input

- Sensing blocks that determine when specified keyboard keys have been pressed, when the mouse button has been pressed, and that retrieve the mouse's X- and Y-coordinates

- A sensing block that reports how loud audio input coming from the computer's microphone is

- Sensing blocks that collect and process input received from the computer's video camera

- Sensing blocks that provide access to a built-in timer that can be used to control the timing of application activity

- A sensing block that retrieves a property value (X position, Y position, direction, costume #, size, or volume) for the stage or a specified sprite

- Sensing blocks that retrieve the current time, number of days since the year 2000, and the user's name

Examples of how to work with each of the sensing code blocks described in this list are provided throughout the rest of this chapter.

DETECTING SPRITE COLLISIONS AND DISTANCE FROM OBJECTS

One key programming requirement of many computer games is the ability to determine when a sprite collides or comes within a certain distance of another sprite, the edge of the screen, or the mouse pointer. Scratch 2.0 provides the ability to perform collision detection and to determine distance using the four sensing blocks shown in Figure 6.1.

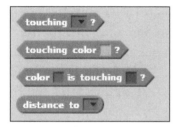

Figure 6.1

You can use these sensing blocks to look for collisions and to determine distance.

You can use the first code block shown in Figure 6.1 to determine when a sprite makes contact with a specified sprite, the edge of the stage, or the mouse pointer. The list of objects that this code block can detect is accessible in the code block's drop-down list. As an example of how to work with this code block, create a new Scratch 2.0 project. Remove the default cat sprite and then create a new sprite by clicking on the Paint New Sprite icon located in the top-right corner of the sprite list. Then create a new sprite made up of a single dot in the center of the canvas area.

Tip

When painting the dot needed for this sprite, all you have to do is click once in the center of the crosshairs that you see displayed in the center of the canvas area.

Next, click on the Scripts tab, and then create the script shown here.

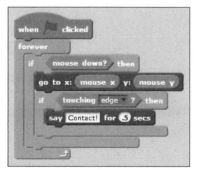

This script demonstrates how to determine when a sprite comes into contact with the edge of the stage. Note that this script includes four sensing blocks, each of which is embedded inside other code blocks. To embed the sensing blocks, drag and drop them from the blocks palette onto the appropriate code block. As you drag a sensing block close to the input area of another code block, a halo appears, indicating that the sensing blocks can be dropped onto the block.

This script executes whenever the green Flag button is clicked and uses a `forever` block to set up a loop that repeatedly executes all embedded code blocks. Within the loop, you'll find a conditional `if` block that executes embedded statements when the mouse's left button is being pressed. When this is the case, a motion block is used to make the application's sprite follow the mouse pointer around the stage. A second sensing code block is used within another conditional `if` code block to detect when the sprite makes contact with the edge of the stage. When this occurs, a looks code block is executed, displaying a text message in a voice bubble.

Figure 6.2 demonstrates the output that is displayed when you run the application with this new script and move the mouse pointer to one of the edges of the stage.

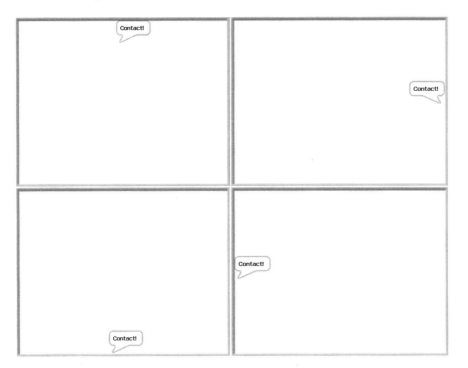

Figure 6.2
An example of the text that is displayed whenever the sprite makes contact with the edge of the stage.

Next, let's take a look at an example of how to work with the second sensing block shown in Figure 6.1. You can use this code block to detect when a sprite makes contact with a specific color on the stage. To see a working example of how to work with this code block, create a new Scratch 2.0 application. Remove the default sprite from the project, and then create and add a new sprite in the shape of a red rectangle (using the Paint Editor), placing it in the middle of the stage. Next, add a second sprite to the application by clicking on the Choose Sprite from Library icon, opening the Sprite Library window. Select the Fantasy category, locate and select the dragon sprite, and then click on OK. The stage for your new application should now look like the example shown in Figure 6.3.

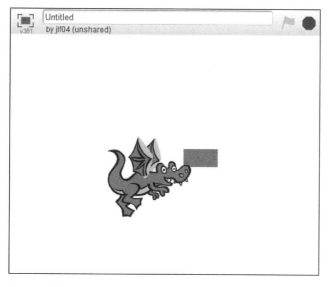

Figure 6.3

This red square demonstrates the ability to detect a collision with a specific color on the stage.

© 2014 Lifelong Kindergarten Group

Click on the thumbnail for the dragon sprite and then click on the Sound tab. Click on the Choose Sound from Library icon, and then scroll down and double-click on the screech sound to add it to the sprite. Add the following script to the sprite representing the dragon. Next, click on the square color area within the touching color ? code block, and then click on the red sprite. This sets the colored square in the code block to precisely match the color of the red sprite. When executed, this script plays an audio file whenever the sprite is moved into contact with the red square in the center of the stage.

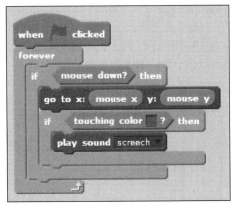

At this point, you should have everything set up and ready to run. Go ahead and run the application. Then press and hold the left mouse button and move the mouse pointer on and off the red rectangle in the middle of the stage, and listen for the audio file to be played.

Using the previous code block, you can set up an application to detect a collision any time any part of sprite comes into contact with a specific color on the stage. In the previous example, this occurs whenever any part of the dragon sprite (head, tail, wings, flames, and so on) comes into contact with the red rectangle sprite.

However, if you prefer, you can use the third sensing code clock shown in Figure 6.1 to set up a more specific type of collision test. Specifically, this code block allows you to specify a color on the sprite that must make contact with another color on the stage for a collision to occur. To get a better understanding of the difference between this code block and the previous sensing code block, look at the following script, which plays an audio file whenever a specified color within a sprite comes into contact with a specified color on the stage.

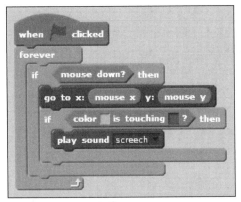

In this example, the sensing code block has been replaced. The new sensing block has been configured so that the color yellow in the dragon sprite must collide with the color red in the rectangle block for a collision to occur. If you were to replace the script in the previous application with this script, the only time a collision would occur is when the yellow portion of the dragon's stomach or wings touches the red rectangle sprite, as demonstrated in Figure 6.4.

No collision   **Collision**

Figure 6.4
Setting up a more restrictive collision test.
© 2014 Lifelong Kindergarten Group

As an alternative to detecting when one sprite collides with another sprite, you may want to detect when one sprite comes within a certain distance of another sprite or the mouse pointer. You can do this using the fourth sensing code block shown in Figure 6.1. To develop an understanding of how to work with this code block, modify the previous Scratch 2.0 application, replacing the dragon sprite's script with the script shown here.

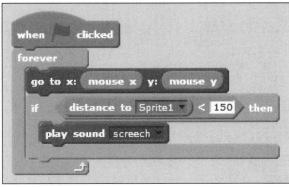

© 2014 Cengage Learning®

Note that this script uses a green operators block to test a less than condition. The operators block is embedded within an if then code block and configured to determine if the distance of the dragon is less than 150 pixels from sprite1 (the red rectangle). Once you have updated the script, run the application, and then move the mouse pointer around the stage. When you do, the dragon sprite follows, and whenever it moves within 150 steps of the red rectangle sprite, an audio file is repeatedly played.

PROMPTING FOR AND COLLECTING USER INPUT

Often computer programs require the ability to interact with and collect user-supplied input. This can come from mouse moment or keyboard input, such as when the space-bar is pressed. In addition to these basic inputs, Scratch 2.0 lets you directly interact with the user and collect his input through the uses of the sensing blocks shown in Figure 6.5.

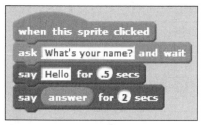

Figure 6.5

These sensing blocks are used to collect user input.

© 2014 Lifelong Kindergarten Group

To demonstrate how to use these two code blocks, consider the following example in which the cat sprite is assigned the following script.

© 2014 Cengage Learning®

This script is executed when the user clicks on the cat sprite. The first thing the script does is display the text What's your name? in a speech bubble and an input field control at the bottom of the stage. The script then waits for the user to type any text he wants and then signal the script that he is done by either pressing the Enter key or clicking on the checkmark icon located at the end of the input field, as demonstrated in Figure 6.6.

Figure 6.6

Prompting the user to enter his name.

© 2014 Lifelong Kindergarten Group

Once provided, the user's input is made accessible via the answer code block, the contents of which are displayed in a speech bubble.

RETRIEVING KEYBOARD INPUT, MOUSE BUTTON, AND COORDINATE STATUS

In many types of applications, the mouse pointer controls the movement of sprites and affects the operation of the application in many other ways. The sensing blocks shown in Figure 6.7 provide access to data about the operation of the mouse pointer.

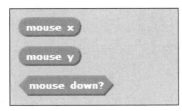

Figure 6.7

These sensing blocks report on the mouse pointer's coordinates and button status.

© 2014 Lifelong Kindergarten Group

The first of these three code blocks retrieves the location of the mouse pointer as it moves along the X-axis. As was stated in Chapter 2, "Getting Comfortable with the

Scratch 2.0 Development Environment," Scratch 2.0 supports a total range of –240 to 240. The second of these code blocks retrieves the location of the mouse pointer as it moves along the Y-axis. Scratch 2.0 supports a total range of 180 to –180 on its Y-axis. The third code block is used to retrieve a `true/false` value that identifies when the mouse's button is being pressed. The following script, which is part of a drawing application, demonstrates how to work with all three of these sensing code blocks.

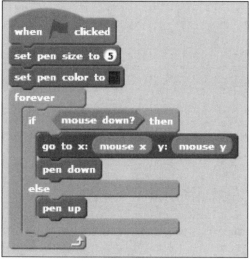

© 2014 Cengage Learning®

To create the drawing application, create a new Scratch 2.0 application project. Remove the cat sprite from it, and then create and add a new sprite that consists of a single black dot. Next, select the thumbnail representing the dot, and then add the script shown above to it.

This application's operation depends on the use of a virtual pen object that Scratch 2.0 makes available to you via pen code blocks, which you learn about in Chapter 12, "Drawing Lines and Shapes." The overall operation of the application is controlled by the script, which automatically begins executing when the green Flag button is clicked. Once started, two pen blocks are used to set the width of the pen and the color used by the pen when drawing. A `forever` code block has been added to repeat the execution of all the code blocks embedded within it.

Within the loop, an `if…else` code block conditionally controls the execution of three additional statements. The `if…else` code block's execution is controlled by examining the value returned by a sensing block that returns a value of `true` when the user presses the mouse's left button and `false` if the mouse's left button is not pressed.

When the user presses the left mouse button, the two statements located at the top of the if…else code block are executed. The first statement moves the sprite to the same location as the pointer, and the second code block places Scratch 2.0's virtual pen in a down position, allowing drawing to begin. As a result, a blue line is drawn anywhere on the stage where the mouse pointer is moved when the left mouse button is pressed. The code block located at the bottom of the if…else code block is executed whenever the user releases the left mouse button, lifting the virtual pen and halting any drawing operations.

Figure 6.8 demonstrates the operation of the drawing application.

Figure 6.8

An example of the drawing application in action.

© 2014 Lifelong Kindergarten Group

One problem with the drawing application is that there is no way to clear the screen and start over should you make a mistake when drawing. You can rectify this easily using the sensing code block shown in Figure 6.9, which retrieves true or false depending on whether a specified key is pressed.

Figure 6.9

This sensing block can be used to detect when the user presses a specified keyboard key.

© 2014 Lifelong Kindergarten Group

To see an example of how to work with this code block, let's modify the previous draw-ing application by editing the script belonging to the application's sprite, as shown here.

```
when ⚑ clicked
set pen size to 5
set pen color to ■
forever
    if   mouse down?   then
        go to x: mouse x  y: mouse y
        pen down
    else
        pen up

    if   key space ▼ pressed?   then
        clear
```

© 2014 Cengage Learning®

As you can see, three new code blocks have been added that clear the stage whenever the spacebar key is pressed. Figure 6.10 shows an example of the drawing application in operation. Here, the application is used to draw the name *Lee* on the stage. Next, the spacebar key is pressed, clearing the stage, after which an image of a tree has been drawn.

Figure 6.10
You can use this enhanced version of the drawing application to draw and erase.
© 2014 Lifelong Kindergarten Group

In addition to detecting keystrokes using a sensing code block, you can use the control code block shown in Figure 6.11. The difference between these two code blocks is that the sensing code block can be used within a loop to continuously determine that a specified keyboard key is being pressed. The events block, on the other hand, executes only once—when the specified key is initially pressed—and is therefore good for initiating an individual action and not for facilitating the repeated execution of an action. You learn more about this code block later in Chapter 9, "Controlling Script Execution."

Figure 6.11

This code block initiates an action whenever a specific keyboard key is pressed.

© 2014 Lifelong Kindergarten Group

Retrieving Audio Data

In addition to sensing mouse pointer and keyboard data, collisions, distance, other stage and sprite properties, and working with the timer, Scratch 2.0 provides access to the sensing block shown in Figure 6.12, which allows you to sense sound input from the computer's microphone (if it has one) and use that input within your Scratch 2.0 applications.

Figure 6.12

This sensing block reports on how loud a sound is being played.

© 2014 Lifelong Kindergarten Group

This sensing block retrieves a number, from 1 to 100, representing the volume of the computer's microphone. The following example demonstrates how to create a script that plays an audio file named pop whenever a loud sound is detected through the computer's microphone.

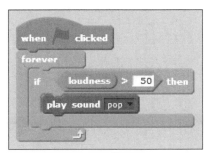

© 2014 Cengage Learning®

Here, an audio file plays whenever the script detects a loud sound from the computer's microphone. Since the loudness code block is a monitor, you can display the results on the stage, as demonstrated in Figure 6.13.

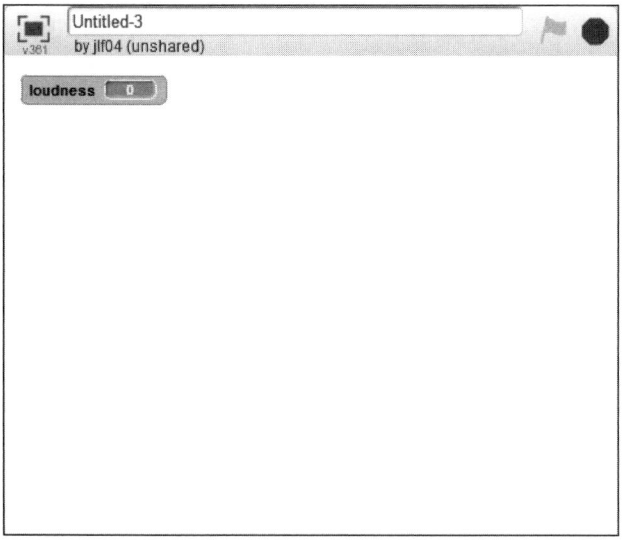

Figure 6.13

Using a monitor to keep track of the loudness of audio playback and input.

© 2014 Lifelong Kindergarten Group

COLLECTING AND PROCESSING VIDEO INPUT

In addition to audio input, Scratch 2.0 can capture and process video input if your computer has a video camera. Scratch 2.0 provides access to the sensing code blocks shown in Figure 6.14, which allows it to sense video input and use that input within your Scratch 2.0 applications.

Figure 6.14

These code blocks integrate video input into your Scratch 2.0 applications.

© 2014 Lifelong Kindergarten Group

To demonstrate how to incorporate video-sensing data into a Scratch 2.0 program, let's create a Scratch program that signals an alert whenever it detects movement in the room after you have gone. This project consists of three sound files and three scripts and requires that your computer has a video camera.

Let's begin by creating a new Scratch 2.0 project and then deleting the default sprite. Next, select the stage thumbnail and click on the Sounds tab. Using the Sound Editor, record three new sounds files. For the first sound, record "Alarm armed! You have five seconds to leave the room" and name it Alarm Armed. For the second sound, record "Intruder alert! Intruder alert! Intruder alert!" and name it Intruder Alert. For the third sound, record "Error. Incorrect passcode had been entered. Alarm not activated." and name it Error.

Next, click on the Scripts tab and add the first of three scripts to the state by adding the following code blocks to the scripts area for the stage. This script lets the user enable the collection of input from her video camera.

© 2014 Cengage Learning®

This script is executed when the user presses the Up Arrow key on her keyboard, at which time the first sensing block turns Scratch video support on. This means that, as long as you have a video camera powered on and attached to your computer, whatever is captured in that camera's view should be displayed as the stage's backdrop. The second sensing block then sets the transparency level at which the camera's video is displayed.

Now add the following script to the stage. This script prompts the user to enter a passcode that, once supplied, triggers the collection of video input. If any significant movement is captured by the video camera that the script is executing, the Intruder Alert sound is played, warning the user that an intruder has entered the room.

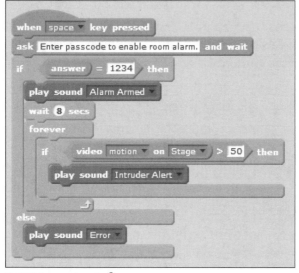

© 2014 Cengage Learning®

This script executes when the user presses the spacebar key, at which time a message is displayed instructing the user to enter a passcode to enable the alarm. The user's input is then analyzed by a control block containing an operators code block in which the user's input, retrieved using the answer sensing block, is checked to see if it equals 1234. If the user enters the correct passcode, a sound block plays the Alarm Armed sound. Script execution is then paused eight seconds to give you time to leave the room, after which another control block is used to repeatedly retrieve video input and play the Intruder Alert sound if the motion in the video input exceeds a given threshold. If, however, the user fails to supply a valid passcode, the Error sound is played and script execution ends.

Finally, add the following script to the stage. It allows the user to disable alert detection by turning off Scratch's collection of video input from the computer's video camera.

© 2014 Cengage Learning®

This script is executed when the user presses the Down Arrow key on her keyboard, at which time the first sensing block turns off Scratch video support. Figure 6.15 shows how the Scratch program might look once started and once the alarm system is enabled.

Figure 6.15
Using a monitor to keep track of the loudness of audio playback and input.
© 2014 Lifelong Kindergarten Group

Working with a Timer

Another pair of sensing code blocks that you need to become familiar with is shown in Figure 6.16. These code blocks let you enable and work with Scratch 2.0's built-in timer.

Figure 6.16
These sensing blocks let you enable and use a timer within your Scratch 2.0 application.
© 2014 Lifelong Kindergarten Group

The first code block resets the timer back to its default value of zero, and the second code block retrieves a number specifying how many seconds have passed since the timer started running. Using Scratch 2.0's timer, you can control the pace of animation and the operation of your Scratch 2.0 applications. For example, you need to use these controls to keep track of time when players are given a certain amount of time in which to make a move.

The following example demonstrates how to use both of these timer code blocks to create a script that repeatedly plays an audio file for five seconds.

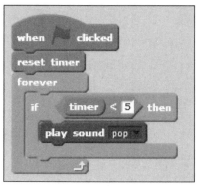

© 2014 Cengage Learning®

RETRIEVING STAGE AND SPRITE DATA

In addition to determining mouse status, sprite collisions, and the distance between sprites, you can use the code block shown in Figure 6.17 to retrieve sprite and stage information.

Figure 6.17
You can use this sensing block to retrieve information about a number of object attributes.
© 2014 Lifelong Kindergarten Group

This code block provides easy access to a number of pieces of information, including

- X position
- Y position
- Direction
- Costume number
- Costume name
- Size
- Volume

As an example of how to work with this code block, take a look at the following script, which retrieves the X-coordinate of a sprite named Sprite1 and plays an audio file whenever that sprite is moved to the right side of the stage (between coordinates 1 and 240).

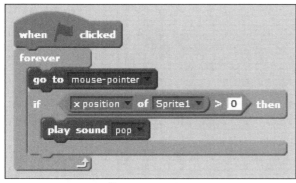

© 2014 Cengage Learning®

RETRIEVING THE DATE, TIME DATA, AND USER'S NAME

In addition to all the status data that sensing blocks let you collect about the mouse, keyboard, video, sound, sprites, and collisions, there are three additional sensing blocks that you can use to retrieve information about the current date and time, the number of days that have passed since the year 2000, and the username of anyone who has logged into the Scratch 2.0 website and is running your Scratch program. All this functionality is provided by the three reporter blocks shown in Figure 6.18.

Figure 6.18
These sensing blocks can retrieve time, date, and username information.
© 2014 Lifelong Kindergarten Group

The first code block shown in Figure 6.18 lets you collect any of the following pieces of information by selecting it from the block's drop-down list:

- Year

- Month

- Date

- Day of week

- Hour
- Minute
- Second

The other two code blocks are self-explanatory. As an example of how to use the code blocks to retrieve sensing data, create a new Scratch project and add the following code blocks to the default sprite.

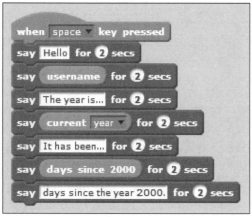

© 2014 Cengage Learning®

When executed, this script causes the cat to say Hello to you by name and then tell you the current year followed by how many days have passed since the year 2000.

CREATING THE FAMILY SCRAPBOOK APPLICATION

The remainder of this chapter guides you through the development of your next Scratch 2.0 application, an electronic family scrapbook. In total, this application consists of one sprite, a blank stage, and three scripts. Once you've created the application, you can use it to display any number of electronic photographs in an automated photo album that displays pictures at three-second intervals. Each picture in the application is actually just a costume added to the application's sprite. Figures 6.19 and 6.20 show how the application looks when displaying two of the photo book's pictures.

Figure 6.19

An example of one of the sprite's costumes.

© 2014 Lifelong Kindergarten Group

Figure 6.20

Another example of one of the sprite's costumes.

© 2014 Lifelong Kindergarten Group

The development of this application project is created by following a series of steps, as outlined here:

1. Create a new Scratch 2.0 application project.

2. Add and remove sprites and costumes.

3. Import a sound file into the application.

4. Add the programming logic required to play backdrop music.

5. Add the programming logic required to manage the display of photographs.

6. Test the execution of your new project.

Step 1: Creating a New Scratch 2.0 Project

The first step in creating the Family Scrapbook project is to create a new Scratch 2.0 application project. Do so by either opening Scratch 2.0, thereby automatically creating a new Scratch 2.0 application project, or clicking on the File menu and then selecting New.

Step 2: Adding and Removing Sprites and Costumes

This application consists of a single sprite, which will be used to display all the application's photographs (as costumes). Therefore, you won't need the default cat sprite, so you should remove it. After removing the cat sprite, click on the Upload Sprite from File icon to open the Select Files(s) to Upload by scratch.mit.edu dialog window. Using this window, navigate to the folder containing the electronic image files (photographs) that you plan to display, select one of these files to be used as the application's sprite, and then click on the Open button.

Click on the thumbnail representing the new sprite (in the sprites list), and then click on the Costumes tab located at the top of the program editor. Next, click on the Upload Costume from File icon, and use the dialog window that is displayed to add another picture to the application. Repeat this process as many times as necessary to add all the image files that you want to be included as part of the family scrapbook, as demonstrated in Figure 6.21.

Figure 6.21

You can add as many pictures as you want to the sprite's list of costumes.

Step 3: Adding a Suitable Audio File to the Stage

To make the Family Scrapbook application more enjoyable, let's add a little background music to help set the mood. To add the music file, select the stage thumbnail in the sprites list and then click on the Sounds tab located at the top of the scripts area. Next, click on the Choose Sound from Library icon to open the Sound Library window. Then double-click on the `Music Loops` folder and locate and select the `GuitarChords1` audio file. Click on OK, adding the sound file to the application project, as shown in Figure 6.22.

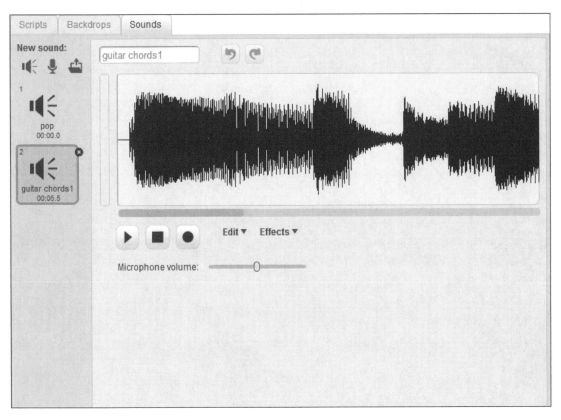

Figure 6.22

Adding background music to be played when the application executes.

Step 4: Playing the Audio File

The next step in the development of the application project is to begin adding the programming logic. In total, you need to add three scripts to the project: one for the stage and two for the application's sprite.

The script to be added to the stage is responsible for playing the application's background music. To create this script, click on the stage thumbnail located in the sprites list and then select the Scripts tab located at the top of the scripts area. Next, add and configure the following code blocks exactly as shown here.

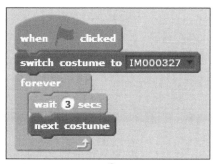

© 2014 Cengage Learning®

This script manages the repeated playback of the application's audio file for as long as the application is run. Audio file playback is performed using a pair of sound blocks, which you learn about in Chapter 11, "Spicing Things Up with Sounds."

Step 5: Adding the Programming Logic Required to Manage the Display of Photographs

Now it is time to add the programming logic that is responsible for displaying all the photographs that make up the Family Scrapbook project. To set this up, you need to add a small script to the application's sprite that specifies the programming logic required to automate the display of all the application's photographs, at three-second intervals. In addition, you will add a second script to the application to allow the user to manually control the display of the application's photographs.

Scripting the Operation of the Family Scrapbook

The code blocks that are responsible for automating the operation of the scrapbook are shown here.

© 2014 Cengage Learning®

This script is automatically executed when the user clicks on the green Flag button. When this happens, a looks block is executed. This block specifies a specific costume to be displayed when the application is started (the first costume in the costume list). Next, a loop is set up that repeatedly executes the two statements embedded within it. The first code block located inside the loop pauses the script's execution for three seconds, after which a second looks block is used to switch the sprite's costume to the next costume in the sprite's costume list.

Allowing for the Manual Operation of the Family Scrapbook

If the user prefers, rather than viewing photographs in the Family Scrapbook project as an automated slideshow, the contents of the scrapbook can be manually browsed by clicking on the application's sprite, which causes the next costumed (photograph) to be displayed. To provide the user with this manual option, add the following script to the application's sprite.

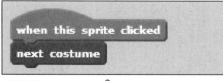

© 2014 Cengage Learning®

Step 6: Saving and Executing Your New Scratch 2.0 Application

Okay, assuming that you have been following along and creating your copy of the Family Scrapbook application as you made your way through this chapter, your copy of the Family Scrapbook application should look something like the example shown in Figure 6.23.

Figure 6.23

The completed application consists of a blank stage and a single sprite with 11 costumes and 2 scripts.

© 2014 Lifelong Kindergarten Group

If you have not done so yet, give your new project a name and then switch to presentation mode, click on the green Flag button, and kick back and enjoy listening to and watching your new application. Alternatively, start clicking on the application's sprite and go through the contents of the Family Scrapbook at your own pace.

CHAPTER 7

STORING AND RETRIEVING DATA

All computer applications require some sort of data with which to work as they execute. This is true of even the simplest applications. The data processed by an application may be embedded within it. Data may also be randomly generated or collected from the user as the application executes. To work with and manipulate data, programmers need the ability to store, retrieve, and modify data when an application runs. Within Scratch 2.0 applications, data is managed using either variables or lists. The goal of this chapter is to teach you everything you need to know to begin developing Scratch 2.0 applications that can collect, store, and process application data.

The major topics covered in this chapter include

- How to create local, global, and cloud variables
- How to use variables as a means of storing and retrieving data
- How to delete variables that are no longer needed
- How to view data stored in local variables belonging to other sprites
- How to manage and process collections of data using lists

LEARNING HOW TO WORK WITH APPLICATION DATA

Like all computer programs, Scratch 2.0 applications need to be able to process and store data. *Data* is any type of information that your Scratch 2.0 applications collect, process, and store when executing. Data can also be collected when the user interacts with the application using the keyboard or mouse. Data may be generated by your applications, such as when you create a Scratch 2.0 project that generates and then uses random numbers (covered in Chapter 8, "Do a Little Math"). Data may also be hard-coded within your Scratch 2.0 application projects. For example, you can use the code block shown in Figure 7.1 to store and display a text string within a script.

Figure 7.1
An example of text embedded within a looks code block.
© 2014 Lifelong Kindergarten Group

When executed, a script containing this looks code block displays the hard-coded text string inside a voice bubble. Like most programming languages, Scratch 2.0 lets you work with a number of different types of data. Scratch 2.0 handles each of these different types of data, listed next, differently.

- String
- Boolean
- Integer
- Real

A *string* is a piece of text data that you hard-code within Scratch 2.0 applications using different types of looks code blocks, which you will learn how to work with in Chapter 10, "Changing the Way Sprites Look and Behave." *Boolean data* is data that Scratch 2.0 automatically generates when you work with different types of operator blocks (which you will learn about in Chapter 8, "Doing a Little Math"). A *Boolean value* represents data that has an assigned value of either True or False. For example, any time you compare one numeric value against another to see if they are equal, Scratch 2.0 returns a Boolean value. Based on the result of that analysis, you can alter the way your Scratch 2.0 applications execute using control blocks, which are covered in Chapter 9, "Controlling Script Execution."

An *integer* is a numeric value that does not include a decimal point (sometimes referred to as a *whole number*). Scratch 2.0 lets you enter integer values as input into numerous types of code blocks. It also allows you to store numeric data inside variables and lists, allowing you to store, retrieve, and manipulate the data as necessary during application execution. A *real* number is a number that includes a decimal number.

Scratch 2.0 handles different types of data differently. For example, string data can only be displayed by embedding it within looks code blocks. Integer and real data can also be embedded within code blocks and displayed in monitors. In addition, integer and real data can be added, subtracted, and manipulated in all the different ways that you would to be able to manipulate numeric data. Scratch 2.0 also allows you to use integers and real numbers interchangeably.

Note

Industrial-strength programming languages Microsoft C++ and Visual Basic support a much wider range of data types. However, they all support the same basic types of data that Scratch 2.0 does.

STORING DATA IN VARIABLES

As has already been stated, you can embed numeric data inside different types of code blocks, using it to control the operation of scripts. You can also store numeric data collected when your applications execute using variables. In Scratch 2.0, *variables* allow you to store, retrieve, and modify numeric data.

Note

Scratch 2.0 can store string or numeric data in variables. Variables cannot, however, be used to store Boolean data.

Creating Scratch 2.0 Variables

To store, modify, and retrieve data in a Scratch 2.0 application, you need to create variables. To work with variables within your Scratch 2.0 applications, you must first define and add them to your application projects. This is done by selecting the Data category in the blocks palette and then clicking on the Variables button located at the top of the blocks palette and clicking on the Make a Variable button, as shown in Figure 7.2.

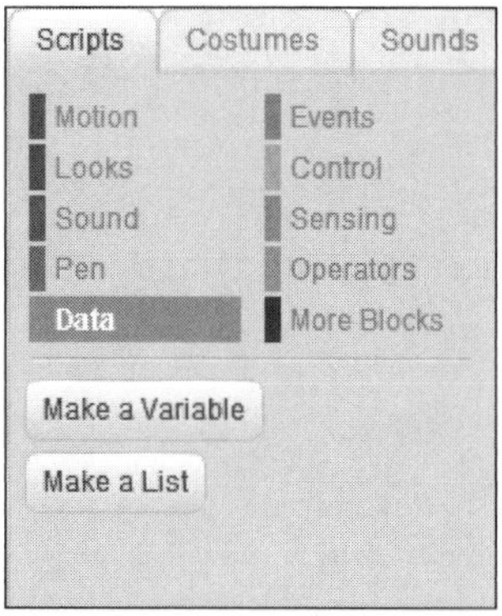

Figure 7.2
Creating Scratch 2.0 variables.
© 2014 Lifelong Kindergarten Group

Once this button has been clicked, Scratch 2.0 displays the window shown in Figure 7.3, allowing you to assign a name to the variable.

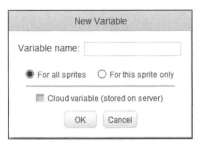

Figure 7.3
Assigning a name to a new Scratch 2.0 variable.
© 2014 Lifelong Kindergarten Group

The name that you assign will be used to create and add five new code blocks to your Scratch 2.0 project, as shown in Figure 7.4.

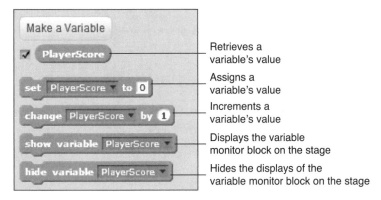

Figure 7.4
Scratch 2.0 creates five new code blocks for each variable that you create.
© 2014 Lifelong Kindergarten Group

In addition, a monitor showing the variables' value is automatically displayed on the stage, as demonstrated in Figure 7.5.

Figure 7.5
Every new variable supports a monitor that displays its value.
© 2014 Lifelong Kindergarten Group

Using the five code blocks created for every variable, you can assign an initial value to the variable, change its value while your application is running, and display a monitor on the stage, which shows the variable's value.

Assigning Variables to Sprites and the Stage

Variables in Scratch 2.0 applications belong to the sprites in which they are defined (or to the stage). Therefore, it is important that when adding new variables to your application, you select the thumbnail for the sprite (or stage) where the variable belongs. For example, variables that need to be accessed by different scripts belonging to different sprites may best be added to the stage, whereas a variable needed only by a specific sprite should be added to that sprite.

Assigning Names to Your Variables

Unlike many programming languages, Scratch 2.0 is flexible when it comes to naming variables. You can make variable names as long or as short as you want. Variable names can include

- Letters
- Numbers
- Special characters
- Blank spaces

Because Scratch 2.0 creates a complete set of code blocks for each new variable that you define, it eliminates any concerns about case-sensitivity, making things a lot easier to work with.

Tip

Make your variable names as descriptive as possible. This helps make your scripts self-documenting. Although Scratch 2.0 variable names can be extremely long, it's a good idea to limit their length to a maximum of 30 characters. This provides you with plenty of room to create descriptive, manageable variable names.

Understanding Variable Scope

One important concept that you need to understand when working with variables is *variable scope*. A variable's scope identifies the location within an application that the variable's value can be modified. Scratch 2.0 supports three levels of variable scope, as outlined here:

- **Local.** Variables that can be modified only by scripts belonging to the sprite in which the variable is defined and created by selecting the For This Sprite Only option when defining the variable's name.

- **Global.** Variables that can be modified by any script in an application and created by selecting the For All Sprites option when defining the variable's name.

- **Cloud.** Variables that store data on Scratch servers that is persistent across multiple executions of your application project and created by selecting the Cloud Variable (Stored on Server) option when creating the variables.

Note

Although local variables can only be modified by scripts belonging to the sprite in which they are defined, their assigned values can be retrieved (not modified) by scripts belonging to other sprites using sensing code blocks, as demonstrated a little later in this chapter.

Creating Local Variables

Local variables can be modified only within the sprite in which they are defined. The following procedure outlines the steps involved in creating a local variable:

1. Select the sprite (or stage) to which the variable is to be added.

2. Click on the Data category located at the top of the blocks palette.

3. Click on the Make a Variable button.

4. Enter the name you want to assign to the variable, and then select the For this Sprite Only option, as demonstrated in Figure 7.6.

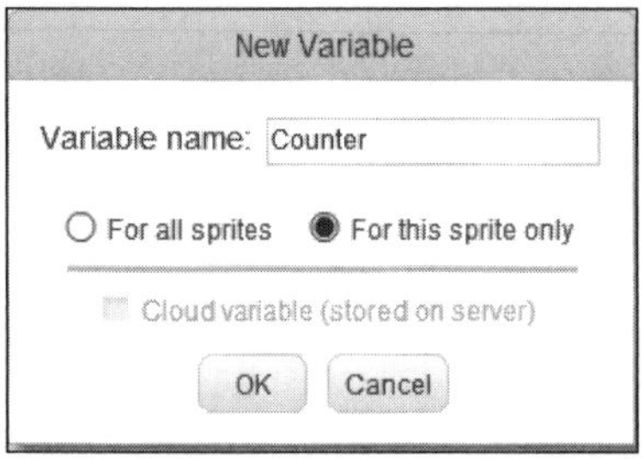

Figure 7.6
Creating a local variable named Counter.
© 2014 Lifelong Kindergarten Group

Since a local variable can only be modified within the sprite in which it has been added, scripts belonging to other sprites cannot modify a local variable. If you need a variable that any script within an application can access, create a global variable as discussed in the next section.

Tip

If you want, you can change the name that you assigned to a variable by right-clicking on the variable block in the blocks palette, clicking on Rename in the menu that appears, and then clicking on the OK button. Once renamed, you should check on any code blocks within your projects scripts that reference the variable because you may have to click on the drop-down list in those code blocks and select the variable's new name to correct the code block's association with the variable.

Creating Global Variables

Unlike local variables, a global variable's value can be modified by any script within the application where it has been defined. You use the same procedure to create a global variable as you do when creating a local variable; the only difference is that you need to leave the default For All Sprites option selected when naming your variable, as demonstrated in Figure 7.7.

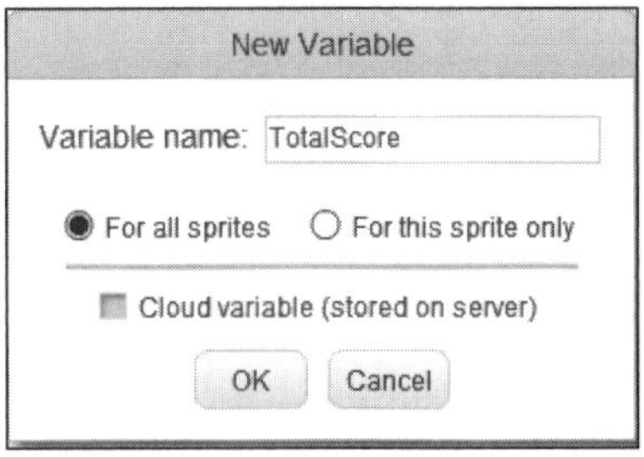

Figure 7.7
Creating a global variable named TotalScore.
© 2014 Lifelong Kindergarten Group

Tip

It is considered a good programming practice to restrict the scope of all variables to local whenever possible. This helps to make your applications easier to maintain and eliminates the possibility that you might accidentally modify the variable's value using scripts belonging to other sprites.

Creating Cloud Variables

Cloud variables are stored on servers maintained as part of the Scratch 2.0 website. Cloud variables are accessible across multiple iterations of program execution. Therefore, they are useful for storing data for things like overall player high scores for a game. Once created, cloud variables are identified within Scratch 2.0 by the presence of a small cloud symbol displayed on the left side of variable code blocks, as demonstrated here.

© 2014 Cengage Learning®

As of the writing of this book, only numeric data can be stored in cloud variables, and Scratchers are limited to a total of 10 cloud variables. Full scratcher status was required to use cloud variables. However, the ability to store string data will eventually follow. You use the same procedure to create a cloud variable as you do when creating local and global variables, but when creating cloud variables, you leave the default For All Sprites option selected and then select the Cloud Variable option, as demonstrated in Figure 7.8.

Figure 7.8
Creating a cloud variable named PlayerHighScores.
© 2014 Lifelong Kindergarten Group

Tip

Cloud variables, like local and global variables, can be renamed and deleted by Shift-clicking on them and selecting either Rename or Delete from the menu that appears.

DELETING VARIABLES WHEN THEY ARE NO LONGER NEEDED

Over time, you may find yourself making numerous changes to your Scratch 2.0 projects. As you do, you may discover that your applications no longer need certain variables. If this is the case, you can clean up your applications by deleting these variables from your projects. Doing so is easy: first, make sure that any references to the variable within the application's scripts have been removed, and then right-click on the variable (in the blocks palette) and select Delete Variable from the menu that is displayed in Figure 7.9. In response, Scratch 2.0 will delete the variable from the sprite to which it was added.

Figure 7.9
Deleting a variable that is no longer needed.
© 2014 Lifelong Kindergarten Group

Caution

If you delete a variable from a sprite without first removing references to the variable in the sprite's scripts, Scratch 2.0 deletes the variable but also leaves in place any code blocks in the application's scripts that reference that variable. As a result, things will not work properly.

ACCESSING VARIABLES BELONGING TO OTHER SPRITES

Data stored in local variables can be changed only by scripts belonging to the sprite the variables have been assigned to. However, Scratch 2.0 does allow scripts belonging to sprites in a project to view data stored in variables belonging to other sprites. To view data stored in another sprite's local variables, you need to use the sensing block shown in Figure 7.10.

Figure 7.10
Using this code block, you can create a script that can view data stored in another sprite's local variables.
© 2014 Lifelong Kindergarten Group

This code block lets one sprite retrieve another sprite's X position, Y position, direction, costume number, size, and volume. It also lets you retrieve values assigned to another sprite's variable. As demonstrated in Figure 7.11, you can click on the code block's right pull-down menu to display a listing made up of the stage and all the sprites in the Scratch 2.0 application.

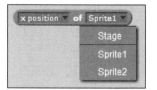

Figure 7.11
Specifying the name of the sprite (or stage) whose variable you want to access.
© 2014 Lifelong Kindergarten Group

After selecting the stage or a sprite, you can use the drop-down menu located on the left side of the code block to select and retrieve information for any of the specified items that are listed. A gray horizontal divider bar located at the bottom of the resulting list denotes the sprite's list of variables, separating the list from other available data, as demonstrated in Figure 7.12.

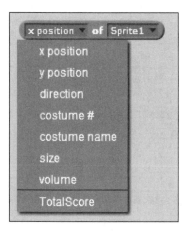

Figure 7.12
Selecting the variable whose data you want to access.
© 2014 Lifelong Kindergarten Group

Using this code block, you can retrieve data stored in any sprite's local variables. However, all you can do is read the value assigned to those variables; you cannot modify them.

A QUICK EXAMPLE

To help you become more comfortable with working with variables, let's look at two quick examples. In the first example, shown next, a script has been created that, when executed, displays the value assigned to a variable named Counter. Remember, by default, every variable that you create has a reporter block with an associated monitor, which Scratch 2.0 displays on the stage.

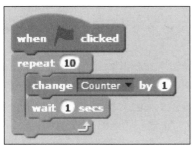

© 2014 Cengage Learning®

Note

To set up and run this example, you must create a new application, add a variable named Counter to it, and then add the script to the application's default script.

This script has been set up to execute whenever the green Flag button is pressed. It uses a control block to set up a loop that repeats the execution of two embedded code blocks a total of 10 times. Each time the loop executes, the value assigned to a variable named Counter is increased by 1. The next statement pauses the loop for one second before allowing it to continue running.

By default, Scratch 2.0 assigns a default value of zero to all new variables, which is why the first time you run the previous script, it counts from 1 to 10. However, if you run it again, you will notice that it counts from 11 to 20. If you want, you can change this behavior by explicitly assigning an initial value to the Counter variable, as demonstrated in the following example.

© 2014 Cengage Learning®

Here, the value of Counter has been set to 0 through the addition of a new variable block at the beginning of the script, immediately after its hat code block. As a result, no matter how many times this script executes, it always counts from 1 to 10.

STORING COLLECTIONS OF DATA IN LISTS

Unlike variables, which store a single piece of data at a time, lists store multiple items, allowing a larger collection of items to be retrieved and processed more efficiently during program execution. Items stored in lists are essentially the same things as variables. Lists can store a theoretically unlimited number of items. Lists can store and retrieve any type of values supported by Scratch 2.0, including

- String
- Boolean
- Integer
- Real

When you're working with lists, items in the list must be referenced based on their location within the list (for example, their numeric index position). Unlike variables, reference by name is not supported. You can add items to and remove them from a list either manually or programmatically.

Note

Lists in Scratch 2.0 are the equivalent of single-dimensional arrays in other programming languages. Scratch 2.0 does not support multidimensional arrays.

Lists are created within the program editor by selecting the Data category at the top of the blocks palette and then clicking on the Make a List button. In response, the dialog window shown in Figure 7.13 is displayed. To finish creating a list, enter a name for it in the List Name field and then specify whether the list should be accessible by all sprites or only by the sprite to which it has been assigned. Then click on OK.

Figure 7.13
Lists are created in much the same way as variables.
© 2014 Lifelong Kindergarten Group

Note

As of the writing of the second edition of this book, Scratch 2.0 only supports the storage of variables in the cloud. However, the developers of Scratch's stated anticipation was that lists would soon be supported in the cloud as well.

Once you've created the list, Scratch 2.0 automatically creates and adds a list of code blocks, like those shown in Figure 7.14, to the blocks palette. These code blocks let you programmatically interact, add, retrieve, and delete list items and information about the list and its contents.

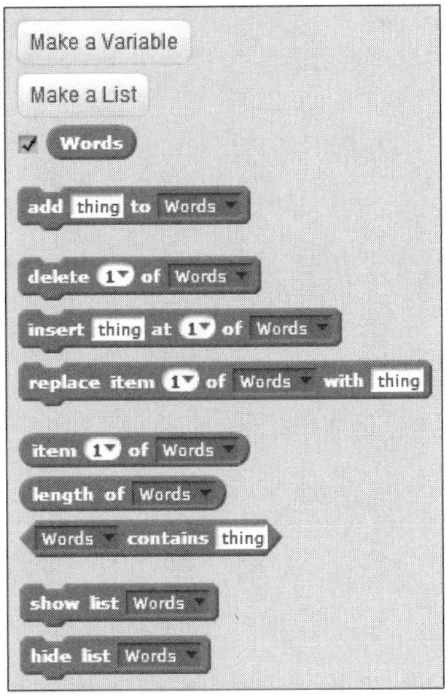

Figure 7.14
Scratch 2.0 generates the following set of code blocks when you create a new list.
© 2014 Lifelong Kindergarten Group

Figure 7.15 shows the stage monitor that Scratch 2.0 automatically displays when you create a new list. As you can see, the list has no items in it.

Figure 7.15

Scratch 2.0 displays an empty stage monitor on the stage when you create a new list.

You can manually add items to a list by clicking on the + icon located in the lower-left corner of the list (see Figure 7.16). You can delete an item by selecting its contents and pressing the Delete key, leaving a blank or empty item behind in the list. You can replace an item in a list by overtyping it with a new item. At the bottom of the list monitor is a count showing the length of the list. Each time you add or remove an item from the list, the length of the list is automatically updated. If you add more items to a list than can be displayed by the stage monitor, a scrollbar is automatically added to the monitor, allowing you to scroll up and down and view its contents.

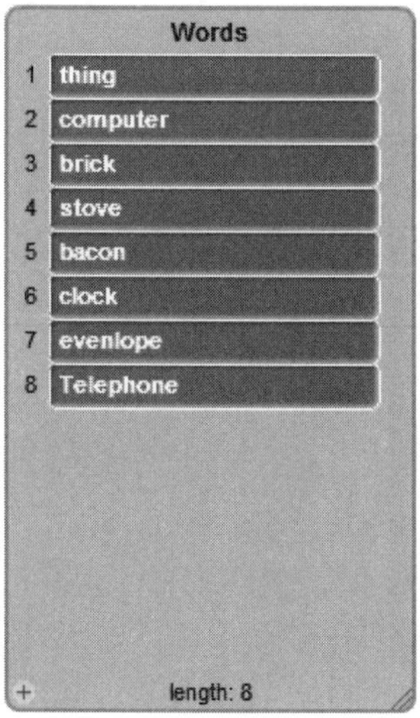

Figure 7.16

An example of a list to which eight entries have been added.

To get a better understanding of how to programmatically interact with lists, let's create a new Scratch 2.0 project as shown in Figure 7.16. Begin by creating a new Scratch application and removing the default sprite. Next, add a new list and manually populate it exactly as shown in Figure 7.17.

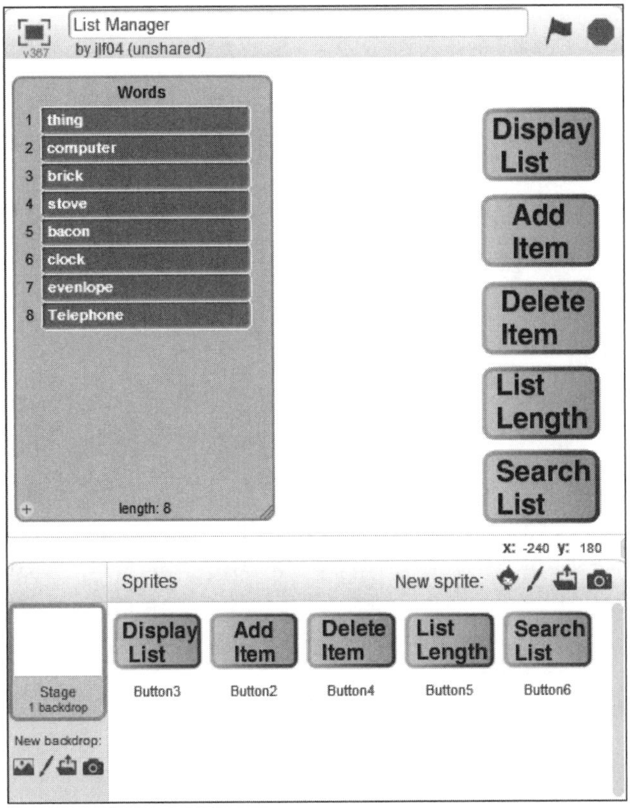

Figure 7.17

The fully assembled List Manager application project.

© 2014 Lifelong Kindergarten Group

Once the list has been added and populated with items, add four sprites (use the `button3` sprite stored in the Things category of the Sprite Library) to the stage and then use the Paint Editor to modify each of these four sprites by adding text labels to them, as shown in Figure 7.17. When clicked, each of these button sprites is used to process items in the list. Add the following script to the uppermost button sprite, labeled Display List. When clicked, it tells you how many items are currently stored in the list.

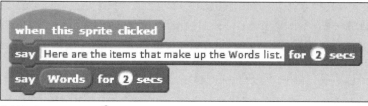

© 2014 Cengage Learning®

Next, add the following script to the next button sprite labeled Add Item. This script executes when the button is clicked and prompts you to type a new entry for the list and then add that entry as a new item at the beginning of the list.

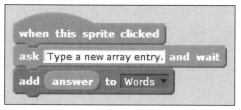

© 2014 Cengage Learning®

Add the following script to the button sprite labeled Delete Item. This script executes when the button is clicked and prompts you to specify the index number of an item you want to delete from the list. The script then removes that entry from the list.

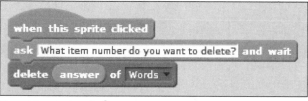

© 2014 Cengage Learning®

Add the following script to the button sprite labeled List Length. This script executes when the button is clicked and tells you how many items are currently stored in the list.

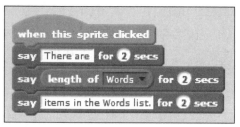

© 2014 Cengage Learning®

Add the following script to the button sprite labeled Search List. This script executes when the button is clicked and lets you search the content of the list by specifying the name of the word you want to search on. It then informs you if the word is or is not stored in the list.

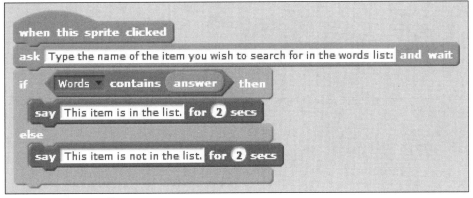

DEVELOPING THE BASKETBALL QUIZ PROJECT

The rest of this chapter is devoted to guiding you through the development of your next Scratch 2.0 application: the NBA trivia quiz. This application makes extensive use of variables to store and retrieve player input and to keep track of the player's quiz results. In total, the application is made up of a backdrop, six sprites, and six scripts.

When executed, this application presents the user with an electronic quiz made up of five questions, designed to evaluate the user's knowledge of NBA trivia. Figure 7.18 shows an example of how the game looks when it's first started. To begin game play, the user must click on the sprite representing the game's hostess, at which point she begins administering the quiz.

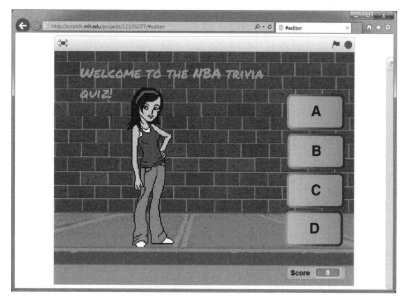

Figure 7.18

The NBA Trivia Quiz presents the user with a series of multiple choice questions.

Figure 7.19 provides an example of how the hostess interacts with the user when administering the quiz.

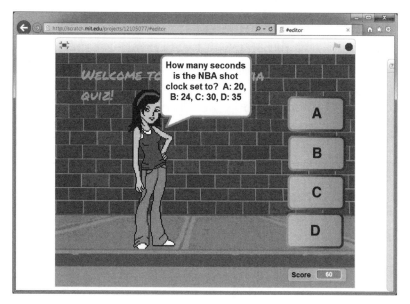

Figure 7.19

The user answers questions by clicking on buttons labeled A, B, C, and D located on the right side of the stage.

The hostess provides the user with immediate feedback after each question is answered, letting the user know if the answer was correct or incorrect. In addition, the user's score is automatically tabulated after each answer is evaluated and displayed in a monitor located at the lower right side of the stage.

You can create the development of this application project by following a series of steps, as outlined here:

1. Create a new Scratch 2.0 application project.
2. Add a backdrop to the stage.
3. Add and remove sprites and costumes.
4. Add the variables that the application needs.
5. Add scripts to each button sprite to collect user answers.
6. Add the programming logic required to administer the quiz.
7. Save and execute your work.

Step 1: Creating a New Scratch 2.0 Project

The first step in creating the NBA trivia quiz application is to create a new Scratch 2.0 application project. Do so by either opening Scratch 2.0, thereby automatically creating a new Scratch 2.0 application project, or clicking on the File menu and then selecting New.

Step 2: Selecting an Appropriate Stage Backdrop

Once you have created your new Scratch 2.0 project, it is time to get to work. Let's begin by adding an appropriate backdrop to the stage. To do so, click on the blank stage thumbnail located in the sprite list. Once selected, modify its backdrop by clicking on the Backdrops tab located at the top of the scripts area. To add a new backdrop to the application, click on the Choose Backdrop from Library icon. When the Backdrop Library window opens, click on the Outdoors folder, select the brick wall thumbnail, and click on the OK button.

Since this application requires only one backdrop, you can remove the default blank backdrop, named backdrop1, from your project.

Step 3: Adding and Removing Sprites

This application consists of a number of sprites, representing a hostess who is responsible for administering the quiz, four buttons on which the user must click when answering quiz questions, and a graphic containing a welcoming text message. Before adding any sprites, go ahead and remove the cat sprite from the application, since you won't need it.

To add the sprite representing the game's hostess, click on the Choose Sprite from Library icon located at the top of the sprite list to open the Sprite Library window. Drill down into the People folder, select the girl4 sprite, and click on the OK button. Enlarge the sprite and reposition it, as demonstrated in Figures 7.18 and 7.19. While you are at it, change the name assigned to the sprite to say host.

Next, click on the Choose Sprite from Library icon, drill down into the Things folder and select the button3 sprite, and click on the window's OK button. Once the button sprite has been added, select it in the sprites list, and click on the Costumes tab located at the top of the scripts area to open the sprite in the Paint Editor program. Click on the Text button located on the Paint Editor's toolbar, and then click in the center of the sprite and type an uppercase letter *A*. Next, rename the sprite A. Drag and drop the sprite to the right side of the stage, as shown in Figures 7.18 and 7.19.

Using the same series of steps outlined in the previous paragraph, add three additional instances of the button3 sprite to the application, naming them B, C, and D. Once added, align all these button sprites along the right side of the stage just under the A sprite, as demonstrated in Figures 7.18 and 7.19. At this point, you only have one last sprite to add. You need to create this sprite from Scratch 2.0. To do so, click on the Paint New Sprite icon, click on the Text button on the Paint Editor toolbar, set the font type to Marker by selecting that font from the drop-down list that is displayed at the bottom-left side of the Paint Editor, and then click on one of the light blue color swatches in the color palette. Finally, click on the top-left corner of the drawing area and type Welcome to the NBA trivia quiz! as demonstrated in Figure 7.20.

Figure 7.20

Creating a new sprite needed by the NBA Trivia Quiz.

© 2014 Lifelong Kindergarten Group

Rename the next text-based sprite `welcome`, and then reposition this new sprite at the top of the stage, as shown in Figures 7.18 and 7.19.

Step 4: Adding Variables That the Application Requires

To execute, this application needs three variables, as shown in Figure 7.21. To add these three variables to the application, click on the Data category in the blocks palette, and then click on the Make a Variable button three times to create three global variables named `Answer`, `Clicked`, and `Score`.

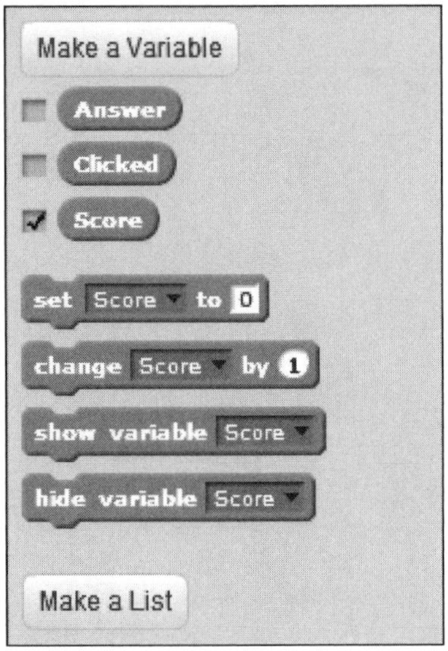

Figure 7.21
The NBA trivia quiz requires the addition of three global variables.
© 2014 Lifelong Kindergarten Group

The variable named Answer keeps track of the user's answers to each quiz question. The variable named Clicked controls application execution, making sure that the script used to administer the quiz pauses and waits each time the user is prompted to answer a new question. The variable named Score keeps track of the user's score (grade).

By default, Scratch 2.0 displays monitors on the stage for all three of these variables. However, the game only needs to display the Score monitor. Therefore, you should clear the monitor check boxes for the Answer and Clicked variables. At this point, the variable code blocks displayed in the blocks palette should be the same as those shown in Figure 7.21.

The monitor for the Score variable needs to be moved to the lower-right corner of the stage, as shown in Figure 7.18 and 7.19.

Step 5: Adding Scripts to Button Sprites to Collect User Input

The programming logic that controls the overall administration of the quiz will be added to the host sprite, which is responsible for displaying quiz questions, collecting user answers, and then grading the results. To answer quiz questions, the user must click on one of the four sprite buttons (A, B, C, or D) when prompted by the hostess. Each of these four sprites has a small script belonging to it, which sets two variables when it is clicked. Following is the script that is executed when the A sprite is clicked.

© 2014 Cengage Learning®

As you can see, this script begins with a hat block that executes whenever the A button is clicked. When this happens, the valued assigned to the Clicked variable is set to 1. The value assigned to the Answer variable is also set to 1.

The Clicked variable is used in the application to keep track of when the user answers a question. This variable's value is set to 1 when the A sprite is clicked, indicating that the user has submitted an answer. Once a script belonging to the host sprite has evaluated the answer, the value of Clicked is set back to 0, making the application ready to process a new question. The Answer variable identifies which button has been clicked. Assigning a value of 1 to this variable indicates that the A sprite has been clicked.

The programming needed by the B sprite is shown next. As you can see, it is almost identical to the code assigned to the A sprite, with the value assigned to the Clicked variable being set to 1 when the button is clicked. Note that the value assigned to the Answer variable is 2, indicating that the second button (the B sprite) has been clicked.

© 2014 Cengage Learning®

The code blocks that make up the C sprite scripts are shown next. As you can see, the third code block is used to identify when it is clicked.

© 2014 Cengage Learning®

As you have probably anticipated, the code blocks that make up the script for the D sprite, shown next, assign a value of 4 to the Answer variable.

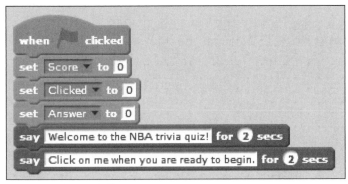

© 2014 Cengage Learning®

Step 6: Automating the Administration of the Quiz

At this point, you should have added scripts to each of the button sprites that indicate when they have been clicked and uniquely identify which of the four buttons was selected. Now it is time to create the two scripts belonging to the host sprite. The first script, shown next, is responsible for starting the application and getting the application ready to administer the quiz.

© 2014 Cengage Learning®

As you can see, this script has been set up to execute when the user clicks on the green Flag button. When this happens, the values assigned to all three of the script's variables are set to 0 (setting the score to zero, indicating that none of the buttons has been clicked, and that no answer has been specified). Next, two looks code blocks are used to display instructions, welcoming the user and then instructing her to click on the hostess when she's ready to begin taking the quiz.

The host sprite's second script, shown here, is responsible for the overall administration of the quiz. As you can see, it is pretty big and is made up of many different types of code blocks, some of which you have not learned about yet. As such, this chapter provides only a high-level overview of the script. Once you have read Chapters 9 and 10, you may want to return and review this script again.

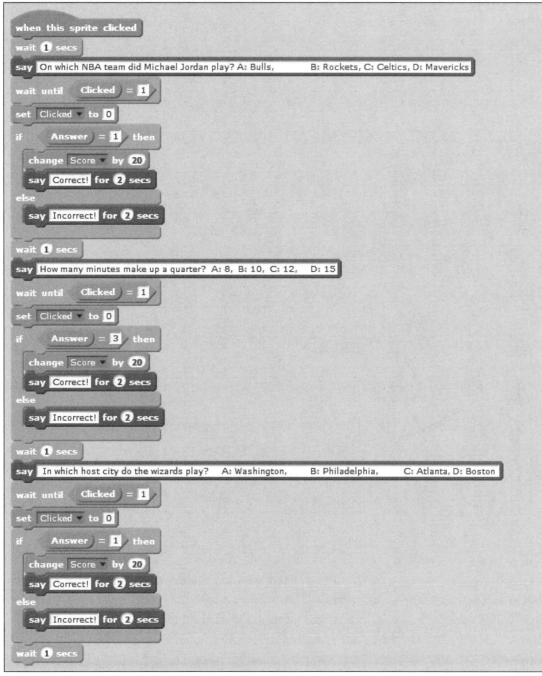

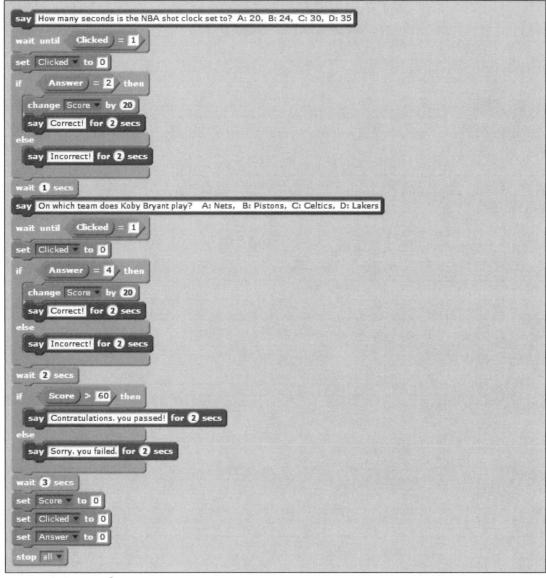

This script begins with a hat code block that executes when the user clicks on the host sprite. Next, the script's execution is paused for one second, and then a looks block is used to display a text message, presenting the user with the quiz's first question. The next code block, which contains a pair of embedded code blocks, pauses script execution and waits until the value assigned to the Clicked variable is set to 1 (which occurs only when the user specifies an answer by clicking on one of the four button sprites).

The value assigned to Clicked is then reset to 0, making the variable ready for the next quiz question. Next, a control code block is used to evaluate the user's answer to the quiz question. This is accomplished by checking to see if the player clicked on the A sprite, as indicated by a value of 1 being assigned to Clicked. If this is the case, the user's score is increased by 20, and a looks block is used to display a text message informing the user that her answer was correct. If this is not the case, the user is notified that the answer provided was incorrect.

The next four quiz questions are administered using programming logic that is identical to that used to administer the first question, the only difference being that a different question is presented and a different answer is required. Finally, once the last quiz question has been processed, the script's execution is paused for two seconds, after which the user's grade (the value assigned to Score) is evaluated to see if it is greater than 60, in which case the hostess announces that the user has passed the quiz. If this is not the case, the hostess announces that the user has failed. Either way, a three-second pause ensues, after which the values assigned to all three variables are reset to their default starting value of 0 to make the quiz ready for the next person. Finally, one last control block is executed, ensuring that all scripts within the application terminate their execution.

Step 7: Testing Your New Application

At this point, you have all the information you need to create your own copy of the NBA trivia quiz. Assuming that you have been following along and creating your copy of the application as you made your way through this chapter, your application project should look something like the example shown in Figure 7.22.

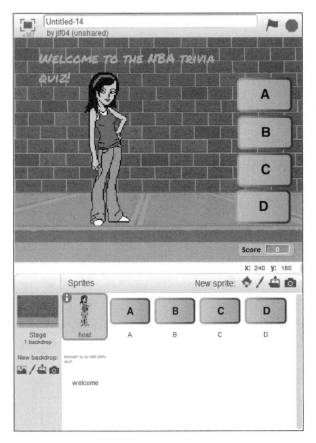

Figure 7.22
The completed application consists of a stage backdrop, six sprites, and six scripts.
© 2014 Lifelong Kindergarten Group

If you have not done so, go ahead and give your new application a name, switch to full screen mode, and start the NBA trivia quiz. As you test your new application, make sure that the feedback the hostess is providing after each answer is correct. In addition, keep an eye on the Score monitor and make sure that the game is correctly tabulating your grade.

CHAPTER 8

DOING A LITTLE MATH

Scratch 2.0 provides robust support for performing mathematical calculations. This lets you develop applications that can manipulate numeric data in a variety of ways. Scratch 2.0 provides this support through operator blocks. Operator blocks are reporter blocks, so you can only use them in conjunction with stack code blocks. This chapter provides a thorough review of each of these code blocks and shows you how to create a new Scratch 2.0 application: the Number Guessing game.

The major topics covered in this chapter include

- Adding, subtracting, multiplying, and dividing programmatically
- Generating random numbers using any range you specify
- Performing different types of numeric comparisons
- Concatenating values, retrieving characters from strings, and retrieving the length of values
- Performing a number of built-in mathematical operations

ADDITION, SUBTRACTION, MULTIPLICATION, AND DIVISION

Like all modern programming languages, Scratch 2.0 allows programmers to add, subtract, multiply, and divide numeric data. This capability is offered through the code blocks shown in Figure 8.1.

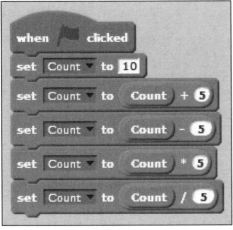

Figure 8.1

These code blocks let Scratch 2.0 programmers perform arithmetic calculations.

© 2014 Lifelong Kindergarten Group

The use of these code blocks is quite intuitive, with each code block clearly identifying its usage. You can embed these code blocks within any Scratch 2.0 code block that accepts numeric input. For example, the following script demonstrates how to use these code blocks to modify the value assigned to a variable named Count.

© 2014 Cengage Learning®

Here, the script begins by assigning an initial value of 10 to Count. Next, four sets of code blocks are executed. Each set consists of one stack block and two reporter blocks. The first set of statements sets the value of Count equal to the value currently assigned to Count plus 5, making Count equal to 15. The second set of code blocks sets Count equal to the value currently assigned to Count minus 5, making Count equal to 10. The third set of code blocks sets Count equal to the current value of Count times 5, making Count equal to 50. The last set of code blocks changes the value of Count to 10 by dividing its current value by 5.

UNDERSTANDING THE MATHEMATICAL ORDER OF PRECEDENCE

As is the case with all programming languages, Scratch 2.0 allows you to string together different combinations of operator blocks so you can create more complicated numeric calculations. For example, take a look at the following script.

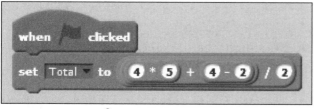

© 2014 Cengage Learning®

Here a small script has been created that evaluates a numeric expression and assigns the result to a variable named `Total`. This equation was created by embedding a series of operator blocks within one another. Specifically, the equation was created by embedding the code blocks shown in Figure 8.2 into one another.

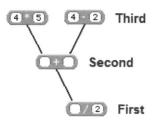

Figure 8.2
Creating complex formulas by assembling different combinations of code blocks.
© 2014 Lifelong Kindergarten Group

As shown in Figure 8.2, the equation was assembled by embedding the division code block into a variable block. Next, the addition code block was embedded within the left side of the division code block. Finally, a multiplication code block and a subtraction code block were embedded within the input fields of the addition code block.

Like all programming languages, Scratch 2.0 evaluates the components of mathematical expressions by following a specific order, referred to as the *order of precedence*.

Specifically, Scratch 2.0 evaluates an expression using a top-down approach. When applied to the example shown in Figures 8.2, Scratch 2.0 evaluates it as follows.

1. First, it calculates the value of the two top code blocks. Therefore, 4 is multiplied by 5 yielding a value of 20, and 2 is subtracted from 4 yielding a value of 2. At this stage, the expression has been evaluated as shown here.

   $20 + 2/2$

2. Next, the expression located in the second-level code bock (the addition block) is evaluated. Therefore, 20 is added to 2 yielding a value of 22. At this stage, the expression has been evaluated as shown here.

   $22/2$

3. Finally, the lowest-level code block is evaluated, dividing 22 by 2 and resulting in a final value of 11.

Generating a Random Number

Some applications, such as computer games, require an element of randomness or chance. For example, a game that needs to simulate the rolling of dice needs to be able to create a pair of random numbers in the range of 1 to 6. Scratch 2.0 provides the capability through the code block shown in Figure 8.3.

Figure 8.3
By default, this code block is configured to generate a number in the range of 1 to 10.
© 2014 Lifelong Kindergarten Group

This code block provides a means of generating random integer (whole) numbers using any specified range of numbers. The default range is 1 to 10, but you may change the input fields to suit your needs. If needed, you can generate negative numbers. In addition to hard-coding a numeric range into the control, you can substitute variable blocks by dragging and dropping them into either or both of this code block's input fields.

To develop an understanding of how this code block works, look at the following example.

© 2014 Cengage Learning®

Here, a script has been created that begins by assigning a variable named Count a starting value of 0. Next, the variable's value is changed by assigning it a randomly selected value in the range of 1 to 5. A loop is then set up to repeat the execution of two embedded code blocks. The loop is designed to repeat a specified number of times and is set up by default to execute 10 times. However, by dragging and dropping an instance of the Count variable block into the loop's input field, the number of times that the loop executes is randomly determined, depending on the randomly assigned value of Count.

Note

Each time the loop executes, it plays an audio file that sounds like a cat meowing. To give the audio file time to finish playing, a control block was added to pause script execution for one second. To see this script in action, create a new Scratch 2.0 application and add the script to the default cat sprite.

COMPARISON OPERATIONS

To work with numbers, you often need to mathematically manipulate them, as demonstrated in the previous section. Doing so ultimately leaves you with a result. Typically, you'll want to do something with this result once it has been calculated. For a simple application, all you may need to do is display its value. However, more often than not, you are going to end up using it to guide the execution of your application in some manner. For example, suppose you want to create a Number Guessing game that automatically generates a random number and then challenges the player to try to guess it. Once the random number is generated and stored in a variable, the player needs to be prompted to try to guess it (perhaps by clicking on one of 10 buttons with numbers printed on them). Once the player's guess is captured, the application needs to compare the player's guess against the value of the variable that stores the game's random number to determine whether the player's guess is correct. To facilitate this type of comparison operation, Scratch 2.0 provides access to the three code blocks shown in Figure 8.4.

Figure 8.4

These code blocks let you compare any two numeric values.

© 2014 Lifelong Kindergarten Group

The first and last code blocks shown in Figure 8.4 allow you to compare one value against a range of values. The first code block checks to see if the numeric value specified in its first input field is less than the value specified in its second input field. The third code block does the opposite, checking to see if the numeric value specified in its first input field is greater than the value specified in its second input field. The middle code block is used to determine if two values are equal.

To develop a better understanding of how to work with each of these three code blocks, let's look at a few examples. In the first example, shown below, a script has been created that executes whenever the green Flag button is clicked. When this happens, the value Count is set equal to 10. Next, an operator block is embedded within a control block to set up a conditional test that evaluates the value assigned to Count and to execute the code block embedded within the control block if the tested condition (for example, Count) is true. Since this is the case, a text string of Hello! is displayed in a speech bubble.

Note

To prove that the embedded operator block is working like it is supposed to, you can change the value assigned to Count to something other than 10 and run the example again. Since the value assigned to Count no longer equals 10, the tested condition would evaluate as false and the text message would not display.

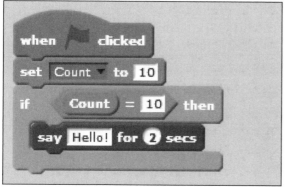

In this next example, the operator block that tests for greater than conditions is used. Again, a script has been set up to execute whenever the green Flag button is clicked. The value assigned to Count is then set to 0, and a control block is used to set up a loop that runs forever (until you provide a means for stopping its execution). A number of code blocks are embedded within the loop. The first block plays an audio file, and the second block pauses script execution for one second to allow Scratch 2.0 time to finish playing the file. Another control block is then used to set up a conditional test that evaluates the value assigned to Count to see if it is greater than 2, and if it is, another control block is used to terminate the script's execution. If the value assigned to Count is not greater than 2, the last code block located at the bottom of the loop is executed, incrementing the value of Count by one. The loop then repeats and executes again.

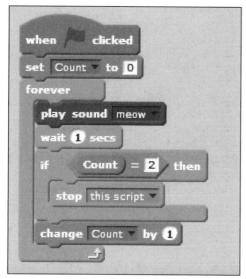

The first time the loop runs, the value assigned to Count is 0. The loop must iterate two times before the value of Count is set to 3, resulting in the termination of the script's execution. Because of this, the audio file plays three times.

In this final example, shown next, the operator block that tests for less than conditions is used. Like the previous two examples, this script is set up to execute whenever the green Flag button is clicked. When this happens, the value of Count is set to 1. Next, a loop is set up that repeatedly executes as long as the value of Count is less than 15. Each time this test evaluates as true, three embedded code blocks are executed. The first code block moves the sprite 25 steps. The next code block increments the value assigned to Count by one, and the last code block pauses script execution for one second.

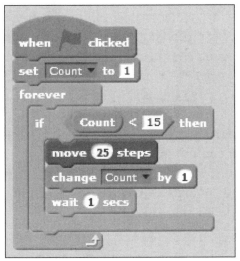

© 2014 Cengage Learning®

The way this script is written, its loop will execute 14 times and will stop executing when the value of Count finally reaches 15.

Creating Different Types of Conditional Tests

While Scratch 2.0 supplies you with only three code blocks for performing conditional tests (equality, greater than, and less than), most programming languages support three additional types of conditional tests, allowing you to perform the following comparison operations:

- Greater than or equal to
- Less than or equal to
- Not equal to

Although Scratch 2.0 does not provide equivalent code blocks, you can easily set up equivalent comparison tests by combining the three code blocks just discussed with Scratch 2.0's logical comparison code blocks, as shown in Figure 8.5.

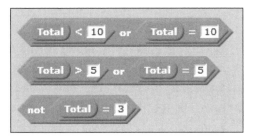

Figure 8.5

Creating customized logical comparisons.

© 2014 Lifelong Kindergarten Group

The first combination of code blocks shown in Figure 8.5 creates a test that determines if the value assigned to a variable named Total is less than or equal to 10. This example is made up of five code blocks—two variable blocks, two operator blocks used to perform less than and equality comparisons, and another operator block that is used to tie everything together. The second combination of code blocks shown in Figure 8.5 is similar and is designed to create a test that checks to see if the value assigned to Total is greater than or equal to 5. The last example is made up of three code blocks and is used to evaluate the values assigned to Total to determine if it is not equal to 3. You will learn more about code blocks that support logical comparisons in the next section.

PERFORMING LOGICAL COMPARISONS

In addition to code blocks designed to perform mathematical and comparison operations, Scratch 2.0 provides access to three code blocks that support logical comparison operations. These code blocks are shown in Figure 8.6.

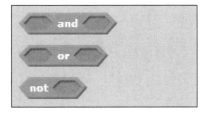

Figure 8.6

Using these code blocks, you can perform more complex comparison operations.

© 2014 Lifelong Kindergarten Group

The first code block is used to test two different sets of values to determine if both are true. The second code block is used to test two different sets of values to determine if at least one is true. And the last code block lets you evaluate two values to determine if the tested condition is false (not true).

To help you better understand how to work with all three of these code blocks, let's review a few examples. The first example, shown next, is a script that executes whenever the green Flag button is clicked. When this occurs, the value assigned to the variable Count is set to 50. Next, a control code block is used to analyze the value assigned to Count. If the value of Count is less than 100 but greater than 10, the end statement embedded within the control block is executed. However, if both tested conditions evaluate as false, the embedded code block is not executed.

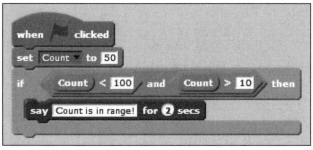

© 2014 Cengage Learning®

Note

Scratch 2.0 is flexible in its support for operator blocks. For example, if you prefer, you can swap the order in which the two embedded operator blocks occur (for example, checking to see that Count is greater than 10 before checking to make sure that Count is also less than 100), and the results would be the same.

This next example is similar to the previous example, except that instead of ensuring that both tested conditions evaluate as being true, the script has been modified so that only one of the tested conditions has evaluated as true in order for the embedded code block to be executed.

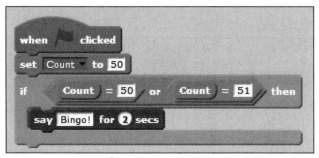

© 2014 Cengage Learning®

This final example shows a script that performs a negative test, checking to see if two values are not equal instead of checking to see if they are equal. As a result, if the value assigned to Count is not equal to 50, which it is not, the code block embedded within the control block is executed.

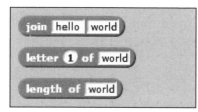

MANIPULATING STRINGS

The operator blocks shown in Figure 8.7 are new in Scratch 2.0 and let you take two strings and concatenate them, retrieve a letter from a string, and determine a string's length.

Figure 8.7

These code blocks concatenate strings, retrieve letters from them, and determine their length.

The following example demonstrates how to work with all three of the code blocks.

```
when      clicked
say  join  Hello  World!  for  2  secs
set  Count ▾  to  1
set  Name ▾  to  William
say  Hello  for  2  secs
repeat  length of  Name
    say  letter  Count  of  Name  for  1  secs
    change  Count ▾  by  1
```

© 2014 Cengage Learning®

This example executes when the user clicks on the green Flag button, at which time the second code block, which contains an embedded join operator block, takes the text strings of Hello and World! and concatenates them into a string with a blank space separator and then has its sprite say the resulting string, as shown in Figure 8.8.

Figure 8.8
The second code block concatenates the string to have the sprite say "Hello World!"
© 2014 Lifelong Kindergarten Group

The remainder of the script sets the value of a variable named Count to 1 and the value of a second variable named Name to William and uses a looks block to have the default sprite say Hello for 2 seconds. Then a loop is set up to repeat one for each letter that makes up the value of the name (for example, seven times since William consists of seven letters). Within the loop, another looks block, with an embedded letter block, is used to retrieve and say one letter from the word stored in Name. The next code block increments the value assigned to Count by one so that the next time the loop repeats, it retrieves the next letter from Name. By the time the loop completes, every letter that makes up the contents of Name (for example, William) is said by the sprite one at time.

ROUNDING NUMBERS AND RETRIEVING REMAINDERS

The next set of operator blocks, shown in Figure 8.9, let you retrieve the remainder portion of any division operation and round any decimal number to the nearest whole number.

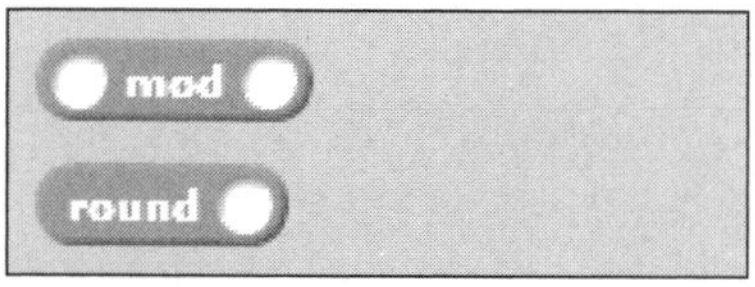

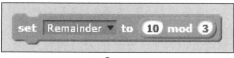

Figure 8.9
These code blocks retrieve remainders and round numbers.
© 2014 Lifelong Kindergarten Group

The first code block shown in Figure 8.9 returns the remainder portion of a division operation, also referred to as *modulus*, as demonstrated in the following example, which divides 10 by 3 and then assigns the modulus (for example, a value of 1) to a variable named Remainder.

set Remainder ▼ to 10 mod 3

© 2014 Cengage Learning®

The second code block shown in Figure 8.9 returns the rounded value for a specified numeric value, rounded to the nearest whole number, as demonstrated in the following examples. These examples return values of 4 and 5, respectively.

set TestValue ▼ to round 4.4

set TestValue ▼ to round 4.6

© 2014 Cengage Learning®

WORKING WITH BUILT-IN MATHEMATICAL FUNCTIONS

In addition to all the mathematical operations that you can put together using the operator blocks previously discussed in this chapter, Scratch 2.0 provides one additional multipurpose code block, as shown in Figure 8.10.

Figure 8.10
This code block can assist you in setting up extremely complex calculations.
© 2014 Lifelong Kindergarten Group

This code block is designed to perform any of 14 different mathematical functions, which can be selected from the code block's drop-down list. The functions that this code block can perform are outlined in the following list:

- **abs.** Returns the absolute, nonnegative value of a number.
- **floor.** Returns the largest integer value of a number that is less than or equal to a specified value.
- **ceiling.** Returns the smallest integer value of a number that is less than or equal to a specified value.
- **sqrt.** Returns the square root of a number.
- **sin.** Returns a value representing the sine of an angle.
- **cos.** Returns a value representing the cosine of an angle.
- **tan.** Returns a value representing the tangent of an angle.
- **asin.** Returns the arc sine for the specified numeric value.
- **acos.** Returns the arc cosine for the specified numeric value.
- **atan.** Returns the arc tangent for the specific numeric value.
- **ln.** Returns the inverse of the natural exponent of a specified value (for example, the opposite of e^).
- **log.** Returns the natural log of a number.
- **e^.** Returns the natural exponent of a specified value.
- **10^.** Returns the value of a number raised to the 10th power.

These code blocks can be real time-savers when developing applications that require the use of any of the mathematical functions supported by the code block, saving you the trouble of implementing the underlying programming logic yourself to retrieve similar results. As a result, not only will you spend less time working on the development of your application, but the programming logic that you have to develop will be simplified and easier to maintain since this code block can do most of the heavy lifting for you.

To specify which function you want to work with, all you have to do is select it from the code block's drop-down list. For example, the following examples demonstrate the use of two different functions provided by this code block.

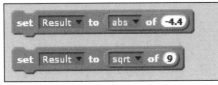

© 2014 Cengage Learning®

This example consists of two sets of code blocks. The first set of code blocks returns the absolute value of –4.4, which is 4.4, and assigns that value to a variable named Result. The second set of blocks returns the square root of 9, which is 3, and assigns that value to a variable named Result.

DEVELOPING THE NUMBER GUESSING GAME QUIZ PROJECT

The remainder of this chapter is focused on the development of your next Scratch 2.0 application: the Number Guessing game. This application uses operator blocks to generate random numbers for the player to guess and to compare the player's guesses against the game's randomly generated number.

In total, the application is made up of a backdrop, 11 sprites, and 12 scripts. When run, the game challenges the player to guess a randomly generated number in the range of 0 to 9 in as few guesses as possible. Figure 8.11 shows an example of how the game looks when it's started.

Figure 8.11
The Number Guessing game is moderated by the cat sprite.
© 2014 Lifelong Kindergarten Group

To enter a guess, the player must click on one of the button sprites located at the bottom of the stage. The cat provides immediate feedback after each guess, as demonstrated in Figure 8.12.

Figure 8.12
The cat lets the player know when guesses are too high or too low.
© 2014 Lifelong Kindergarten Group

Figure 8.13 shows how the game looks once the player finally manages to guess the game's secret random number.

Figure 8.13
The player guessed the secret number in five guesses.
© 2014 Lifelong Kindergarten Group

The game automatically generates a new random number at the end of each game so the game is ready to be played again. The development of this application project is created by following a series of steps, as outlined here:

1. Create a new Scratch 2.0 application project.
2. Add a backdrop to the stage.
3. Add and remove sprites.
4. Add variables that the application needs.
5. Add an audio file to the application.
6. Add scripts to each button to collect player guesses.
7. Add the programming logic required to process player guesses.
8. Test your work.

Step 1: Creating a New Scratch 2.0 Project

The first step in the development of the Number Guessing game is to create a new Scratch 2.0 application project. Do so by either opening Scratch 2.0, thereby automatically creating a new Scratch 2.0 application project, or clicking on the File menu and then selecting New.

Step 2: Adding a Stage Backdrop

The next step in the development of the Number Guessing game is to add a backdrop to the stage. To do so, click on the blank stage thumbnail located in the sprite list and then change its backdrop by clicking on the Backdrops tab located at the top of the scripts area. Next, click on the Choose Backdrop from Library icon. When the Backdrop library window opens, click on the Outdoors folder. Then select the `brick-wall1` thumbnail and click on the OK button. Since the application needs only one backdrop, remove the default blank backdrop, named `backdrop1`, from your project.

Step 3: Adding and Removing Sprites

The Number Guessing game is composed of the default cat sprite plus 10 button sprites and a variable monitor, as shown in Figure 8.14.

Figure 8.14

An overview of the different parts of the Number Guessing game.

To add the first of the sprites representing the 10 input buttons, click on the Choose Sprite from Library icon to open the Sprite Library window. Click on the Things category and locate the Button1 sprite. Then click on the OK button. Select the thumbnail for this sprite, and then click on the Costumes tab to display it in the Paint Editor. The sprite is currently too big for the projects purposed. Click on the image until it becomes enclosed within an orange square box. With the sprite selected, click on the Shrink icon, located at the top of the program editor in the menu bar, 12 times to return the size of the sprite to the size needed. Rename this sprite Button0. Right-click in the sprite list and select Duplicate from the menu that appears. Make sure the sprite is named Button1. If it is not, change its name accordingly. Duplicate Button1 eight additional times, creating Button2 through Button 9. Using the Paint Editor, select each of the 10 button sprites, starting with Button0, and paint its number on it, so that Button0 is labeled 0, Button1 is labeled 1, and so on.

When you're finished painting the button sprites, arrange them in order from left to right across the bottom of the stage, as shown in Figure 8.14. At this point, all that is left in the design of the application's user interface is the display and reposition of the monitor, which you do in the next step.

Step 4: Adding Variables That the Application Requires

To execute, the Number Guessing game requires three variables, as shown in Figure 8.15. To add these variables to the application, click on the Variables category located at the top of the blocks palette, and then click on the Make a Variable button three times to define global variables named Guess, No Of Guesses, and RandomNo.

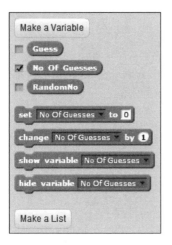

Figure 8.15

The Number Guessing game requires three variables.

© 2014 Lifelong Kindergarten Group

The variable named Guess is used to store the most recent guess the player made. The variable named No Of Guesses is used to keep track of the number of guesses the player made during each game. The variable named RandomNo stores the game's randomly generated secret number. Once you've added them, clear the check box controls belonging to the Guess and No Of Guesses variables to prevent their monitors from being displayed. Lastly, drag and drop the monitor for the No Of Guesses variable to the upper-right side of the stage.

Step 5: Adding an Audio File to the Application

The Number Guessing game uses two audio files that are played as sound effects when the player makes incorrect and correct guesses. The audio file played when the player enters a missed guess is the default pop sound, which is automatically included as part of each of the button sprites used in the application. The second audio file is the Fairydust sound, which is played whenever the player manages to correctly guess the mystery number.

To add the Fairydust audio file, select the cat sprite thumbnail in the sprites list and then click on the Sounds tab located at the top of the scripts area. Next, click on the Choose Sound from Library icon to display the Sound Library window, click on the Electronic folder, select the Fairydust sound, and click on OK.

Step 6: Adding Scripts to Capture Player Input

The programming logic that drives the Number Guessing application is divided into a series of scripts belonging to the application's sprites. Specifically, you must add small scripts to each of the button sprites to capture and save player guesses. In addition, you must add two scripts to the cat sprite. These two scripts, which are responsible for starting the game and processing player guesses, are covered in Step 7.

To begin work on each of the scripts belonging to the button sprites, select the sprite representing the 0 button, and then add the following code blocks to it.

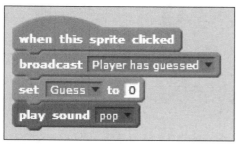

The script begins with a hat block that executes whenever the sprite is clicked (for example, when the player clicks on it as a guess). When this occurs, the second code block in the script sends a `Player has guessed` broadcast message to the other sprites as a signal that the player has submitted a guess. The `Player has guessed` must be typed into the control block exactly as shown. A third code block is then used to assign a value to the `Guess` variable, recording the player's guess. Note that in this example, setting `Guess` to 0 indicates that the player has submitted a guess of 0. The last code block in the script plays the default pop audio file, which lets the player know that the guess has been processed.

Note

A *broadcast message* is a message exchanged between sprites that signals when an event of some type has occurred within an application. Broadcast messages are generated by and received using various control code blocks, which you learn about in Chapter 9, "Controlling Script Execution." For now, all you need to know is that this application uses broadcast messages to coordinate activity and keep track of what is occurring within the game.

The scripts that need to be added to the rest of the button sprites are almost identical to the script that you just added. The only difference is that you need to modify the value that is set in the third code block to properly reflect which button sprite each script belongs to. The easiest way to add these scripts to the other nine button sprites is to drag and drop an instance of the first script onto each of the nine other sprites and then select each sprite, one at a time, and modify the value of the third code block accordingly.

Step 7: Processing Player Guesses

Once scripts have been added to all 10 of the button sprites, it is time to create the two scripts belonging to the cat sprite. The first of these scripts is shown next and is responsible for initializing the game and getting it ready to play.

This script is executed when the player clicks on the green Flag button. It begins by assigning an initial value of 0 to No Of Guesses and then assigns a randomly generated value in the range of 0 to 9 to a variable named RandomNo. Lastly, it displays a pair of messages that inform the player that the cat is thinking of a number and challenges the player to try to guess it.

The second and final script to be added to the cat sprite is shown next. This script is automatically executed whenever the Player has guessed broadcast message is received. This happens when the player clicks on one of the 10 button sprites. First, the script modifies the value assigned to No Of Guesses by increasing it by one. This allows the application to keep track of the number of guesses that the player has made in the current game.

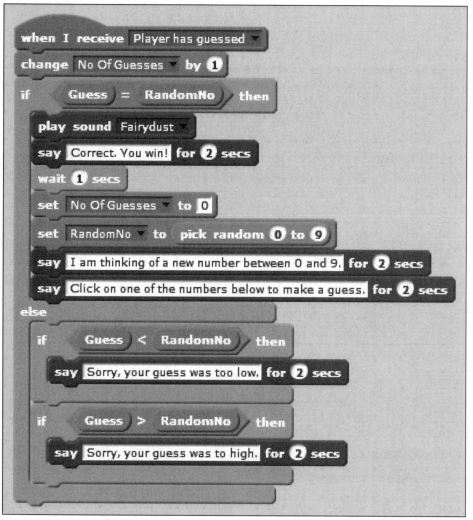

The rest of the script is made up of code blocks embedded within a control block. The control block begins by evaluating the value assigned to the Guess variable to see if it is equal to the value assigned to the RandomNo variable. If this is the case, a series of code blocks embedded within the upper portion of the control block are executed. If this is not the case, code blocks embedded in the bottom of the control block are executed.

The code statements located in the upper half of the control block, which execute when the player enters a correct guess, perform the following actions:

- Play the Fairydust audio file that was added to the cat sprite back in Step 5.
- Notify the player that the game has been won.
- Pause script execution for one second.
- Reset the value of No Of Guesses to 0.
- Select a new random number for the game.
- Challenge the player to play again.

If, on the other hand, the player enters an incorrect guess, the code blocks embedded at the bottom of the script are executed. These code blocks are organized into two separate control blocks. The first control block evaluates the value assigned to Guess to see if it is less than RandomNo. If it is, a message is displayed that informs the player that the guess was too low. The second control block determines if the value assigned to Guess is less than RandomNo. If it is, a message is displayed that informs the player that the guess was too high.

Step 8: Saving and Executing Your New Scratch 2.0 Application

At this point, you have all the information you need to create your own copy of the Number Guessing game. If you have not already done so, give your new project a name. Switch to Presentation mode, run the game, and put your new game through its paces. Remember to begin game play by clicking on the green Flag button and following the instructions that the cat sprite provides.

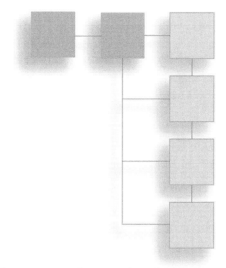

CHAPTER 9

CONTROLLING SCRIPT EXECUTION

To create a script, you must know how to work with events and control code blocks. Events blocks let you initiate and coordinate script execution. Control blocks let you implement loops and conditional programming logic, which are the building blocks of advanced and complex applications. Control blocks can pause and halt script execution. They also allow you to clone and manage cloned copies of sprites.

The major topics covered in this chapter include

- How to use control blocks to initiate script execution
- How to use broadcast to coordinate script execution
- How to pause and halt script execution
- How to set up different types of loops and implement conditional programming logic

INTRODUCING SCRATCH EVENTS AND CONTROL BLOCKS

Scratch control blocks offer programmers many different capabilities, all of which are geared toward controlling script execution. Without events and control blocks, scripts can't execute. Nor can they pause, loop, or execute conditional logic when evaluating data. Through events and control blocks, Scratch can perform all the actions listed here:

- Program events
- Pause script execution
- Create loops

- Send and receive broadcast messages
- Execute conditional logic
- Halt script execution

You have already seen events and control blocks in action in every script presented in the first eight chapters of this book. Now it is time to learn more about these two powerful categories of code blocks and the programming features they provide.

EVENT PROGRAMMING

Code blocks belonging to the Events category initiate script execution and send and receive broadcast messages. They enable you to develop scripts that you can execute in response to a variety of circumstances, such as when the user does something with the mouse or keyboard. Through message broadcasting, events code blocks also allow you to coordinate and synchronize script execution.

Initiating Script Execution

Events control blocks initiate script execution, which is critical to the execution of Scratch applications. They do this with hat blocks, including those shown in Figure 9.1.

Figure 9.1
Hat blocks automate the execution of scripts.
© 2014 Lifelong Kindergarten Group

As you have seen in many examples in this book, the first code block shown in Figure 9.1 initiates a script's execution whenever the green Flag button is clicked, and it is the most common means of starting an application's execution. For example, if you were to add the following script to any sprite or backdrop in a Scratch application, it would automatically play a specified audio file (provided that file has been imported).

© 2014 Cengage Learning®

The second code block shown in Figure 9.1 initiates a script's execution whenever a specified keyboard key is pressed. The key that is used as the trigger is selected by clicking on the code block's drop-down list and making a selection of one of the following keystrokes:

- Up, down, right, and left arrows keys
- The space key
- a–z
- 0–9

For example, the following script demonstrates how to move a sprite by 50 steps whenever the keyboard's space key is pressed.

© 2014 Cengage Learning®

The third code block shown in Figure 9.1 initiates script execution whenever the sprite to which it belongs is clicked. The following script demonstrates how to use this code block to automate the display of text in a speech bubble whenever the sprite to which it has been added is clicked.

© 2014 Cengage Learning®

The fourth code block shown in Figure 9.1 initiates script execution whenever the program switches to a specified backdrop. The following script demonstrates how to use this code block to automate the display of text in a speech bubble when the sprite to which it has been added is clicked.

© 2014 Cengage Learning®

The last code block shown in Figure 9.1 initiates script execution whenever a sound captured from the computer's microphone exceeds a specified volume level as specified by a numeric value, displaying a message via a speech bubble.

© 2014 Cengage Learning®

Note

Scratch provides a fourth hat control block, which is covered in the next section of this chapter. This code block initiates script execution when broadcast messages are received.

Sending and Receiving Broadcasts

Because Scratch applications can be made up of many different sprites, each of which may consist of many different scripts, coordinating the activity of all the different parts of the application can be challenging. By providing access to the three code blocks shown in Figure 9.2, Scratch allows you to send and receive broadcast messages as a means of coordinating script execution.

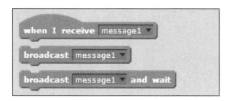

Figure 9.2
Broadcast messages enable one script to notify other scripts that an event has occurred.
© 2014 Lifelong Kindergarten Group

Using the second and third code blocks shown in Figure 9.2, you can pass messages to any script within an application that begins with the hat code block shown at the top of Figure 9.2. For example, the following script demonstrates how to send a broadcast message of jump to all sprites within the application.

© 2014 Cengage Learning®

To specify the message that the control code block sends, all you have to do is click on the block's drop-down list and then either select a previously typed message or create a new message by clicking on New Message and then typing in the message in the New Message window, as shown in Figure 9.3.

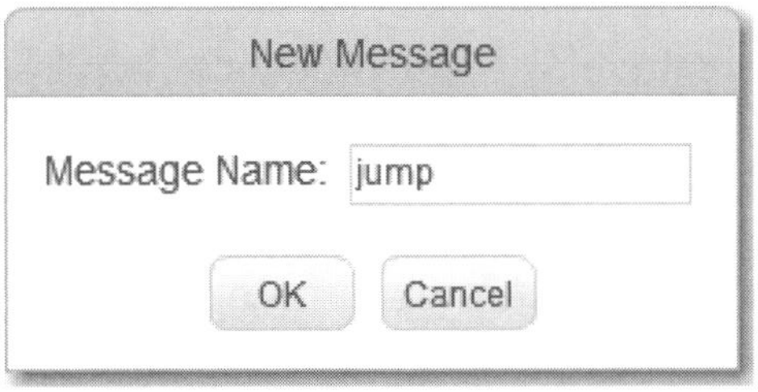

Figure 9.3
Keying the message to be broadcast to all sprites in the application.
© 2014 Lifelong Kindergarten Group

This particular code block sends its message and then allows the script in which it is embedded to continue executing. Alternatively, the following script not only sends a broadcast message but also waits until every script in the application, which has been set up to execute when the message is sent, has finished executing.

© 2014 Cengage Learning®

Using the hat block, you can set up a script to execute whenever a specified message is received.

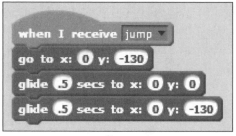

© 2014 Cengage Learning®

Note

Using the three previous scripts, you can create a new application made up of two button controls and the default cat sprite. By assigning the first script to the first button sprite, the second script to the second button sprite, and the third script to the cat sprite, you can make the cat sprite jump up and down on the stage any time you click on one of the button sprites.

CONTROLLING SCRIPT EXECUTION

Code blocks belonging to the Control block category provide essential controls over script execution. You can use the code blocks to pause script execution, establish loops to repeatedly and efficiently process large amounts of information, or control game play. Control blocks also let you implement conditional programming logic and halt script execution. In addition, new control blocks in Scratch 2.0 allow you to create, delete, and clone sprites during program execution and trigger script execution when clones are started.

Pausing Script Execution

Once they're started, scripts execute without pause until they are done. However, sometimes you need to temporarily pause a script's execution for a specified period. The code block that you need to use in this type of situation is shown in Figure 9.4.

Figure 9.4

Using this control block, you can pause script execution for as long as necessary.

© 2014 Lifelong Kindergarten Group

This code block adds brief pauses to your Scratch applications. For example, you might want to pause a script's execution for a second or two after the player scores a point. This brief pause allows the player a moment to review the score and to get ready for the next point. Another reason for pausing a script's execution is to help manage the playback of audio files, as demonstrated in the following example.

© 2014 Cengage Learning®

Here, you see a script that plays two audio files. To allow the first audio file time to play back, the script is paused for two seconds, after which execution resumes and the second audio file is played. If you were to remove the control block that pauses the script from this example, both audio files would play simultaneously, interfering with one another.

TIP

It you want to continuously play an audio file without pausing a script's execution, consider putting the code statements that are responsible for audio file playback in their own script and adding that script to the stage.

The control block shown in Figure 9.5 also pauses script execution, waiting until a specified condition becomes true. This code block is covered a little later in this chapter, when conditional programming logic is discussed.

Figure 9.5

This code block provides another way of conditionally pausing script execution.

© 2014 Lifelong Kindergarten Group

Executing Loops

Most computer applications and games are interactive, meaning that they respond to user input and react accordingly. That's why it is often necessary to execute collections of code statements repeatedly. For example, an arcade-style computer game might require the continuous playback of background music and sound effects. This would require the repeated execution of programming logic required to manage sound playback for as long as the game was played. To manage this type of interaction, you need to add loops to your applications. In Scratch, a *loop* is a collection of one or more code blocks embedded with a control block that are repeatedly executed.

Without loops, programmers would have to create extremely large scripts filled with repeated series of duplicate statements to perform certain tasks. For example, to create a Scratch application that bounces the cat sprite up and down four times without a loop, you would have to add a script like the one shown next to the sprite.

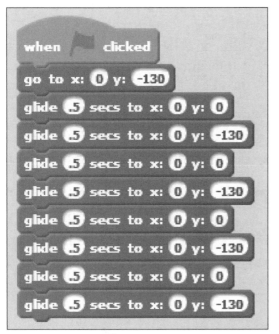

© 2014 Cengage Learning®

The script begins by positioning the sprite at the bottom center of the stage. Two sets of motion blocks are needed to bounce the sprite one time. To bounce the sprite up and down four times, you have to repeat these two code blocks four times. Suppose you wanted to make the sprite bounce 10, 100, or 1,000 times. Clearly, in this situation, a loop is needed.

Scratch supplies access to two code blocks that you can use to set up loops, as shown in Figure 9.6.

Note

Scratch also supplies two additional control blocks that offer the capability to conditionally execute loops. These two code blocks are discussed a little later in this chapter when conditional logic is covered.

Figure 9.6
Using these code blocks, you can create loops that repeat the execution of any code blocks you embed within them.
© 2014 Lifelong Kindergarten Group

You can set up the first of the two code blocks shown in Figure 9.6 as a loop that executes forever, which really means that the loop repeatedly executes until the script in which it resides is halted. For example, the following script uses this code block to set up a loop that bounces a sprite over and over again, until the Stop Everything button is clicked.

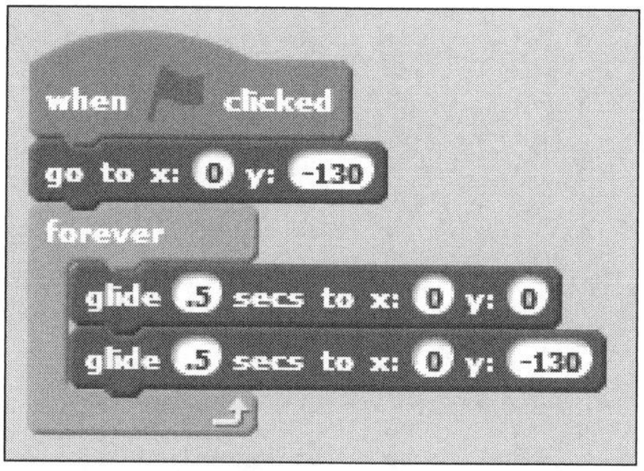

© 2014 Cengage Learning®

The first statement moves the sprite to the bottom center of the stage. The two statements within the loop bounce the sprite, in a gliding motion, up and down from the bottom to the middle of the stage.

Note

In Scratch, there are two ways to force an immediate termination of a script. First, you can halt a script by stopping the execution of the application when you click on the red Stop Everything button. However, this option can often be a bit of overkill. As a less extreme option, Scratch offers a control block that allows you to halt only the script in which it is used, halt all scripts except for the script in which it is used, or halt every script in the program. This control block is reviewed a little later in this chapter.

Rather than repeating the execution of a loop forever, you can use the second code block shown in Figure 9.6 to set up a loop that executes a predetermined number of times. For example, the following script demonstrates how to bounce a sprite up and down a total of 10 times.

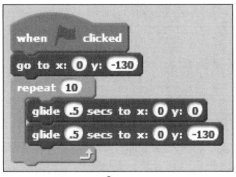

© 2014 Cengage Learning®

Obviously, the fewer code blocks you use when developing scripts, the more streamlined and easier to support your applications will be. Loops make programming a lot easier and provide a tool that you can use to repeat the execution of any number of code statements with as little fuss as possible.

Conditional Programming Logic

The next set of control code blocks provided by Scratch is shown in Figure 9.7. These code blocks allow you to apply conditional programming logic to your scripts.

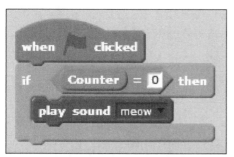

Figure 9.7

These four code blocks let you conditionally execute collections of code blocks.

© 2014 Lifelong Kindergarten Group

Using these code blocks, you can analyze data within your applications and make decisions based on this analysis, resulting in the conditional execution of collections of code blocks. The key concept to understand when working with these types of code blocks is that conditional logic involves an evaluation as to whether a condition is `true` or not. If the condition being analyzed is `true`, the code blocks embedded within the control block are executed. However, if the condition being analyzed proves `false`, the embedded code blocks are not executed.

The following script demonstrates how to use the first code block shown in Figure 9.7 to set up a loop that conditionally executes the playback of an audio file. When executed, this script examines the value assigned to a variable named `Counter` to see if it is equal to 0, and if it is, the audio file is played.

© 2014 Cengage Learning®

Sometimes you may want to execute either of two sets of code blocks based on the results of a tested condition. You can accomplish this using the second code block shown in Figure 9.7.

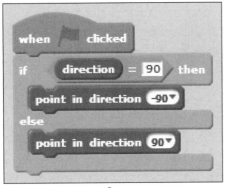

© 2014 Cengage Learning®

Here, a conditional test is performed that checks to see if the direction that a sprite is facing is 90 degrees. If it is, the direction that the sprite is pointing is reversed. If you run the script repeatedly, the direction that the sprite is pointing is continuously reversed.

This next example demonstrates how to use a control block that pauses script execution and waits for a specified condition to become true.

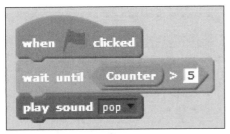

© 2014 Cengage Learning®

Here, a script has been set up that, once run, checks on the value assigned to Counter to see if it is greater than 5. If it is, an audio file is played. If Counter is not greater than 5, the script pauses its execution, waiting until the value of Counter exceeds 5 before finishing its execution.

Finally, the last example demonstrates how to work with the last of the control blocks shown in Figure 9.7. Here, a loop is set up to execute repeatedly until the value assigned to Counter is set to equal 3, at which time the loop stops running. Each time the loop runs, it moves, or bounces, its associated sprite up and down on the stage.

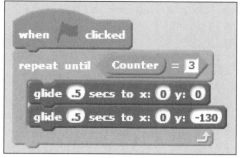

Nesting Conditional Control Code Blocks

As powerful as the control blocks are that facilitate conditional execution, they are limited to analyzing a single condition at a time. To develop more complex programming logic, you can embed one control block within another, as demonstrated in the following example.

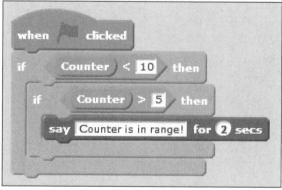

Here, one control block has been embedded within another control block to further analyze the value assigned to Counter. If necessary, you can embed control blocks many levels deep. However, the deeper you go, the more difficult your scripts are to understand and maintain.

Preventing Endless Loops

Loops are extremely powerful tools, providing the capability to perform repetitive tasks with ease. However, if you are not careful when setting them up, you can accidentally set up an endless loop. An *endless loop* is a loop that, because of a logical error on the programmer's part, never ends. For example, you might want to set up a loop that plays an audio file five times. But suppose when setting up the loop that you made a mistake that prevented the loop from terminating, as shown here.

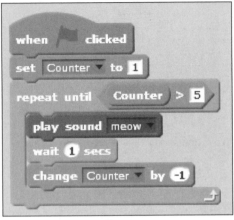

© 2014 Cengage Learning®

Here, the intention was to set up a loop that would execute five times. The loop has been set up to execute for as long as the value assigned to Counter is less than 5. Counter is assigned an initial value of 1, and its value is supposed to be incremented by 1 each time the loop executes. However, instead of incrementing the value of Counter by 1 at the end of the loop, the value of Counter is decremented by a value of −1. As a result, the loop never terminates, forever repeating the playback of the audio file. To prevent endless loops from occurring, you need to take extra care when setting up loops and test your scripts thoroughly when developing your applications.

Terminating Script Execution

The control block shown in Figure 9.8 lets you terminate script execution. This code blocks programmatically halts script execution within your Scratch applications.

Figure 9.8
Using this code block, you can halt the execution of scripts within an application.
© 2014 Lifelong Kindergarten Group

This control block has a drop-down list that lets you choose any of the following options:

- **All.** Halts the execution of every script in the application.

- **This Script.** Halts the execution of the script that contains the code block.

- **Other Scripts in Sprite.** Halts the executions of every script belonging to the sprite except for the sprite that contains this block.

Using this code block, you can halt the execution of the scripts where the code block is placed, as demonstrated in the following example.

© 2014 Cengage Learning®

Here, the script checks to see if the value assigned to a variable named Counter is equal to 3, and if it is, an audio file is played. If Counter is not equal to 3, a different audio file is played, and the script's execution is halted. Halting a script this way forces its immediate termination, even if the script contains additional code blocks that have not been executed.

This next example demonstrates how to use this code block to not only halt the execution of the current script but halt the execution of every script in the application. For example, the following script executes a loop three times and then halts the execution of every script in the application in which it resides.

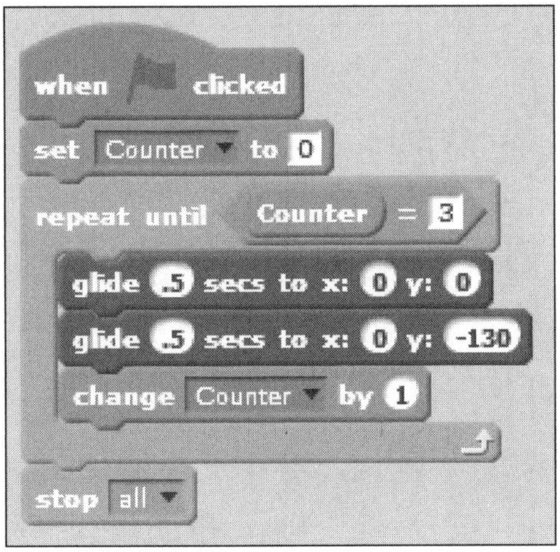

© 2014 Cengage Learning®

Cloning Sprites

Cloning is a new capability in Scratch 2.0. It lets you make an identical copy of any sprite in your Scratch 2.0 project. Cloning can greatly simplify program development. For example, let's say you wanted to create a game in which 10 sheep are to follow their shepherd around the stage. Rather than create the first sheep and then duplicate it repeatedly when designing your project and perhaps hide them until it is time to show them on the stage, you can instead create and program a single sheep and then make copies or clones of the sheep on-the-fly during program execution.

The three control blocks shown in Figure 9.9 are used to create, delete, and initiate clone execution.

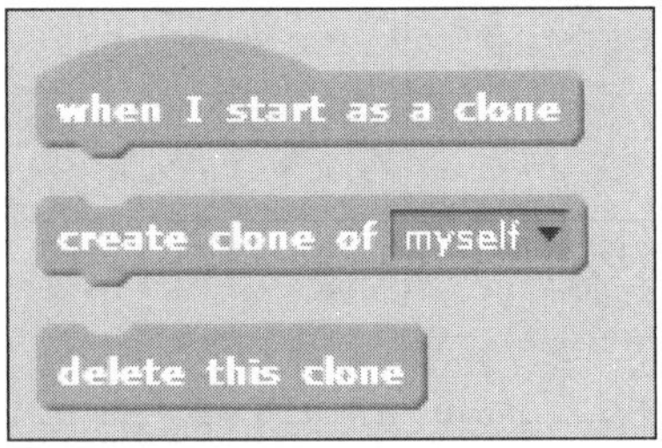

Figure 9.9

These control blocks let you programmatically work with sprite clones.

© 2014 Lifelong Kindergarten Group

To understand how to work with these three control blocks, let's create a new Scratch project named Butterfly Clones. To begin, create a new project and remove its default sprite, replacing it with the Butterfly2 sprite found in the sprite library. Place the new sprite in the center of the stage. Now add the following script to the sprite.

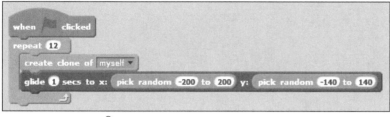

© 2014 Cengage Learning®

This sprite executes when the user clicks on the green Flag button, at which time it executes a loop 12 times, creating 12 clones of the Butterfly2 sprite at random locations around the stage. When done, there will be 13 butterfly sprites scattered at different locations on the stage.

Next, add this second script to the Butterfly2 sprite. When executed, it deletes all cloned instances of the Butterfly2 sprite from the stage, leaving only the original sprite.

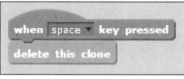

© 2014 Cengage Learning®

That's all there is to this project. If you have not done so, give it a name of Butterfly Clones, and then test its execution. Figure 9.10 shows how the program looks after the 12 cloned sprites are added to the stage.

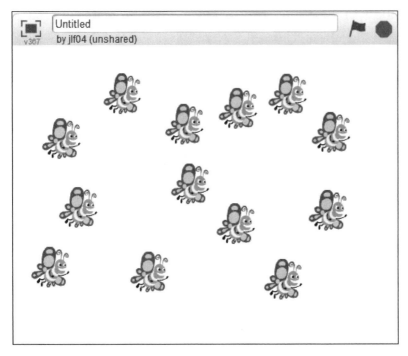

Figure 9.10
An example of how the stage looks once all 12 clones have been added.

You can press the spacebar at any time to delete and clear the clones from the stage.

DEVELOPING THE BALL CHASE GAME

The rest of this chapter is dedicated to teaching you how to create your next Scratch application: the Ball Chase game. This application makes heavy use of different control blocks to control the movement of the ball and the cat that chases it around the stage. In total, the application is made up of four sprites and nine scripts. The object of the game is to try to prevent the cat from catching the ball as it chases it around the stage. If you can keep the ball out of the cat's reach for 30 seconds, you win. Figure 9.11 shows how the game looks when it's started.

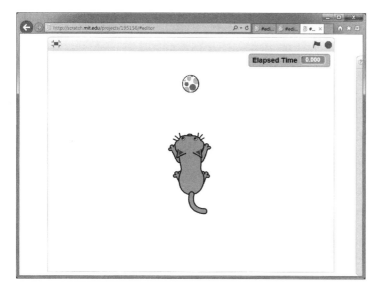

Figure 9.11
The object of the game is to prevent the cat from catching the ball.
© 2014 Lifelong Kindergarten Group

To play, all you have to do is move the mouse pointer around the stage; the ball automatically follows. If the cat manages to catch the ball before 30 seconds is up, the game ends, as demonstrated in Figure 9.12.

Figure 9.12
The game ends if the cat catches the ball.
© 2014 Lifelong Kindergarten Group

Figure 9.13 shows how the game looks when the player successfully manages to evade the cat for the entire 30 seconds.

Figure 9.13
The player wins if the ball can be kept away from the cat for 30 seconds.

You accomplish the development of this application by following a series of steps, as outlined here:

1. Create a new Scratch project.

2. Add and remove sprites.

3. Add variables that the application needs.

4. Add an audio file to the application.

5. Add a script to control ball movement.

6. Add scripts that display game over messages.

7. Add the scripts required to control and coordinate game play.

8. Save and test the execution of your new Scratch project.

Step 1: Creating a New Scratch Project

The first step in the development of the Ball Chase game is to create a new Scratch project. Do so by either opening Scratch 2.0, thereby automatically creating a new Scratch 2.0 application project, or clicking on the File menu and then selecting New.

Step 2: Adding and Removing Sprites

The Ball Chase game is made up of the default cat sprite plus three other sprites and a variable monitor, as shown in Figure 9.14.

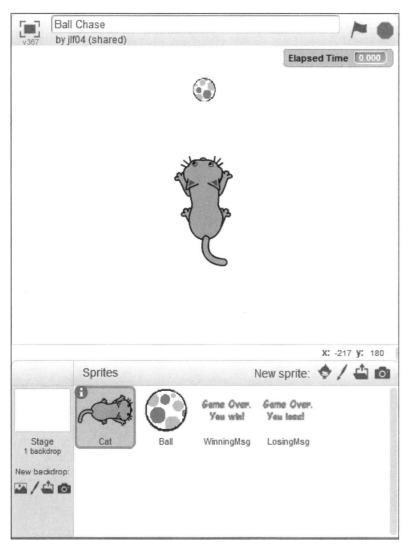

Figure 9.14

An overview of the different parts of the Ball Chase game.

© 2014 Lifelong Kindergarten Group

Because you don't need the default cat sprite in this application, go ahead and remove it. In its place, you need to add a different sprite, representing a top-down view of a different cat sprite. To add this sprite, click on the Choose Sprite from Library icon in the sprites area. When the Sprite Library window opens, click on the Animals category, and then select the cat2 sprite and click on the OK button. By default, the sprite is placed in the middle of the stage and faces a 90-degree direction. Leave this sprite in its default location in the middle of the stage, change its direction to 0, and then change its assigned name to Cat. Next, locate and add the Ball sprite (located in the Things category under the name of Beachball). Change the sprite's name to Ball and place it at the top center of the stage.

To add the application's remaining two sprites, which will be nothing more than text strings saved as sprites, you must create them using Scratch's built-in Paint Editor program. Both of these sprites consist of text messages. For the first of these two sprites, type the following text over two lines: Game over, You lose!. For the second of the two sprites, type the following message over two lines: Game over, You win!. Assign the first sprite a name of LosingMsg and assign a name of WinningMsg to the second sprite.

Step 3: Adding Variables That the Application Needs

To execute, the Ball Chase game requires one variable, as shown in Figure 9.15. To add this variable to the application, click on the Data category located at the top of the blocks palette, and then click on the Make a Variable button to define a variable named Elapsed Time.

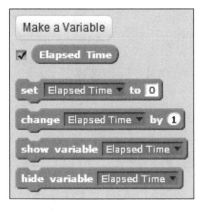

Figure 9.15
The Ball Chase game requires one variable.
© 2014 Lifelong Kindergarten Group

This variable is used to display the amount of time remaining in the game. Make sure that you leave the check box for this variable selected and that you reposition the variable's corresponding monitor to the upper-right corner of the stage.

Step 4: Adding an Audio File to the Application

The Ball Chase game uses one sound effect, which simulates the meowing of the cat as it chases the ball around the stage. To add this audio file, select the `Cat` sprite thumbnail in the sprites list and then click on the Sounds tab located at the top of the scripts area. Next, click on the Choose Sound from Library icon to display the Import Sound window, click on the Animal category, select the `Meow` audio file, and click on OK to add the audio file to the sprite.

Step 5: Adding a Script to Control Ball Movement

The objective of the game is to try to keep the ball out of the reach of the cat for 30 seconds. The following script, which should be added to the `Ball` sprite, is responsible for controlling the movement of the ball on the stage.

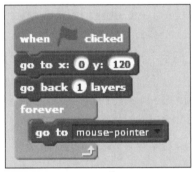

© 2014 Cengage Learning®

This script begins with a hat block. Next, a motion block is used to position the ball in the upper-middle portion of the stage. A looks block then moves the sprite back one layer, ensuring that if the `Ball` sprite encounters the `Cat` sprite, the `Ball` sprite will be displayed under the `Cat` sprite instead of on top of it. (You will learn about looks blocks in Chapter 10, "Changing the Way Sprites Look and Behave.")

The rest of the script consists of a loop that repeatedly executes another motion block. The motion block is responsible for moving the `Ball` sprite around the stage to where the mouse pointer is.

Step 6: Adding Scripts That Display Game Over Messages

You will add the script that is responsible for making the cat chase the ball around the stage in the next section. Before doing so, add the following pair of scripts to the `WinningMsg` sprite. These scripts are responsible for displaying and hiding the game's winning message.

© 2014 Cengage Learning®

The first of the two scripts shown here is responsible for hiding the display of the sprite to which it has been added. The second script, on the other hand, is responsible for displaying the sprite whenever a broadcast message of You win is received. Note that this script includes a looks block that pushes the sprite to the front of any other sprites that it may happen to overlap. This ensures that the message is completely visible once it's displayed.

Once you have created and added these two scripts to the WinningMsg sprite, drag and drop both of them onto the LosingMsg sprite and then edit the second script so that it executes whenever a broadcast message of You lose is received.

Step 7: Adding Scripts Needed to Control and Coordinate Game Play

To wrap up your work on the Ball Chase game, you need to add four scripts to the Cat sprite. The first of these scripts is shown next and is responsible for ensuring the cat chases the ball around the stage.

© 2014 Cengage Learning®

This script begins by moving the Cat sprite to the center of the stage and pointing it in its default upward direction. Next, it pauses for one second and then enters into a loop, which repeatedly executes the embedded code blocks. The first of these three code blocks points the Cat sprite toward the Ball sprite. The second code block pauses the loop's execution for .15 seconds, after which the third block moves the Cat sprite 66 steps in the direction of the Ball sprite.

Note

The reason for imposing the .15 second delay in the script's loop is to slow down things enough to give the player a chance to keep the ball from the cat. If the little extra delay were removed from the loop, the speed at which the cat moves would easily overcome even the fastest player.

The second of the four scripts to be added to the Cat sprite is shown next. This script is set to execute when the player starts the game by clicking on the green Flag button. The script begins by setting the value at which the audio is played to 50% of the level of the computer's current sound level. The rest of the script is controlled by a loop that repeatedly runs two embedded code blocks. The first code block pauses script execution for five seconds. The second code block plays the Meow audio file. The result is that the cat meows every five seconds as it chases the ball around the stage.

© 2014 Cengage Learning®

The third script to be added to the Cat sprite is responsible for halting the execution of all scripts in the application in the event that the cat manages to touch the sprite during game play. The code blocks that make up this script are shown here.

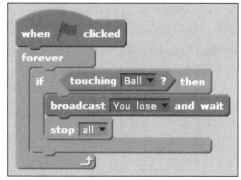

This script is executed when the player starts the game by clicking on the green Flag button. The script's overall execution is controlled by a loop. Within the loop, a conditional test is performed that checks to see if the Cat sprite has made contact with the Ball sprite. If this is the case, a broadcast message of You lose is sent. Once the other scripts in the application have received and processed this message, the last code block in the loop is executed, halting all script execution.

The last script to be added to the Cat sprite is shown next. This script is responsible for keeping track of time as the application executes and for halting game play after 30 seconds, should the player manage to keep the cat at bay for that long.

When started, this script begins by resetting Scratch's internal timer and then assigning the current value of the timer (for example, 0.0) to a variable named Elapsed Time.

A loop controls the rest of the script. Each time the loop executes, it updates the value assigned to the `Elapsed Time` variable to reflect the timer's current value. Next, a check is made to see if the timer's value has exceeded 30 seconds, and if it has, a broadcast message of `You win` is sent. Once processed by the other scripts in the application, the execution of all scripts in the application is halted. If, on the other hand, the timer's value is less than 30 seconds, the loop simply executes again. Accordingly, if the cat does not manage to catch the ball within 30 seconds, thus ending the game, the fourth script ends the game and declares the player to be the winner.

Step 8: Saving and Executing Your Scratch Project

All right! Assuming you have followed along closely with each of the steps presented in this chapter, your copy of the Ball Chase game should be ready for testing. If you have not done so yet, name your new Scratch project. Switch over to Full screen mode and execute the game. Remember that game play begins when you click on the green Flag button and that your objective is to keep the ball out of the cat's reach for 30 seconds.

CHAPTER 10

CHANGING THE WAY SPRITES LOOK AND BEHAVE

By its very nature, Scratch 2.0 lends itself to the development of graphical applications that involve the manipulation of sprites. This includes taking actions that affect the appearance and behavior of both sprites and the stage. Sprite and stage appearance and behavior are controlled using looks blocks. Looks blocks are used to affect sprite appearance through the application of special effects, to make sprites visible or invisible as applications execute, and even to change sprite costumes and stage backdrops. This chapter provides an overview of all of Scratch 2.0's looks blocks and guides you through the creation of your next Scratch 2.0 project: the Crazy Eight Ball game.

The major topics covered in this chapter include

- Learning how to display text in speech and thought bubbles
- Making sprites appear and disappear during application execution
- Learning how to programmatically change a sprite's costume and the stage's backdrop
- Discovering how to apply a range of special graphical effects to sprites and the stage's backdrop
- Learning how to change a sprite's size
- Specifying how sprites that overlap one another should be displayed
- Learning how to retrieve a costume's number and size and a backdrop's name and number

Looks Blocks That Affect Sprites Versus the Stage

Looks blocks affect the way sprites and the stage appear. As shown in Figure 10.1, different looks blocks are displayed in the blocks palette depending on whether you have selected a sprite's thumbnail or the stage thumbnail in the sprite list.

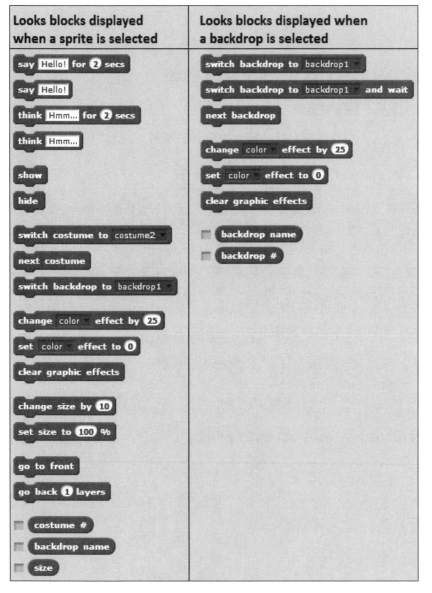

Figure 10.1

The code blocks on the left are displayed when you are working with a sprite, and the code blocks on the right are displayed when you are working with the stage.

© 2014 Lifelong Kindergarten Group

MAKING SPRITES TALK AND THINK

The following set of looks blocks, shown in Figure 10.2, are applicable only to sprites and are used to display text in speech and thought bubbles, making a sprite look like it is talking or thinking.

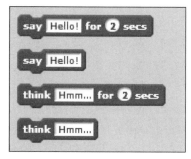

Figure 10.2

Using these code blocks, you can display text in both speech and thought bubbles.

© 2014 Lifelong Kindergarten Group

Figure 10.3 provides examples of what speech and thought bubbles look like.

Figure 10.3

Speech and thought bubbles resemble callouts used to display captions in cartoons found in many popular newspaper comic strips.

© 2014 Lifelong Kindergarten Group

The first two code blocks shown in Figure 10.2 are used to display text in speech bubbles. The difference between these two code blocks is that the first code block displays its text for a specified number of seconds, and the second code block permanently displays its text (until the text is overridden by another speech or thought bubble). For example, you can use the following script to display the text Hello! for two seconds in a speech bubble.

TIP

Any text displayed using the second and fourth code blocks shown in Figure 10.2 does not automatically go away. However, you can clear out the text displayed in a speech or thought button by executing a speech or thought code block with no text typed in it.

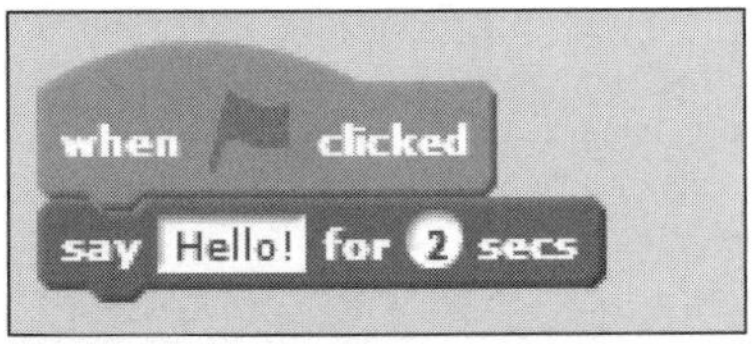

© 2014 Cengage Learning®

Similarly, the following script demonstrates how to display a text message of Hmm... in a thought bubble.

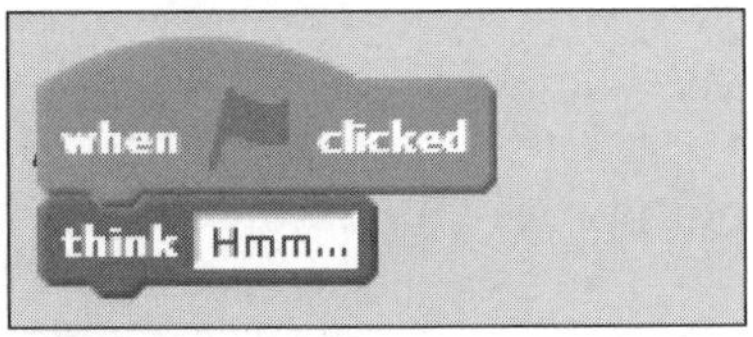

© 2014 Cengage Learning®

MAKING SPRITES APPEAR AND DISAPPEAR

The next two looks code blocks, shown in Figure 10.4, apply only to sprites. As the text displayed on these the blocks indicates, they are used programmatically to display or hide a sprite.

Figure 10.4
With these two code blocks, you can control when sprites appear on the stage.
© 2014 Lifelong Kindergarten Group

Since they do not accept input, these two code blocks are easy to work with. For example, you can add the following script to any sprite to make it disappear and then reappear after a one-second pause.

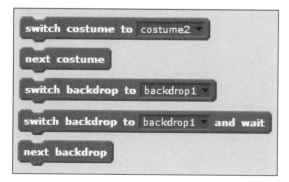

CHANGING SPRITE COSTUMES AND STAGE BACKDROPS

Every sprite that is added to a Scratch 2.0 application is capable of changing its appearance by changing its costume. You can assign sprites any number of costumes and switch between them at any time. To add a costume to a sprite, all you have to do is select the sprite's thumbnail, click on the Costumes tab located at the top of the scripts area, and then click on the Choose Costume from Library icon. This opens a window that allows you to locate and select a graphics file to be used as a new costume for the sprite.

Using looks blocks, you can programmatically change a sprite's appearance by changing its costume. Similarly, you can modify the stage's backdrop or add additional backdrops to it and change between them during program execution. The looks blocks that facilitate these actions are shown in Figure 10.5.

Figure 10.5

These code blocks are used to programmatically change sprite costumes and stage backdrops.

Changing Sprite Costumes

Every costume that is added to a sprite is automatically assigned a number and a name (based on the graphic's filename). The first costume in the costume list represents the sprite when the application is started. However, using drag and drop, you can rearrange the order in which costumes are listed. In addition, you can programmatically replace a sprite's current costume by specifying the name of a different costume.

For example, the following script demonstrates how to use the first looks block shown in Figure 10.5 in a loop to repeatedly change a sprite's costume 10 times at half-second intervals.

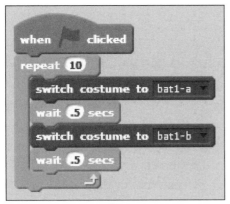

© 2014 Cengage Learning®

If this script were added to a sprite that had two costumes, named as shown in Figure 10.6, the script would make the bat appear to flap its wings and fly for five seconds whenever it was clicked. Note that the names of the sprite's costumes are automatically populated in the code block's drop-down list. Once they're added to the script, it is easy to configure the looks block to work with the costumes.

Figure 10.6
Bat costumes.
© 2014 Lifelong Kindergarten Group

Scratch 2.0 automatically assigns costume numbers as you import new costumes into a sprite. The first costume assigned to a sprite is given a costume number of 1. Each successive costume is assigned a higher number, as demonstrated in Figure 10.7.

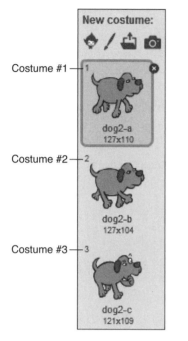

Figure 10.7

Three costumes have been added to a sprite, each of which depicts a slightly different version of a dog. These costumes are numbered 1, 2, and 3 and are named dog2-a, dog2-b, and dog2-c, respectively.

© 2014 Lifelong Kindergarten Group

Using the second code block shown in Figure 10.5, you can change a sprite's costume to the next costume in the costume list. For example, the following script automatically changes a sprite's costume whenever the sprite is clicked.

```
when this sprite clicked
next costume
```

© 2014 Cengage Learning®

When executed, the script changes the sprite's costume to the next costume in the list. By clicking on the sprite repeatedly, you can continue to change the sprite's costume. Once the last costume in the costume list has been displayed, Scratch 2.0 goes back to the top of the costume list and starts over, as depicted in Figure 10.8.

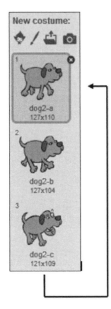

Figure 10.8
Scratch 2.0 loops back to the beginning of the sprite's costume list as necessary to fulfill additional costume switches.
© 2014 Lifelong Kindergarten Group

Changing a Stage's Backdrop

The last three looks blocks in Figure 10.5 let you switch the stage's backdrop. They work in much the same manner as the first two blocks, which switch sprite costumes. For example, the following script demonstrates how to randomly set the stage's backdrop to one of three options.

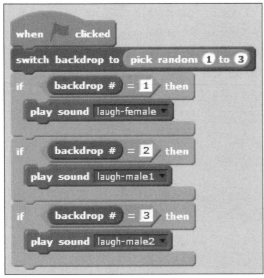

© 2014 Cengage Learning®

Note that in addition to changing the stage's backdrop, this example plays one of three audio files depending on which of the three backdrops is randomly selected.

APPLYING SPECIAL EFFECTS TO COSTUMES AND BACKDROPS

The next three looks blocks, shown in Figure 10.9, apply to both sprites and the stage and can be used to set and clear different graphical special effects.

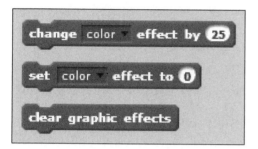

Figure 10.9
These code blocks allow you to set and clear different graphics effects on sprites.
© 2014 Lifelong Kindergarten Group

The first and second code blocks shown in Figure 10.9 are used to apply one of the following special effects to a sprite's costume or to the stage's backdrop:

- **Color.** Modifies the costume's or backdrop's color.
- **Fisheye.** Magnifies a portion of a costume or backdrop.
- **Whirl.** Twists and distorts a portion of a costume or backdrop.
- **Pixelate.** Displays a sprite or backdrop at a lower resolution than the resolution at which the image was created.
- **Mosaic.** Creates an image made up of repeated instances of a sprite or backdrop.
- **Brightness.** Modifies an image by increasing or decreasing its intensity of light.
- **Ghost.** Fades the appearance of a costume or backdrop to make it look transparent.

An example of each of these graphic effects when applied to a sprite is shown in Figure 10.10.

Figure 10.10

A demonstration of how special effects influence a sprite.

© 2014 Lifelong Kindergarten Group

To develop a better understanding of how to work with these two code blocks, let's look at a couple of examples. In this first example, a sprite's appearance is changed by executing a loop four times. Each time the loop executes, it applies the ghost effect to the sprite to which it belongs.

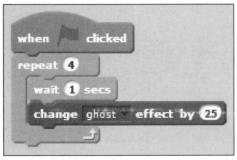

© 2014 Cengage Learning®

Note that the value specified in the input field for the code block in the previous script is 25, which represents a percentage value. As such, for each of the four times that the loop repeats, the sprite fades away until at the end of the last execution of the loop, the sprite completely disappears.

This next example applies the whirl special effect to its sprite. Specifically, it begins by clearing any previous whirl effect that may have been applied to the sprite. Then, over a period of four seconds, it slowly modifies the appearance of the sprite by applying an increased application of the whirl effect.

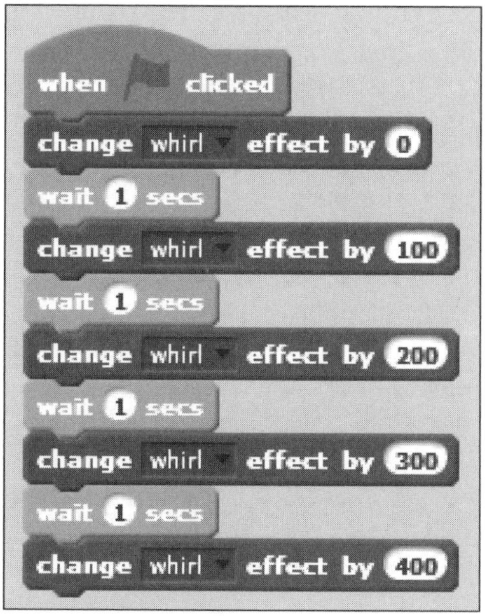

© 2014 Cengage Learning®

The last looks block restores a costume or backdrop to its original appearance regardless of how many different graphical effects may have been applied to it. For example, the following statement demonstrates how to restore a costume or backdrop's appearance when the green Flag button is pressed.

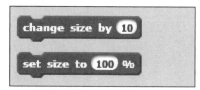

© 2014 Cengage Learning®

CHANGING A SPRITE'S SIZE

The next two looks blocks, shown in Figure 10.11, apply only to sprites. They allow you to change a sprite's size.

Figure 10.11

With these code blocks, you can modify a sprite's size.

© 2014 Lifelong Kindergarten Group

The first code block modifies a sprite's size by specifying a relative value. Using this code block, as demonstrated next, you can slowly increase a sprite's size and then reduce its size just as quickly.

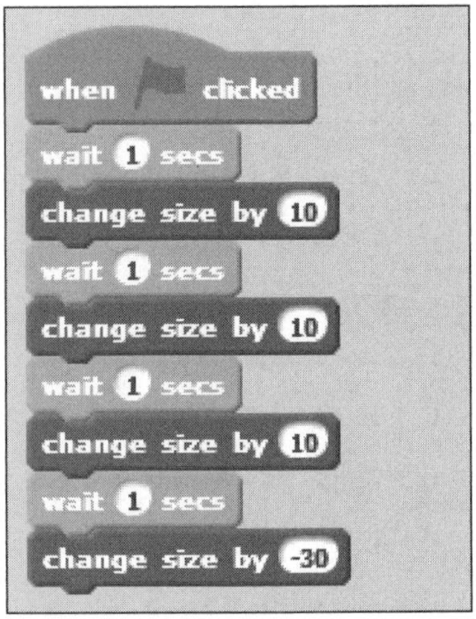

© 2014 Cengage Learning®

The second code block shown in Figure 10.11 lets you set a sprite's size to a specific percentage of its current size (larger or smaller). For example, the following script begins by doubling the size of a sprite. It then pauses for a second and reduces the sprite to 50% of its original size. After another brief pause, the sprite is restored to its original size.

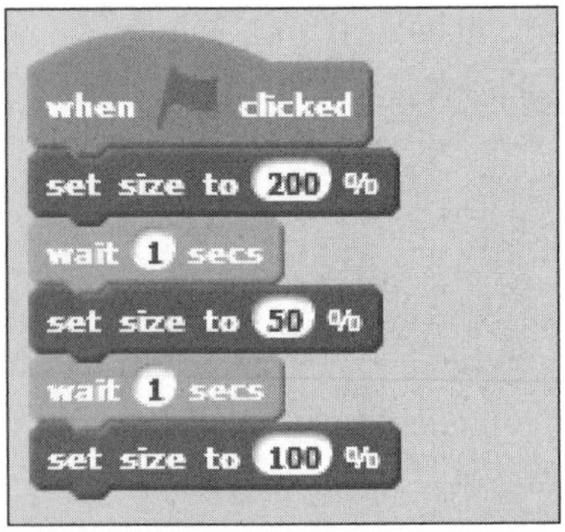

© 2014 Cengage Learning®

DETERMINING WHAT HAPPENS WHEN TWO SPRITES OVERLAP

The next two Scratch 2.0 looks blocks, shown in Figure 10.12, specify what happens when all or part of a sprite is covered by another sprite.

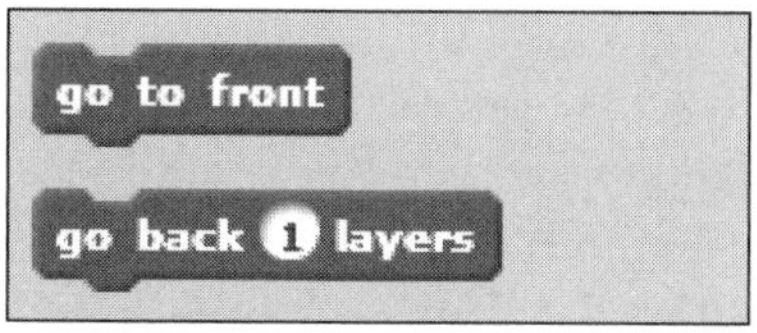

Figure 10.12

With these code blocks, you can determine what happens when two sprites overlap.
© 2014 Lifelong Kindergarten Group

In Scratch 2.0, each sprite that you add to an application is assigned to a layer. For example, suppose you created an application with multiple sprites. When you add the first sprite to the application, it is placed at the topmost layer. When you add the application's second sprite, it is added to the top layer, and the previous sprite is moved back one layer. Each additional sprite that you add starts off at the top layer and stays there until you either add another new sprite or click on one of the sprites that were previously added, which moves the selected sprite back to the topmost layer.

By default, the first sprite is placed on the top layer. The second sprite added to the application is placed on the second layer, and the third sprite is placed on the third layer.

Understanding the layer on which a sprite has been placed is important because the sprite's layer assignment determines whether it remains on top or is displayed underneath another sprite when they overlap one another. Sprites at higher levels remain on top of sprites at lower levels.

Note

To better understand the importance of levels, consider what happens when you place five pieces of paper on top of one another on a desk. The piece of paper sitting on top (at the top layer) is visible, and your view of the other pieces of paper is obstructed. Now reach into the middle of the stack of paper, pull out a sheet, and place it on top of all the other pages. By altering the page's layer position, you have now made it visible.

In addition to controlling what happens to sprites by adding them to applications in a specific order, controlling their layer position, you can use the code blocks shown in Figure 10.12 to programmatically control a sprite layer location. For example, using the first code block, you can move a sprite to the top layer, ensuring that it remains visible at all times on the stage, even when other sprites come into contact with it.

As an example of how to work with both of these code blocks, revisit the Ball Chase game that was presented in Chapter 9, "Controlling Script Execution," in which both of these two code blocks were used to ensure that end-of-game messages were displayed on top of all other sprites. In addition, the application used these blocks to ensure that the cat overlaps the ball when it catches it.

RETRIEVING COSTUME AND BACKDROP DATA

The looks blocks shown in Figure 10.13 are used to display stage monitors that display sprite costumer number, stage backdrop number, and name, as well as sprite size as a percentage. Alternatively, you can use these code blocks as input to any code block that accepts numeric input.

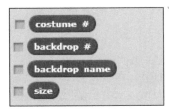

Figure 10.13

With these code blocks, you can retrieve information about sprites and backdrops.

© 2014 Lifelong Kindergarten Group

DEVELOPING THE CRAZY EIGHT BALL GAME

Now it is time to turn your attention to the development of a new Scratch 2.0 application: the Crazy Eight Ball game. This game simulates the operation of a crazy eight ball fortune-telling toy. As you work on the development of this game, you will get additional experience with different looks blocks. In total, the application is made up of three sprites and three scripts. Figure 10.14 shows how the game looks when it's started.

Figure 10.14

To play, you must ask questions that can be answered with yes/no style answers.

© 2014 Lifelong Kindergarten Group

To play the game, think of a question, and then click on the image of the cat located in the center of the eight ball. Once clicked, the image of the cat is replaced with an 8, as demonstrated in Figure 10.15, and over the next four seconds, you can hear the sounds of bubbles.

Figure 10.15

It takes a few moments for the crazy eight ball to come up with an answer.

The crazy eight ball displays any of five randomly selected answers in response to player questions. The range of answers supported by the game includes

- Maybe!
- No!
- Yes!
- Ask a different question!
- Maybe…but then maybe not!

Figure 10.16 shows how the game looks once it has finally decided on an answer to the player's question.

Figure 10.16
The crazy eight ball has decided not to answer the player's question.
© 2014 Lifelong Kindergarten Group

The development of this application project is created by following a series of steps, as outlined here:

1. Create a new Scratch 2.0 application project.

2. Add and remove sprites.

3. Add the variable that the application needs.

4. Add an audio file to the application.

5. Add a script to control the display of the 8 in the eight ball.

6. Add the programming logic required to operate the eight ball.

7. Save and execute your work.

Step 1: Creating a New Scratch 2.0 Project

Begin the creation of the Crazy Eight Ball game by creating a new Scratch 2.0 project. Do so by either opening Scratch 2.0, thereby automatically creating a new Scratch 2.0 application project, or clicking on the File menu and then selecting New.

Step 2: Adding and Removing Sprites

The Crazy Eight Ball game consists of three sprites and three scripts, as shown in Figure 10.17.

Figure 10.17

An overview of the different components that make up the Crazy Eight Ball game.

© 2014 Lifelong Kindergarten Group

The first sprite that you need to add to the game is that of an empty eight ball. The second sprite is that of a graphic number 8. You will find copies of the graphics for both of these sprites located in the Crazy Eight Ball application, which you can find in the Scratch Programming for Teens by Jerry Ford studio on the Scratch 2.0 website. Use your backpack to make copies of these two sprites, and add them to your own Scratch project.

Once added to the sprite list in your project, reposition these two sprites so that the eight ball is centered in the middle of the stage and the number is centered in the middle of the eight ball.

The application's third sprite is that of a cat's face. You can create this sprite by using the Paint Editor program to edit the application's default sprite, removing the cat sprite's body, leaving just its face in place. Once you've modified the sprite, click on the Grow Sprite button located on Scratch 2.0's toolbar, and then click on the image of the cat sprite 12 times to increase the size of the cat's face. Next, reposition the cat sprite, moving it onto the center of the eight ball so that it overlaps the Number sprite. At this point, the overall design of the Crazy Eight Ball game is complete.

Before moving on to the next step, rename these three sprites Cat, EightBall, and Number, as shown in Figure 10.17.

Step 3: Adding a Variable Required by the Application

To execute, the Crazy Eight Ball game requires the definition of the variable shown in Figure 10.18. To add this variable, click on the Variables category in the blocks palette, click on the Make a Variable button, and then define a new variable named RandomNo.

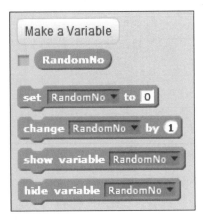

Figure 10.18
The Crazy Eight Ball game requires one variable.
© 2014 Lifelong Kindergarten Group

This variable stores a randomly generated number that the game uses when generating answers to player questions.

Step 4: Adding an Audio File to the Application

The Crazy Eight Ball game uses a single sound effect, which sounds like bubbles being blown in water. This sound is played for four seconds preceding the display of the eight ball's answer. The audio file that is played should be added to the Cat sprite. To add this sound file, select the Cat sprite thumbnail in the sprites list and then click on the Sounds tab located at the top of the scripts area. Next, click on the Choose Sound from Library icon to display the Sound Library window, click on the Effects folder, and then select the Bubbles sound and click on OK.

Step 5: Creating a Script to Control the Display of the 8 in the Eight Ball

Of the application's three scripts, two belong to the Number sprite. These scripts, shown next, are automatically executed based on the receipt of broadcast messages. Specifically, when a message of Show 8 is received, the Number sprite is made visible. When the message Hide 8 is received, the Number sprite is hidden. The receipt of these messages serves as a trigger that controls when the Number sprite is visible (which occurs only when the eight ball is in the process of preparing to generate an answer).

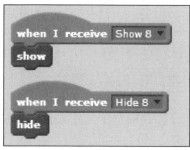

© 2014 Cengage Learning®

As you can see, these two scripts use a looks block to control sprite visibility. Since the game begins by displaying only the image of the Cat sprite, go ahead and click on the second script belonging to the Number sprite, hiding it from view.

Step 6: Adding the Programming Logic Needed to Control the Eight Ball

The last script in the application, shown next, belongs to the Cat sprite. It is executed whenever the player thinks of a question and clicks on the Cat sprite for an answer.

© 2014 Cengage Learning®

Once started, the script begins by assigning a random number in the range of 1 to 5 to the RandomNo variable. Next, a looks block is executed, hiding the Cat sprite, and then the broadcast message Show 8 is sent. This message triggers the execution of a script belonging to the Number sprite. Next, the Bubbles audio file is played, and the script's execution is paused for four seconds, allowing Scratch 2.0 time to finish playing the audio file. Once the four seconds is up, a second broadcast message of Hide 8 is sent, triggering the hiding of the Number sprite.

Next, the Cat sprite is redisplayed on the stage and the value assigned to RandomNo is analyzed. Depending on the value assigned to RandomNo, one of five different text messages is displayed in a speech bubble. After two seconds, the bubble is closed, and the game waits on the player to ask another question.

Step 7: Saving and Executing Your Scratch 2.0 Project

At this point, you have all the information you need to create your own copy of the Crazy Eight Ball game. If you have not already done so, assign a name to your new project and then test it to make sure that you do not run into any problems. If you have not done so yet, switch over to Full screen mode and test the operation of the Crazy Eight ball game.

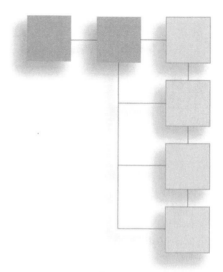

CHAPTER 11

SPICING THINGS UP WITH SOUNDS

Many different types of applications, especially computer games, rely on sound as a means of conveying meaning and excitement. Through the addition of background music and sounds effects, applications can really come alive, providing users with a deeper and more meaningful experience. In Scratch 2.0, sound effects and music are integrated into applications using sound blocks. This chapter teaches you how to work with all of Scratch 2.0's sound blocks and demonstrates how to incorporate sounds (audio files), drum notes, and musical notes into your applications. On top of all this, you learn how to create a new application called the Family Picture Movie, which demonstrates how to create a slideshow complete with accompanying background music.

The major topics covered in this chapter include learning how to

- Control the playback of sounds
- Play drum beats and pause drum play
- Set and control the volume at which sounds, notes, and musical instruments are played
- Set and change the tempo of drum and note play

PLAYING SOUNDS

To add the playback of music and sound effects to your applications, you need to learn how to use the sound code blocks shown in Figure 11.1. These code blocks provide everything you need to play or stop the playback of MP3 and wave files in your Scratch 2.0 applications.

Figure 11.1

These code blocks control sound playback.

© 2014 Lifelong Kindergarten Group

The first two code blocks shown in Figure 11.1 let you play any MP3 or wave file that you add to your Scratch 2.0 project. The third code block lets you stop the playback of all the sounds belonging to a sprite. To play a sound, you must first add it to a sprite or to the stage. You can add one of the sounds provided by Scratch 2.0 by selecting the stage or a sprite in the sprite list, clicking on the Sounds tab located at the top of the scripts area, and then clicking on the Choose Sound from Library icon. Once you've imported the sound, you can play it using a script belonging to the stage or sprite, as demonstrated here.

© 2014 Cengage Learning®

Here, a sound named meow is played when the green Flag button is pressed. To play the sound, you must select it from the code block's drop-down list. The drop-down list is automatically populated by Scratch 2.0 with all the audio files that have been added to the sprite to which the script belongs.

The sound code block used in the previous script allows the script to which it has been added to continue running. If the script containing the sound block has additional code block left to be executed, the playback of the sound is cut short when the script continues executing. This was not a problem in the previous example because the sound block was the last code block in the script.

When you want to pause script execution to allow time for the entire sound to finish playing, you have two choices. First, you can add a control block to the script immediately following the sound block that pauses script execution for a specified number of seconds (for example, the number of seconds needed to play the sound). Better yet, you can use the second code block shown in Figure 11.1 as demonstrated in the following script.

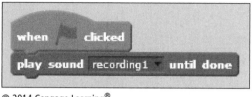

© 2014 Cengage Learning®

The sound code block used in this example plays a sound that has been previously added to your Scratch 2.0 application, pausing script execution until the sound has finished playing. Once playback is complete, the rest of the script is permitted to finish its execution.

Tip

If you want to add the repeated playback of background music or sound effects to an application, create a script specifically for this purpose. This keeps the programming logic needed to play the sound separate from other scripts and eliminates the need to pause other scripts' execution to support sound playback.

Depending on what your applications are designed to do, there may be times that you want to stop the playback of sounds belonging to a sprite or the stage. You can achieve this using the third code block shown in Figure 11.1, as demonstrated in the following example.

© 2014 Cengage Learning®

Here, the playback of any sounds belonging to the sprite is immediately halted when the space key is pressed.

PLAY A DRUM

Using the two code blocks shown in Figure 11.2, you can add the playing of a drum to your Scratch 2.0 application and, when necessary, pause drum play for a specified number of beats.

Figure 11.2

These code blocks let you control the playing of a drum within your applications.

© 2014 Lifelong Kindergarten Group

The first code block shown in Figure 11.2 plays a drum sound for a specified number of beats. This code block lets you choose from among 18 different types of drums, each of which is easily selected by clicking on the code block's drop-down list, as demonstrated in Figure 11.3.

Figure 11.3

This code block supports the playing of 18 different types of drum sounds, numbered from 1 to 18.

© 2014 Lifelong Kindergarten Group

The second code block shown in Figure 11.2 lets you momentarily pause drum play for a specified number of beats. Using both of the code blocks, you can play a wide assortment of drums within your applications.

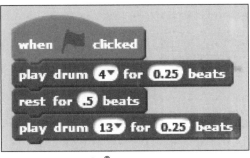

© 2014 Cengage Learning®

In this example, the first sound block plays a drum beat for .25 beats using a crash cymbal. The second sound block rests for .5 beats, and the third code block uses a bongo to play a drum for .25 beats.

PLAYING MUSICAL NOTES

In addition to allowing you to play sounds and different types of drum beats, Scratch 2.0 lets you play musical notes with various instruments using the sound blocks shown in Figure 11.4.

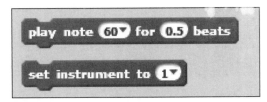

Figure 11.4
These sound blocks let you play notes using musical instruments.
© 2014 Lifelong Kindergarten Group

The first code block plays a note for a particular number of beats. You can specify a note by typing it into the code block's first input box. The range of available notes is from 0 to 127, with 60 representing the middle C note. Alternatively, you can click on the drop-down list located inside the code block's input field and select a note from the list that is displayed, as demonstrated in Figure 11.5.

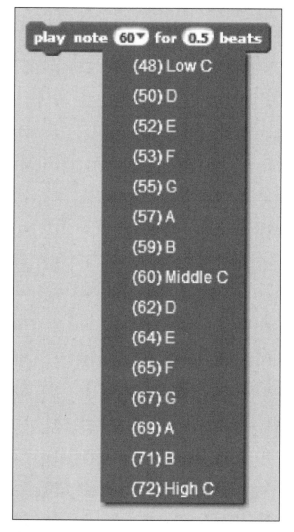

Figure 11.5
Selecting a note and specifying the number of beats that it is to be played.
© 2014 Lifelong Kindergarten Group

The second code block shown in Figure 11.4 specifies the instrument to be used and is designed to be used in conjunction with the first control block. It supports a total of 21 different instruments, numbered 1 to 21. You can select an instrument by keying its number into the block's input field or selecting an instrument from the block's drop-down list, as demonstrated in Figure 11.6.

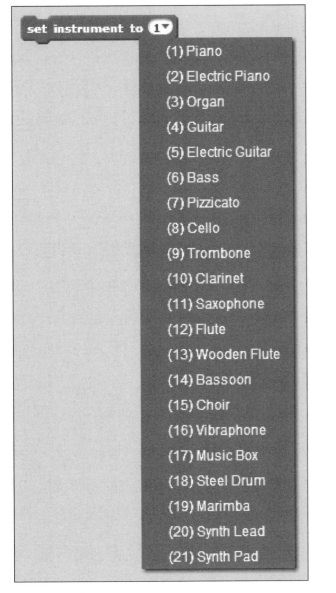

Figure 11.6
Selecting the instrument you want to play within your Scratch 2.0 application.
© 2014 Lifelong Kindergarten Group

The following script demonstrates how to use both of the code blocks shown in Figure 11.5 to play a middle C note followed by a D note using an organ. Each note is played for .5 beats.

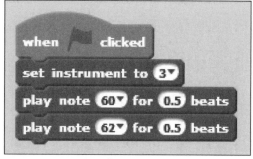

© 2014 Cengage Learning®

CONFIGURING AUDIO VOLUME

Rather than playing sounds, drum beats, and musical notes at whatever volume the computer is set to, you can use the sound blocks shown in Figure 11.7 to change or set the volume at which sounds, drum beats, and musical notes are played.

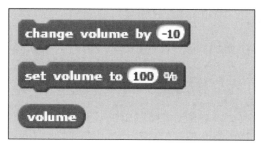

Figure 11.7
Using these code blocks, you can take control of the volume of music and sound effects played by any sprite in your application.
© 2014 Lifelong Kindergarten Group

The first code block shown in Figure 11.7 changes the volume of sound playback for an individual sprite. Using this code block, you can change a sprite's volume by a specified percentage, with 0 being no volume and 100 being the maximum volume. The second code block lets you assign a specific value to a sprite in the range of 0 to 100. Using the third code block, you can retrieve a sprite's volume and optionally display this value in a monitor on the stage.

Note

Volume is set individually for each sprite in an application. Therefore, you can assign different volume levels to each sprite in your application.

An example of how to work with the first of these control blocks is provided here.

© 2014 Cengage Learning®

Here, a sound named meow is played at the computer's default volume level. Next, the volume setting for the sprite to which the script has been added is reduced by 80%. The meow file is then played a second time, this time much quieter.

In this next example, the sprite's volume is set to 10 percent of its default volume level, after which a sound named meow is played.

© 2014 Cengage Learning®

Note

You can use the third code block shown in Figure 11.7 to retrieve a sprite's current volume level. In addition, by selecting its check box, you can enable a monitor that displays the volume level of the sprite on the stage.

SETTING AND CHANGING TEMPO

The last three sound blocks provided by Scratch 2.0 are shown in Figure 11.8. Using these blocks, you can set, change, and report on the tempo at which drum beats and musical notes are played.

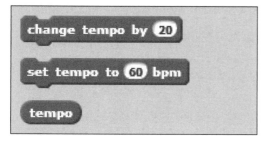

Figure 11.8
These code blocks allow you to modify and report on the tempo used by a sprite to play beats and notes.
© 2014 Lifelong Kindergarten Group

The first code block shown in Figure 11.8 changes the tempo used to play a drum or note. *Tempo* is a measurement of the speed, in beats per minute, at which a drum or note is played. The larger the tempo value, the faster the drum or note is played. The second code block lets you set the tempo used to play a drum or note to a specific number of beats per minute. Using the third code block, you can retrieve a sprite's currently assigned tempo and optionally display this value in a monitor on the stage.

The following script demonstrates how to set and modify a sprite's tempo when playing musical notes.

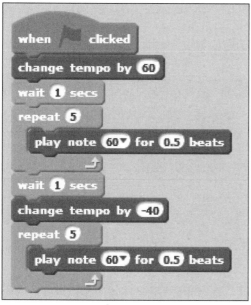

© 2014 Cengage Learning®

Here, the tempo used to play notes is set to 60 beats per minute and then, after a one-second pause, a C note is played five times in a row, each time for half a beat.

After another one-second pause, the sprite's tempo is slowed down to 20 beats per minute and another C note is played five times.

CREATING THE FAMILY PICTURE MOVIE

The rest of this chapter is dedicated to showing you how to develop your next application project: the Family Picture Movie. The development of this application provides the opportunity to work further with different sound blocks, controlling sound volume, playback, and playback termination. In total, the application is made up of 8 sprites and 13 scripts. Figure 11.9 shows how the application looks when it's started.

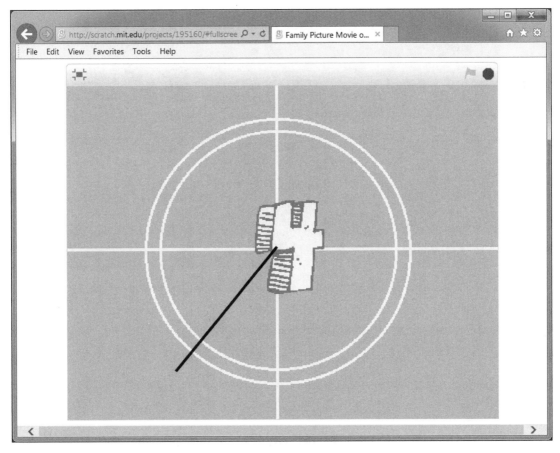

Figure 11.9

The application begins by displaying a series of numbers, from five to one, on an orange radar screen.

© 2014 Lifelong Kindergarten Group

To run the application and view its picture show, all you have to do is click on the green Flag button. Once you've clicked it, the application begins an animation sequence that counts down from five and then starts displaying a series of pictures representing the contents of the movie, as demonstrated in Figure 11.10.

Figure 11.10
As the movie plays, a series of pictures is displayed at three-second intervals.
© 2014 Lifelong Kindergarten Group

Background music is played to help set a friendly tone as the pictures are displayed. The Family Picture Movie is capable of displaying any number of pictures. Once the movie ends, credits are displayed.

The development of this project is accomplished by following a series of steps, as outlined here:

1. Create a new Scratch 2.0 project.

2. Add and remove sprites and backdrops.

3. Add the variable needed by the application.

4. Add a sound to the application.

5. Add the programming logic to control application execution.

6. Name and test your Scratch 2.0 project.

Step 1: Creating a New Scratch 2.0 Project

To begin the development of the Family Picture Movie, you must create a new Scratch 2.0 project. Do so by opening Scratch 2.0 and by clicking on the File menu and then selecting New.

Step 2: Adding and Removing Sprites and Backdrops

The Family Picture Movie is made up of 8 sprites, as shown in Figure 11.11.

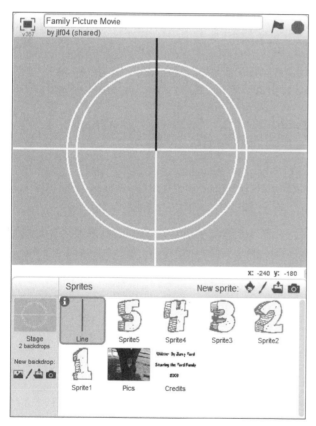

Figure 11.11

An overview of the different components that make up the Family Picture Movie application.

© 2014 Lifelong Kindergarten Group

The application consists of two separate backdrops: Counter, which is displayed when the application is started and begins its countdown, and the default blank stage backdrop. You will find a copy of the graphic for the Counter backdrop located in the Family Picture Movie application, found in the Scratch Programming for Teens by Jerry Ford studio on the Scratch 2.0 website. Use your backpack to make a copy of this backdrop and add it to your own Scratch project. To add it, click on the Stage thumbnail located in the sprites list and then click on the Backdrops tab located at the top of the scripts area. After that, drag and drop the Counter backdrop from your backpack onto the Backdrops list located in the middle of the Project Editor window. Since the Counter backdrop is going to be used as the application's initial backdrop, drag and drop its thumbnail from the bottom of the list of backdrop files to the top position.

In addition to the backdrop, the Family Picture Movie uses a number of sprites. As shown in Figure 11.11, the first of these sprites is a black line. You will find a copy of this graphic and all the graphics for all of this project's sprites located in the Family Picture Movie application, which can be found in the Scratch Programming for Teens by Jerry Ford studio on the Scratch 2.0 website. Use your backpack to make copies of these sprites and add them to your own Scratch project. Once you've added them, you need to position the line sprite exactly as shown in Figure 11.11.

Note

If you elect to create your own version of the line sprite, you need to set the rotation center for the sprite as shown in Figure 11.12.

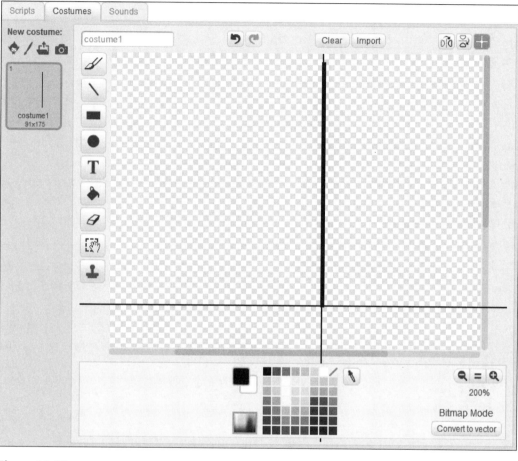

Figure 11.12
Assigning a rotation center to the line sprite.

Next, you need to add five sprites representing numbers displayed during the application's opening animation sequence. Copies of graphics for these five sprites are located in the Family Picture Movie application, which can be found in the Scratch Programming for Teens by Jerry Ford studio on the Scratch 2.0 website. You can use your backpack to make copies of these sprites to add them to your own Scratch project. Alternatively, you can use the Paint Editor to create them for yourself. Once you've added them to your project, center each sprite in the middle of the stage.

Once the initial animation sequence has finished, the Family Picture Movie begins displaying a series of graphics pictures. To add the first of these pictures, click on the Choose Sprite from Library icon and then add any graphics file that you want. If you do not have a suitable graphics file handy, you can acquire a graphic (picture) from the Family Picture Movie application. You can locate that application in the Scratch Programming for Teens by Jerry Ford studio on the Scratch 2.0 website and use your backpack to make a copy of it and add it to your own Scratch project.

The rest of the pictures shown in the application are stored as costumes and are displayed by changing this sprite's costume. If you elected to acquire a graphic (picture) from the Family Picture Movie application located on the Scratch Programming for Teens by Jerry Ford studio on the Scratch 2.0 website, that sprite already has 11 costumes (pictures) assigned to it. Otherwise, you need to add additional costumes to the sprite by selecting the sprite, clicking on the Costumes tab located at the top of the scripts area, and then clicking on the Upload Costume from File icon. This displays a dialog window that you can use to locate and upload graphics (pictures) of your own from your computer.

The last sprite to be added to the application is a graphics file that displays the application's credits, which you should create and customize using the Paint Editor. Once you've added this sprite, the stage should be filled with different sprites. However, of all these sprites, only the line sprite needs to remain visible. To temporarily remove each of the remaining sprites from view, select each sprite one at a time, click on the Looks button located at the top of the blocks palette, and then double-click on the Hide code block. By the time you are done, the stage should look like the example shown in Figure 11.11.

Step 3: Adding a Variable That the Application Requires

To execute, the Family Picture Movie requires that you define a single variable. To add this variable, click on the Data category located at the top of the blocks palette, click on the Make a Variable button, and then create a new variable named Counter, as shown in Figure 11.13.

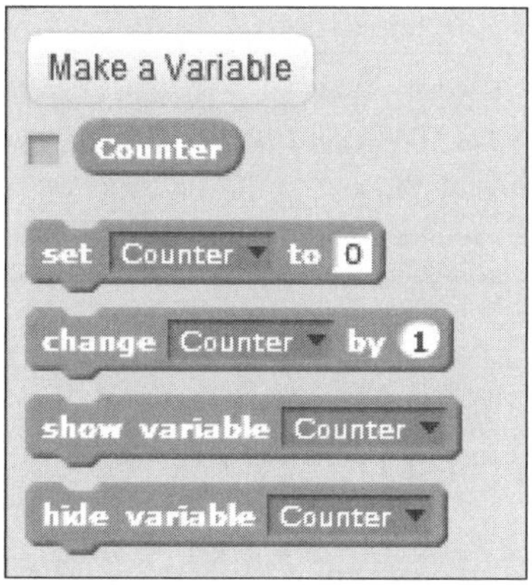

Figure 11.13

The Family Picture Movie uses one variable to help control the opening animation sequence.

© 2014 Lifelong Kindergarten Group

The application uses the variable to control the execution of the application's opening countdown sequence, coordinating the display of the numbers used during the countdown process.

Step 4: Adding a Sound to the Application

As it executes, the Family Picture Movie plays backdrop music to set the mood for the application. The script responsible for playing this music belongs to the Pics sprite. To add this sound to the pics sprite, select the sprite's thumbnail in the sprites list and then click on the Sounds tab located at the top of the scripts area. Next, click on the Choose Sound from Library icon to open the Sound Library window, locate and click on the GuitarChords2 sound, and then click on OK.

Step 5: Developing the Application's Programming Logic

The programming logic that drives the execution of the Family Picture Movie is organized into 13 separate scripts, assigned to each of the application's sprites and to its backdrop. The overall execution of all of this application's scripts is coordinated through the use of broadcast messages and through the use of control blocks that monitor the value assigned to the application's variable, executing only when the variable reaches a predefined value.

Note

If you elected to acquire copies of the backdrop and the sprites needed for this application from the Family Picture Movie application located on the Scratch Programming for Teens by Jerry Ford studio on the Scratch 2.0 website, you already have the scripts the application needs. When a sprite or backdrop is added to your backpack, everything associated with it is included (their sounds, costumes, scripts).

Setting Up the Opening Animation Sequence

The Family Picture Movie begins running when the player clicks on the green Flag button. When this occurs, a number of the scripts within the application begin executing. One of these scripts is responsible for managing the animated sequence that plays when the application begins executing. This script, shown next, must be added to the line sprite.

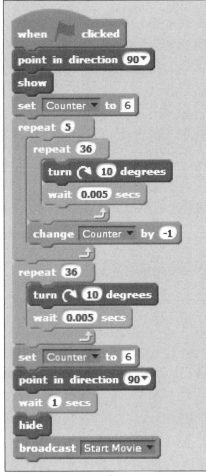

As you can see, this script begins by setting the direction of the line sprite and then makes it visible. Next, the `Counter` variable is assigned a starting value of 6, after which a loop is set up to execute five times. Within this loop, a second loop executes 36 times (for a total of 360 degrees), rotating the line sprite by 10 degrees and pausing .005 second after each turn. The value assigned to `Counter` is then decremented by a value of −1.

By the time the outer loop has executed five times, five other application scripts, monitoring the value assigned to `Counter`, are executed. Each of these five scripts is responsible for displaying a number on the stage. The result is an animated sequence that emulates the countdown that is often displayed at the beginning of old movie reels. Once the countdown has been completed, a second loop executes, rotating the line sprite one final time around the center of the stage. Once the last loop has finished, the value of `Counter` is reset to 6 and pointed back to its initial direction. A one-second pause then ensues, and the line sprite is hidden. Lastly, a control block is used to send a broadcast message of `Start Movie`. This broadcast message triggers the execution of two scripts belonging to the pics sprite, which is responsible for displaying the pictures that make up the application's picture show.

Displaying the Numeric Countdown

As the previous script executes, it modifies the value assigned to the `Counter` variable, changing its value from 6 to 1, one number at a time. Each of the five sprites representing the numbers displayed during the opening animation sequence is displayed by scripts belonging to those sprites. The scripts belonging to each sprite are nearly identical. The following script belongs to the `Sprite5` sprite.

© 2014 Cengage Learning®

As you can see, the script starts executing when the player clicks on the green Flag button, which begins by making sure that the sprite is hidden from view. The script then goes into a loop that waits until the value of Counter is set to 5. Once this occurs, the script displays the sprite for 1.6 seconds and then hides it again. After creating this script, drag and drop an instance of it onto the Sprite4, Sprite3, Sprite2, and Sprite1 sprites, and then modify the scripts belonging to each sprite by changing the value that is looked for to 4, 3, 2, and 1, respectively.

Switching Costumes and Playing Backdrop Music

As has been previously stated, the application displays different pictures by changing costumes. In addition, backdrop music is played to set the mood as the picture show begins. Two separate scripts, belonging to the pics sprite, are responsible for managing the switching of costumes and the playing of the sprite's sound. Both of the scripts are automatically executed when the Start Movie broadcast message is received.

The first of these two scripts, shown next, manages costume switches. It begins by displaying the first costume belongings to the pics sprite on the stage. Next, a loop is set up that pauses three seconds and then switches the sprite's costume to the next costume in the list.

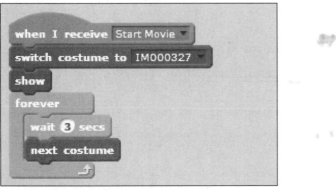

© 2014 Cengage Learning®

The second script, shown next, begins by sending out its broadcast message of Clear backdrop and then sets the sprite's value to half its current level. Next, a loop is set up that executes 10 times. Each time the loop executes, a sound named GuitarChords2 is played. At the end of its tenth execution, the loop halts and the pics sprite is hidden. The script ends by sending out a broadcast message of Show Credits.

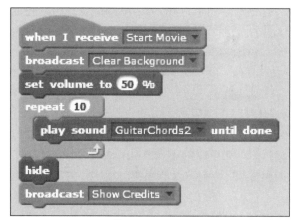

Note

The Show Credits broadcast message is used as a trigger that executes a script belonging to the credits sprite.

Displaying the Closing Credits

The credits sprite has two scripts, as shown next. The first script executes when the green Flag button is pressed and is responsible for removing the display of the sprite from the stage.

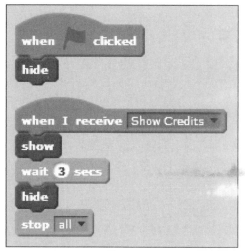

The second script is automatically executed when the Show Credits broadcast message is received. It displays the credits sprite, waits three seconds, and then hides the sprite, leaving the stage blank. The script ends by executing a control block that halts the execution of the application's scripts.

Switching Backdrops

The last two scripts belong to the stage. These scripts are shown next. The first script executes when the green Flag button is clicked. Its job is to switch the stage's backdrop to Counter, readying the application to begin its five-second countdown sequence.

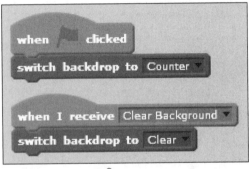

© 2014 Cengage Learning®

The second of the stage's scripts automatically executes when the Clear Backdrop broadcast message is received. Once executed, it switches the stage back to the default Clear backdrop.

Step 6: Naming and Testing Your Scratch 2.0 Project

Assuming you have followed along carefully with the instructions that have been provided, your copy of the Family Picture Movie should be ready for testing. If you have not already named your new application, do so now. When you are ready, click on the green Flag button to run the application and watch the movie. If you run into any problems, go back and recheck your work against the instructions outlined in this chapter.

CHAPTER 12

DRAWING LINES AND SHAPES

In addition to displaying sprites with different costumes and different stage backdrops, Scratch 2.0 draws custom lines, shapes, and other graphics using pen code blocks. Using a virtualized pen, these code blocks allow you to set the color, width, and shade used in drawing operations. This chapter reveals how to work with all of Scratch 2.0's pen blocks and ends by demonstrating how to use them to create a paint drawing application.

The major topics covered in this chapter include learning how to

- Draw using Scratch 2.0's virtual pen
- Set the color used when drawing
- Set pen shade and size
- Stamp a copy of a costume on the stage
- Clear the stage of any drawing operations

CLEARING THE STAGE AREA

The first of Scratch 2.0's pen code blocks, shown in Figure 12.1, is designed to let you clear out any drawing operations that you may have made on the stage.

Figure 12.1
This pen block clears out any drawing operations that you may have made on the stage.
©2014 Lifelong Kindergarten Group

Anything you draw or stamp on the stage's current backdrop does not actually change the backdrop. Therefore, when you clear out any drawing, the costume that makes up the backdrop remains unchanged. The following script demonstrates how easy it is to use this code block.

©2014 Cengage Learning®

By adding a script like this to a Scratch 2.0 application, you can reset the stage to its original state (erasing any drawing made to the stage).

STAMPING AN INSTANCE OF A COSTUME ON THE STAGE

Scratch 2.0 provides the code block shown in Figure 12.2 to allow you to capture a sprite's costume and use it to add, or stamp, copies of the sprite on the stage.

Figure 12.2
This code block lets you use a sprite's costume as the basis for creating a stamp.
©2014 Lifelong Kindergarten Group

As an example of how to work with this code block, create a new Scratch 2.0 application, remove the default cat sprite from it, and then add a copy of the crab sprite to it. You will find this sprite in Scratch 2.0's Animals category of the Sprite Library. Once you've added it, shrink the sprite to about a third of its default size, and then add the following script to it.

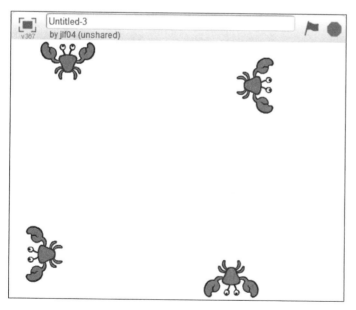

©2014 Cengage Learning®

When executed, this script clears the stage of any previous drawing, which also includes stamps, moves the sprite to the upper-left corner of the stage, and sets its direction. Next, a loop is executed four times, stamping the image of the sprite four times as it is moved around the stage. Figure 12.3 shows how the stage looks once the script has finished executing.

Figure 12.3

Decorating the stage using a sprite as the basis for generating stamps.

©2014 Lifelong Kindergarten Group

DRAWING WITH THE PEN

Within Scratch 2.0 applications, drawing is performed using a virtual pen. This pen works much like a real pen. When the pen is placed in a down position, you can use it to draw on the stage. When it's placed in an up position, drawing ceases. To draw or stop drawing, you must be able to programmatically control the pen's up and down position, which you do using the code blocks shown in Figure 12.4.

Figure 12.4
Using these pen blocks, you can control when the pen can be used to draw.
©2014 Lifelong Kindergarten Group

Using the first code block, you can easily create a simple drawing application. To create this application, start a new Scratch 2.0 project and then delete the default cat sprite and replace it with a new sprite made up of a small black dot (easily created using the Paint Editor). Once you have created your new application as described, select its sprite and add the following script to it.

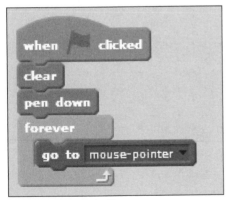

©2014 Cengage Learning®

When executed, this script clears the stage and then places Scratch 2.0's virtual pen in a down position, enabling drawing to occur (whenever the sprite to which the script belongs is moved). Next, the script sets up a loop that uses a motion block to make the sprite follow the pointer around the stage. As a result, whenever you move the mouse around the stage, the sprite follows, and a line is drawn. Once you create and run your own copy of this application, it should become immediately clear that you do not have enough control over the pen. Specifically, you cannot control when and when not to draw. This situation is easily remedied by modifying the script so that you can place the pen in a down or up position based on the status of the mouse pointer's left mouse button, as shown next.

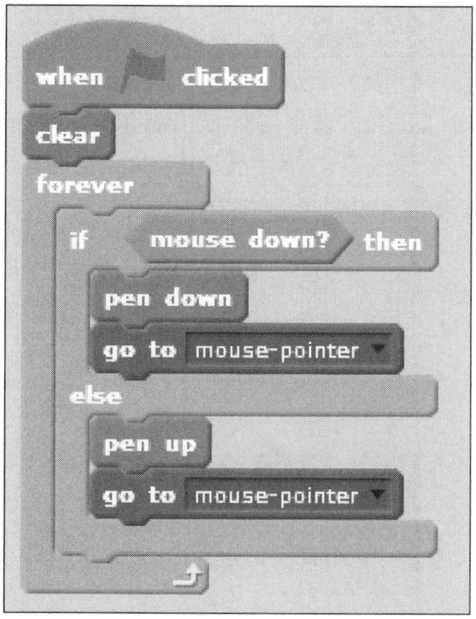

©2014 Cengage Learning®

By controlling when the pen is in a down position, you can produce a precise drawing.

SETTING PEN COLOR

In addition to being able to clear the stage and control when the pen is up or down, Scratch 2.0 provides three code blocks that specify the color to be used in drawing operations, as shown in Figure 12.5.

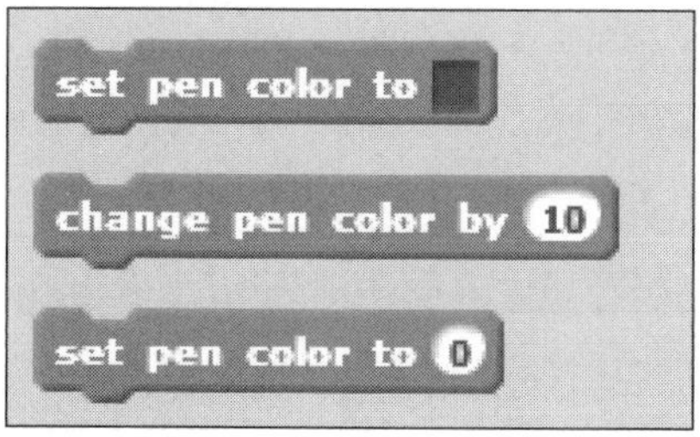

Figure 12.5
The code blocks let you control the color used when drawing.
©2014 Lifelong Kindergarten Group

The first code block shown in Figure 12.5 lets you set the color to be used when drawing. Scratch 2.0 limits your color selection to the colors currently displayed in the Code Editor. To pick a color, click on the color swatch located on the right side of the code block, move the mouse pointer over any color currently displayed anywhere on the Scratch 2.0 Project Editor, and click on it. Once specified, the color you selected is displayed in the code block's input area.

Previous versions of Scratch displayed a color palette (hue) when you clicked on the square color swatch on the code block. This let you select from a rainbow-like range of colors by clicking on the desired color in the hue. Scratch 2.0 dropped this capability. One way to get this feature back is to use your web browser to search on the term *color hue* and then download and save a color hue like the one shown in Figure 12.6.

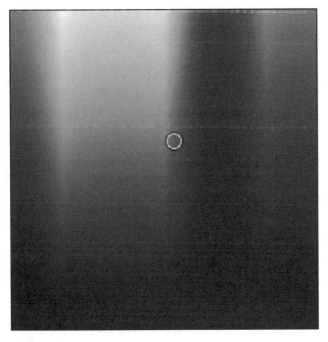

Figure 12.6
An example of a color hue available on the Internet.
©2014 Colblindor

You can then use the color hue as the basis for adding a temporary sprite to your Scratch 2.0 application by clicking on the Upload Sprite from File icon and selecting the color hue graphic. Now when you click on the color swatch, you can move the mouse pointer over any portion of the color hue sprite in the sprite list to select the color you want. Once you have selected the color you desire, you can remove the temporary sprite from your project.

The following script demonstrates how to use this code block to specify the color you want to use.

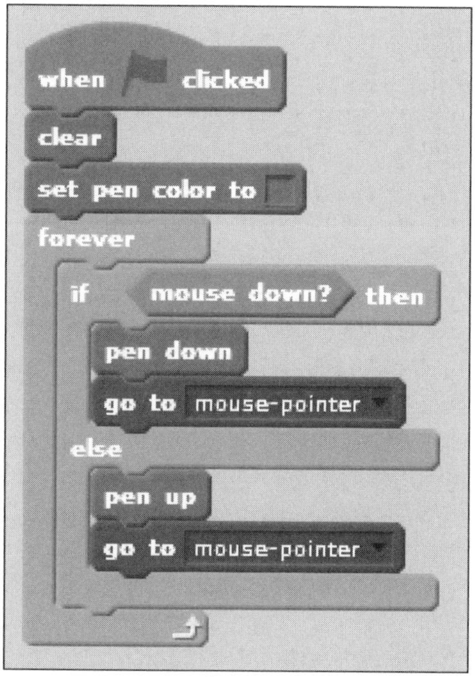

©2014 Cengage Learning®

Here, the stage is cleared, and the pen's color is set to red. Otherwise, the application operates no differently than before.

Scratch 2.0 also lets you specify the color to be used when drawing by specifying a number. For example, the following list identifies numbers that you can use to specify a range of commonly used colors:

- 0 = red
- 70 = green
- 130 = blue

By experimenting with other numbers, you identify a host of different colors. For example, using the second code block shown in Figure 12.5, you change the color used when drawing relative to its currently assigned value.

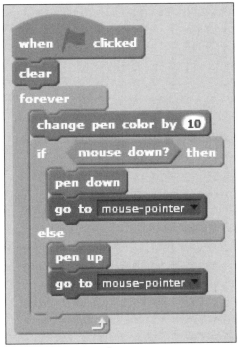

Here, the pen block has been added to the beginning of the script's loop. Each time the loop repeats, it changes the pen's current color assignment by a value of 10. The result is that a rainbow effect is applied as you draw, with the color changing across a full spectrum of color supported by Scratch 2.0 as you move the mouse and draw on the stage.

Using the third code block shown in Figure 12.5, you can identify the color to be used when drawing by specifying its associated numeric value. For example, you can modify the application's script to draw using red with this code block by passing it a value of 0, as demonstrated here.

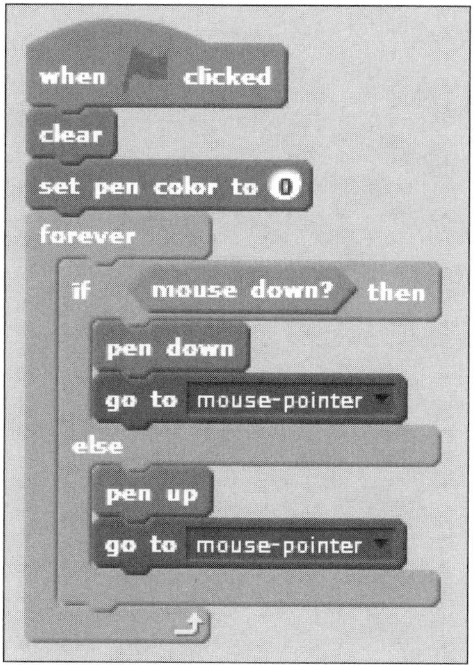

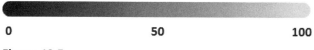

©2014 Cengage Learning®

CHANGING PEN SHADE

In addition to selecting color, Scratch 2.0 allows you to select the level of shading applied when drawing. The range of values supported by the pen shade is 1–100, as demonstrated in Figure 12.7.

0   50   100

Figure 12.7
Shading affects the application of light to a color.
©2014 Lifelong Kindergarten Group

By default, Scratch 2.0 applies a shading value of 50 when drawing colors. A shade value of 0 results in black. A shade value of 100 results in white. Scratch 2.0 lets you specify the level of shading to be applied when drawing using either of the pen blocks shown in Figure 12.8.

Figure 12.8
You can change the value used to apply shading by varying its current value or by setting an entirely new value.
©2014 Lifelong Kindergarten Group

As an example of how to work with the first code block shown in Figure 12.8, let's modify the drawing example again, as shown here.

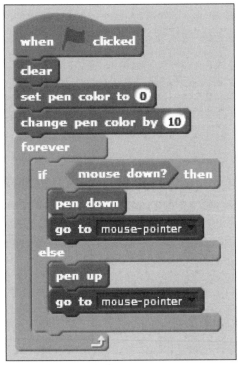

©2014 Cengage Learning®

Here, the shading level has been increased by a value of 10. Rather than change the shading level relative to its current value, you can use the second code block shown in Figure 12.8 to specify a specific shade level, as demonstrated in the following script.

```
when [flag] clicked
clear
set pen color to 0
set pen shade to 60
forever
    if < mouse down? > then
        pen down
        go to mouse-pointer
    else
        pen up
        go to mouse-pointer
```

WORKING WITH DIFFERENT SIZE PENS

In addition to setting color and shading values, Scratch 2.0 lets you change the size of the pen. You can accomplish this using either of the two pen blocks shown in Figure 12.9.

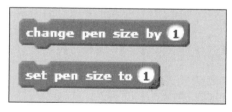

Figure 12.9

Scratch 2.0 supports a range of pen sizes from 0–255.

By default, Scratch 2.0 draws using a pen size of 1. You can change the pen size relative to its current size using the first code block, as demonstrated in the following script.

```
when [flag] clicked
clear
set pen color to (0)
set pen shade to (60)
change pen size by (1)
forever
    if < mouse down? > then
        pen down
        go to [mouse-pointer ▼]
    else
        pen up
        go to [mouse-pointer ▼]
```

Here, the size of the pen used in the drawing application in increased by 1, making it twice its default size. If you prefer, you can simply assign a specific pen size using the second code block, which can then, if desired, be changed at any time during program execution. To demonstrate, take a look at the following script, which sets the pen initial size to 0 and then uses a loop to increase the pen size across the entire range of pen sizes that Scratch 2.0 supports.

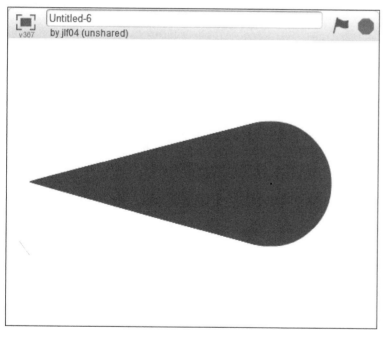

©2014 Cengage Learning®

Figure 12.10 shows the drawing produced when this script is run.

Figure 12.10

An example of a drawing made using Scratch 2.0's entire range of pen sizes.

©2014 Lifelong Kindergarten Group

CREATING THE DOODLE DRAWING APPLICATION

At this point, you have completed your review of all of Scratch 2.0's pen blocks and have learned how to put them all to work. Now it is time to work on the chapter's application project: the Doodle Drawing application. This paint-like application expands on the examples you have been working on throughout this chapter, making extensive use of the pen blocks and allowing you to draw by selecting from a range of predefined colors. The application allows you to draw using a range of different pen sizes. There is also a Clear feature that lets you start over any time you want so that you can begin working on a new drawing.

In total, the Doodle Drawing application is made up of 12 sprites and 3 scripts.

To create a drawing, click on one of buttons shown on the left side of the stage to pick a color, hold down the mouse's left button, and move the mouse pointer around the stage to draw. If you want, you can use different-sized lines when drawing by pressing keyboard keys 1 through 9. Pressing the 1 key results in a thin line, whereas pressing the 9 key results in a line that is approximately a quarter of an inch thick. If you make a mistake or want to start over, you can do so at any time by clicking on the Clear button located at the lower-left side of the stage.

Figure 12.11 shows the Doodle Drawing application in action. Here, the application has been used to draw a snowman, complete with a black top hat and red scarf.

Figure 12.11
You can use any of 10 colors and 9 different pen sizes when drawing.
©2014 Lifelong Kindergarten Group

This application project develops by following a series of steps, as outlined here:

1. Create a new Scratch 2.0 application project.

2. Add and remove sprites.

3. Create the scripts that control the application.

4. Name and test your Scratch 2.0 project.

Step 1: Creating a New Scratch 2.0 Project

To begin work on the Doodle Drawing application, you need to create a new Scratch 2.0 project. Do so by either opening the Scratch 2.0 Project Editor, thereby automatically creating a new Scratch 2.0 application project, or clicking on the File menu and then selecting New.

Step 2: Adding and Removing Sprites

The Doodle Drawing application is made up of 12 sprites, as shown in Figure 12.12.

Figure 12.12
An overview of the different parts of the Doodle Drawing application.
©2014 Lifelong Kindergarten Group

This application does not need the default cat sprite, so you should begin by removing that sprite from the application. You will find a copy of all the graphics for this project's sprites in the Doodle application, found in the Scratch Programming for Teens by Jerry Ford studio on the Scratch 2.0 website. Use your backpack to make copies of these sprites and add them to your own Scratch project.

Alternatively, you can use the Paint Editor and the Button3 sprite located in the sprite library as the basis on which to create each of the application's 11 buttons. If you choose this approach, once added, select the buttons sprites, one at a time, and then click on the Costumes tab. Using the Fill tool feature located on the Paint Editor's toolbar, change the entire surface of the sprite to red. Change the next 9 button sprites by assigning them the following colors:

- Yellow
- Green
- LightBlue
- NavyBlue
- Purple
- Pink
- Black
- White

Open the eleventh button sprite, and then use the Paint Editor to give it a label of Clear. Next, rename all eleven of these button sprites, as shown in Figure 12.12. Lastly, create one additional sprite for your application, consisting of a single dot. Make sure the dot's rotation center is established in the center of the dot. Assign this sprite a name of Drawing Point. Finally, arrange the buttons controls on the stage, as shown in Figure 12.12.

The default blank backdrop will be used in this application to provide it with white space on which to draw. Assuming that you have created all the sprites as instructed, you should be ready to begin the coding process.

Step 3: Creating Scripts to Control the Doodle Drawing Application

Most of the Doodle Drawing application's programming logic resides within a single script belonging to the Drawing Point sprite. This script is responsible for all drawing operations, including determining which color and what size pen the user wants to use. The remaining logic revolves around the clearing of the stage, which is handled by two small scripts: one belonging to the Clear sprite and the other to the stage.

Developing the Drawing Point Sprite's Programming Logic

The programming logic that controls the overall execution of all drawing within the Doodle Drawing application belongs to a script that must be added to the Drawing

Point sprite. Do not let the length of the code deceive you; the programming logic is simple.

To help make things easy to follow, the scripts are developed in three parts. For the first part, create and add the following script to the Drawing Point sprite.

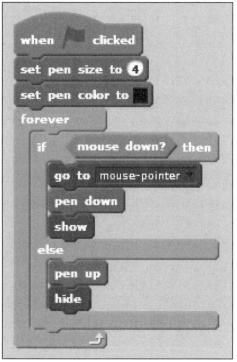

©2014 Cengage Learning®

As you can see, the script executes when the green Flag button is pressed. It starts by setting a default pen size of 4 and a default color of black. Next, a loop is set up that will be used to manage the execution of all the remaining code blocks. The first set of code blocks to be embedded within the loop is already present. It consists of a control block that checks to see if the left mouse button is being pressed, and if it is, the Drawing Point sprite is moved to the mouse pointer, the pen is placed in a down position, and the Drawing Point sprite is displayed. If the left mouse button is not being pressed, the pen is placed in an up position, and the Drawing Point sprite is hidden from view.

The programming logic outlined here is responsible for the overall management of the drawing process and is, in fact, all that you need to create a simple drawing application. If you want, you can switch to Presentation mode and run the application and use it to draw. Of course, as currently written, the application only allows the user to draw using a color of black and a pen size of 4. To enhance the application so that the user can select different colors by clicking on one of the color buttons located on the left side of the stage, add the following code block to the end of the script, placing it inside and at the bottom of the script's loop.

As you can see, these code blocks are organized using 10 separate conditional code blocks, each of which checks to see if the Drawing Point sprite has been moved over one of the 10 color buttons. (For the sprite to be moved over one of the buttons, the Drawing Point sprite must be visible, which occurs only when the left mouse button is pressed.) If it has, the pen's color is changed to reflect the button upon which the user has clicked.

Note

> The application only switches color when the Drawing Point sprite is moved over a color button and the left mouse button is clicked. The Drawing Point must be visible for this to work, and this is the case only when the left mouse button is being pressed. Therefore, to select a color, the user must click on the color. Simply moving the mouse over a color does not select it.

In addition to allowing the user to choose a color by clicking on one of the application's 10 colored button controls, the application allows the user to change pen size by clicking on keyboard keys 1–9. To enable support for different pen sizes, add the following code block to the script, inside and at the bottom of the script's loop.

```
if    key 1 ▼ pressed?   then
    set pen size to 1

if    key 2 ▼ pressed?   then
    set pen size to 2

if    key 3 ▼ pressed?   then
    set pen size to 3

if    key 4 ▼ pressed?   then
    set pen size to 4

if    key 5 ▼ pressed?   then
    set pen size to 5

if    key 6 ▼ pressed?   then
    set pen size to 5

if    key 7 ▼ pressed?   then
    set pen size to 6

if    key 8 ▼ pressed?   then
    set pen size to 8

if    key 9 ▼ pressed?   then
    set pen size to 9
```

As you can see, these code blocks are organized using nine separate conditional control blocks, each of which monitors the keyboard looking for a specific key to be pressed and changing pen size accordingly.

Clearing the Stage

In addition to facilitating drawing by using different colors and pen sizes, the Doodle Drawing application allows the user to clear the stage at any time to ready it for a new drawing. The programming logic that allows the user to clear the stage to start a new drawing is managed by the Clear sprite in conjunction with the stage. The process of clearing the stage is initiated whenever the user clicks on the Clear sprite. When this happens, the following script, which needs to be added to the Clear sprite, is executed.

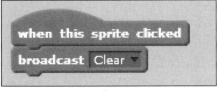

©2014 Cengage Learning®

As you can see, this script sends a broadcast message of Clear, indicating that the user wants to clear the stage. This broadcast message serves as a trigger that initiates the execution of the following script, which you must add to the stage.

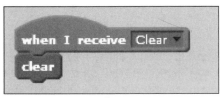

©2014 Cengage Learning®

As you can see, this script is straightforward. It executes a pen code block that clears off the stage whenever the Clear broadcast message is received.

Step 4: Naming and Testing Your Scratch 2.0 Project

All right! You now have all the information you need to create and execute the Doodle Drawing application. Assuming that you followed along carefully with all the instructions that were provided, you should be ready to test your new application. If you have not already done so, name the new Scratch 2.0 application project, and then switch over to Full Screen mode and click on the green Flag button.

As you work with the Doodle Drawing application, be sure to click on every one of its buttons to make sure the pen switches its color when drawing. Also, experiment with each of the application's line sizes to ensure they are working properly.

CHAPTER 13

IMPROVING CODE ORGANIZATION

The purpose of this chapter is to teach you different ways of improving how the scripts that make up your Scratch 2.0 projects are written and organized. This chapter covers three ways in which you can improve your scripts. You learn how to use more blocks to create custom code blocks that function as procedures within Scratch 2.0 projects. Procedures help you enhance project organization and maintainability and can significantly reduce the length and number of scripts in your projects. You learn how to improve your scripts through the addition of comments, allowing you to document critical programming logic and make it easier for others to understand why you developed a script the way you did. Lastly, you learn how to clone sprites, which not only reduces the size of your projects but cuts down on the number of scripts that you have to update and maintain.

The major topics covered in this chapter include learning how to

- Create specialized custom code blocks
- Use custom code blocks as the basis for developing procedures
- Enhance programs through the addition of comments
- Clone sprites as a means of simplifying project design and size

SIMPLIFYING SCRIPT ORGANIZATION THROUGH PROCEDURES

As you learn more about Scratch and how to program, it is inevitable that you will develop more challenging projects with larger and more complex scripts. The larger and more numerous the scripts that make up your projects become, the more important script organization and efficiency become. The development and organization of scripts using procedures is an essential programming technique that can reduce both the size and the number of scripts in your projects.

In Scratch 2.0, procedures are created using more blocks. Procedures can receive and process data that is passed to them as arguments from calling code blocks. *Procedures are shared scripts belonging to the same sprite that you can call upon to execute and perform a repetitive task.* Use of procedures alleviates the need to develop duplicate programming logic in the process in different scripts belonging to the same sprite.

Creating Custom Blocks

Procedures are created and executed using more blocks. There are two types of more blocks, although by default none are visible when you first look at the More Block category in the blocks palette. Only the Make a Block button is displayed.

Clicking on the Make a Block button displays the pop-up dialog windows shown in Figure 13.1. The first step in the creation of a new more block is to assign it a name, which you do by typing into the pink shaded portion of the code block.

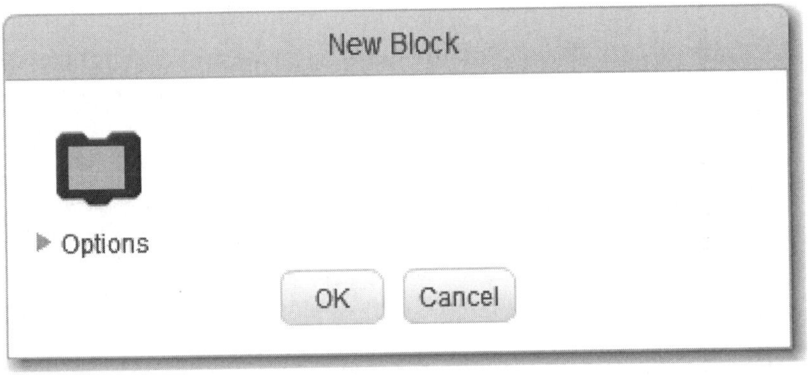

Figure 13.1
The first step in creating a custom block is to provide it with a name.
© 2014 Lifelong Kindergarten Group

More blocks are capable of processing argument data that is passed to them when they're called upon to execute. Argument data can be any of the following:

■ Number

■ String

■ Boolean

Argument data is mapped out against parameters that you have to define when creating the more block. As an example of how to create a custom block, let's develop a more block named AddAndSayThem that accepts two numbers as input. When creating a more block that needs to accept and process arguments, you must click on the Options link located just beneath the purple code block in the pop-up dialog window. This expands the window, as shown in Figure 13.2. You can skip this step if your custom more block does not need to process arguments.

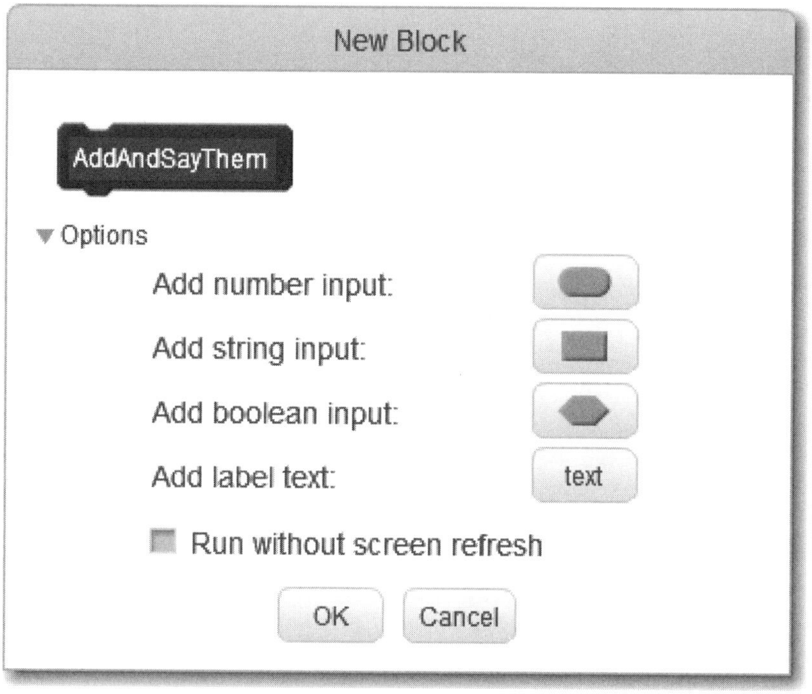

Figure 13.2

You can configure more blocks to process argument input.

© 2014 Lifelong Kindergarten Group

As shown in Figure 13.2, a new more block named AddAndSayThem is being created. You can configure the block to display descriptive text by clicking on the Text button. When clicked, a text entry field is added to the purple code block, allowing you to key in the text. Figure 13.3 shows what the block looks like when the text 1st #: has been added to it.

Note

If you make a mistake when defining text or arguments in your more block, you can click on the offending entry, which displays a small circular *x* icon over it. Clicking on this icon removes the text or argument from the block.

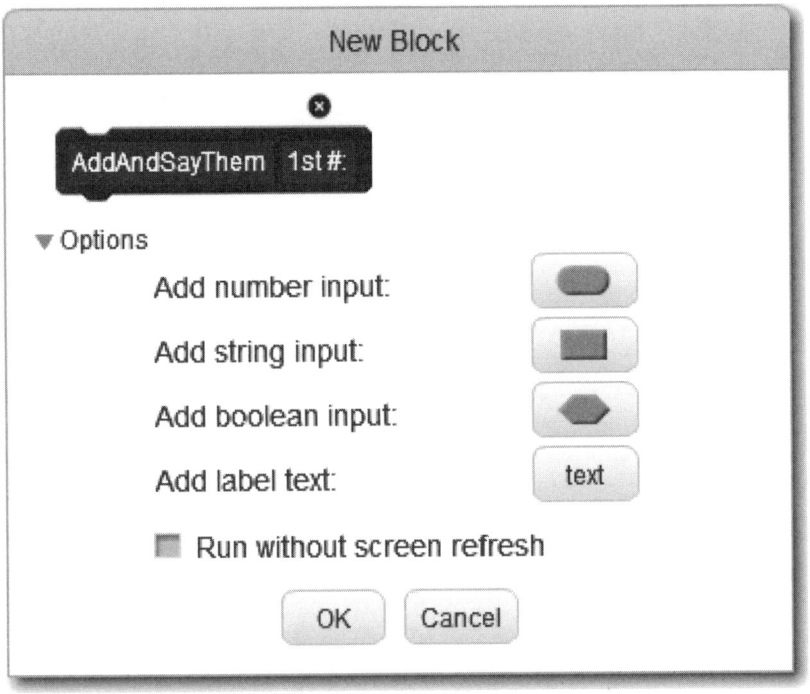

Figure 13.3
An example of a more block configured to display a text label.
© 2014 Lifelong Kindergarten Group

Next, click on the Add Number Input button to add a numeric field to the block. To finish off the block, add a second text label of 2nd #: followed by another numeric input field, as shown in Figure 13.4.

New Block

AddAndSayThem   1st #:   number1   2nd #:   number2

▼ Options

Add number input:

Add string input:

Add boolean input:

Add label text: text

☐ Run without screen refresh

OK   Cancel

Figure 13.4

An example of a more block configured to process two numeric arguments as input.

© 2014 Lifelong Kindergarten Group

The last option on the New block pop-up dialog window, not needed in this example, enables the block to run without screen refresh. In Scratch 2.0, an exceptionally small pause occurs between the execution of code blocks. When this last option is enabled, this block and blocks connected to it are executed without this delay. The lack of delay allows for the faster execution, which can be important when complex and resource intensive operations are performed.

Leave the Run Without Screen Refresh option cleared, and click on OK to tell Scratch 2.0 to build your new more block, as shown here.

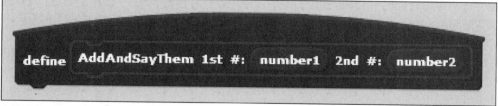

define   AddAndSayThem 1st #:   number1   2nd #:   number2

© 2014 Cengage Learning®

The code block shown here is referred to as a *define block*. As you can see, it is a hat block with its own unique shape. This block and any code blocks that you attached to it to create a script represent a procedure. You may create as many define blocks as you want to a sprite; each represents a unique procedure.

Note

If you need to, you can edit the define block, once created, by Shift-clicking on it and then clicking on Edit from the pop-up menu that appears.

In addition to the more block in the scripts area, you see that a second more block has been added to the More Blocks category in the blocks palette. This block looks like the example shown here.

© 2014 Cengage Learning®

This block has one function: to call upon its partner block for execution and to pass it argument data for processing. In order words, you use this block to call and execute its corresponding procedure.

Note

You can delete a define block, but only if you've removed every instance of its associated code block from the sprite's scripts first.

Using a Define Block to Create a Procedure

As has been stated, define blocks can process argument input. In the case of the custom block whose creation was just demonstrated, two numeric parameters were defined. Their parameters were named number1 and number2. You can click on either of these oval-shaped parameters and drag and drop an instance of them onto other code blocks, allowing the argument data to be used as necessary throughout the procedure. For example, the following script is a procedure created using the previously defined block. When it's called, the procedure takes two numeric values passed to it and adds them together. It then uses a looks block to have its sprite report the result of this calculation.

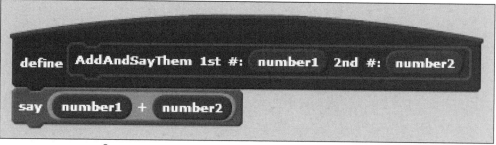

© 2014 Cengage Learning®

Any script belonging to its sprite can call the procedure. For example, the following script calls on the AddAndSayThem procedure and passes it two numeric values.

© 2014 Cengage Learning®

ADDING CLARITY THROUGH COMMENTS

As your scripts grow larger and more complex, they become more difficult to update and maintain. One way of mitigating this complexity is by documenting your program code using comments. Comments are configurable text boxes that you can attach to code blocks or freely place anywhere in the script area. As demonstrated in Figure 13.5, comments come in two forms: single lined and multilined.

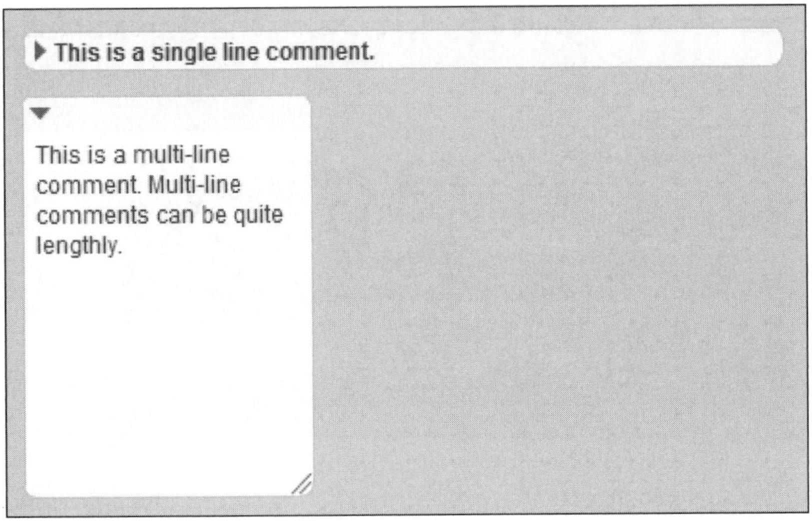

Figure 13.5

Example of floating single-lined and multilined comments.

© 2014 Lifelong Kindergarten Group

To add floating line comments to your scripts, all you have to do is Shift-click on a free area of the scripts area and select Add Comments from the pop-up menu that appears. You can also attach comments directly to code blocks. To do so, just Shift-click on a code block and select Add Comment from the pop-up menu that appears. This adds the comment to the scripts area with a yellow connector or line linking the comment to the code block, as demonstrated here. All you have to do to fill in a comment is to overtype the default text that is displayed.

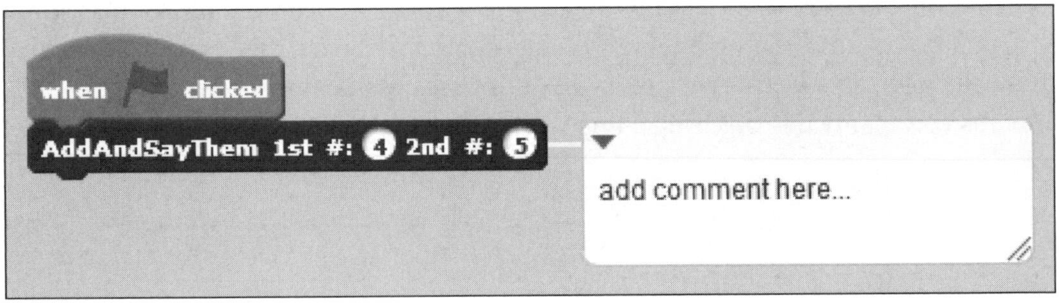

© 2014 Cengage Learning®

Comments linked to a code block remain attached even if you drag the script around the scripts area. By default, new comments are added to your scripts as multiline comments. However, if you click on the small downward-pointing triangle icon in the upper-left corner of the comment, you can change it to a single-line comment.

If there is insufficient room to display the text of a comment, the text is truncated. In similar fashion, you can change a single-line comment to a multiline comment by clicking on the right-facing triangle icon in its left corner.

You can also resize comments when displayed as multiline comments by clicking and holding down the right mouse button on the two gray lines located in the lower-right corner of the comment and dragging the mouse pointer to a new location and then releasing the mouse button. The script shown here provides a more detailed example of how comments can enhance and document the programming logic in a script.

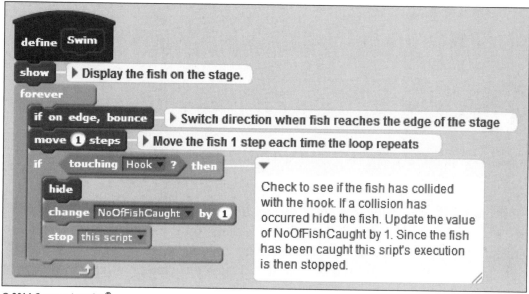

SIMPLIFYING THE PROJECT AND REDUCING THE PROJECT SIZE WITH CLONING

Another important programming technique supported by Scratch 2.0 is the ability to clone sprites. This is helpful in programs when multiple instances of the same sprite are needed. For example, suppose you were working on a program in which you wanted to be able to make it rain by dropping a graphics raindrop from the sky. Without cloning, you would be forced to add dozens if not hundreds of instances of raindrop sprites to your Scratch 2.0 project to produce a rain shower. If there were any scripts associated with the raindrop sprite, they would have to be added to each instance of the raindrop. If you decided to make a change to the raindrop's scripts, you would have to make that same change over and over again in every script belonging to every instance of the raindrop. Cloning overcomes this challenge by allowing you to add a single raindrop sprite to your project and then make an unlimited number of copies (clones) of it. To modify raindrop behavior, all you have to do is edit the script(s) belonging to the one raindrop sprite. The result is a significantly small and easy-to-manage project.

Cloning is implemented in the Scratch 2.0 project using the three control blocks shown in Figure 13.6.

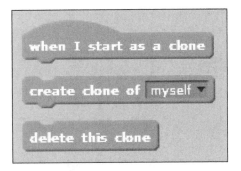

Figure 13.6

These code blocks are used to create, manage, and delete cloned sprites.

© 2014 Lifelong Kindergarten Group

To understand how to take advantage of cloning, let's take a look at an example in which 10 soccer balls are placed at random locations on the stage and then made to bounce around in random directions. Begin by creating a new Scratch 2.0 project. Remove the default sprite and then add a new sprite by clicking on the Choose Sprite from Library icon, clicking on the Things category in the Sprite Library and then double-clicking on the soccer ball sprite. Configure the sprite by selecting it, clicking on the small *i* icon located in the upper-left corner of the Soccer Ball thumbnail, and clearing the Show option.

To complete the cloning project, you need to add two scripts to the soccer ball sprite. The first of these two scripts is shown here.

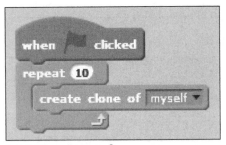

© 2014 Cengage Learning®

This script executes when the green Flag is clicked. It executes a loop 10 times, each time creating a new clone of the sprite to which it belongs (for example, soccer ball sprite). Next, add the following script to the soccer ball sprite.

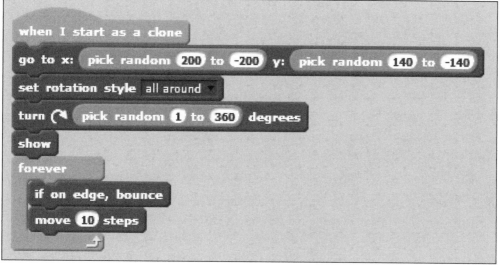

© 2014 Cengage Learning®

Here, the when I start as a clone block is used to control script execution. Specifically, it automatically executes every time a new clone is created, at which time it randomly places the new clone on the stage. The script then sets the rotational style to All Around and sets the clone in a random direction. Once the clone's rotation style and direction have been set, it is made visible. Lastly, a loop is set up that moves the clone 10 steps and bounces the clone (soccer ball) off the stage whenever it comes into contact with the edge of the stage.

Each time you run the project, 10 soccer balls are displayed in random locations on the stage and begin to bounce around in different directions, as demonstrated in Figure 13.7.

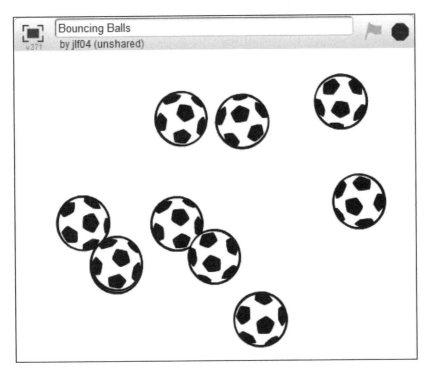

Figure 13.7

The 10 soccer balls shown on the stage are all clones of the soccer ball sprite.

© 2014 Lifelong Kindergarten Group

Now that you have completed this project, consider how much more complex this project would have been to create and maintain if you had to add 10 different instances of the soccer ball sprite to it.

CREATING THE GONE FISHING APPLICATION

At this point, you have seen how to enhance Scratch 2.0 projects through the use of procedures, the addition of comments, and the use of cloning. The result of implementing these programming techniques is smaller, easier-to-maintain-and-understand projects with fewer sprites and fewer and small scripts. Let's put all these new programming techniques to use in the development of a new Scratch 2.0 project called Gone Fishing, shown in Figure 13.8.

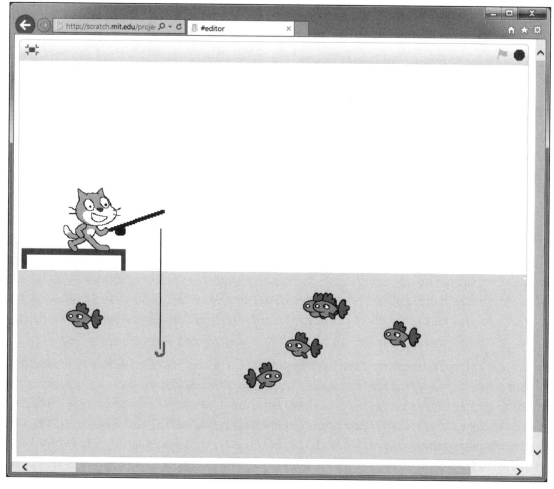

Figure 13.8

The Gone Fishing project when it's started.

© 2014 Lifelong Kindergarten Group

Game play begins when the player clicks on the green Flag icon. To operate the game, the player uses the Up and Down arrow keyboard keys to raise and lower the fish hook in the water. Each time the hook makes contact with the fish, the fish is caught and disappears from the water. Game play continues until all the fish have been caught.

You can develop this application project by following a series of steps, as outlined here:

1. Create a new Scratch 2.0 application project.

2. Add an appropriate backdrop.

3. Add your application's sprites.

4. Define an application variable.

5. Create scripts that control the application.

6. Test your Scratch 2.0 project.

Step 1: Creating a New Scratch 2.0 Project

To begin work on the Gone Fishing project, you need to create a new Scratch 2.0 project. Do so by either opening the Scratch 2.0 Project Editor, thereby automatically creating a new Scratch 2.0 application project, or clicking on the File menu and then selecting New.

Step 2: Adding an Appropriate Backdrop

The next step in the development of the Gone Fishing game is to add a suitable backdrop to the stage. The application has a backdrop that shows a fishing dock and fishing reel over a body of clear, blue water. You can use the Paint Editor to draw this backdrop yourself, or you can get a copy of it from the Gone Fishing application found in the Scratch Programming for Teens by Jerry Ford studio on the Scratch 2.0 website.

To acquire the backdrop, use your backpack to make a copy of this backdrop and add it to your Scratch project. Once you have a copy of the backdrop in your backpack, click on your project's stage thumbnail (located in the sprites list) and then click on the Backdrops tab located at the top of the scripts area and then drag and drop the FishingPond backdrop from your backpack onto the Backdrops list. Since the FishingPond backdrop is the application's only backdrop, you should either move it to the top of the list of backdrop files in your project or remove the default backdrop altogether.

Step 3: Adding Your Application's Sprites

In total, the Gone Fishing application is made up of a backdrop and 3 sprites, as shown in Figure 13.9.

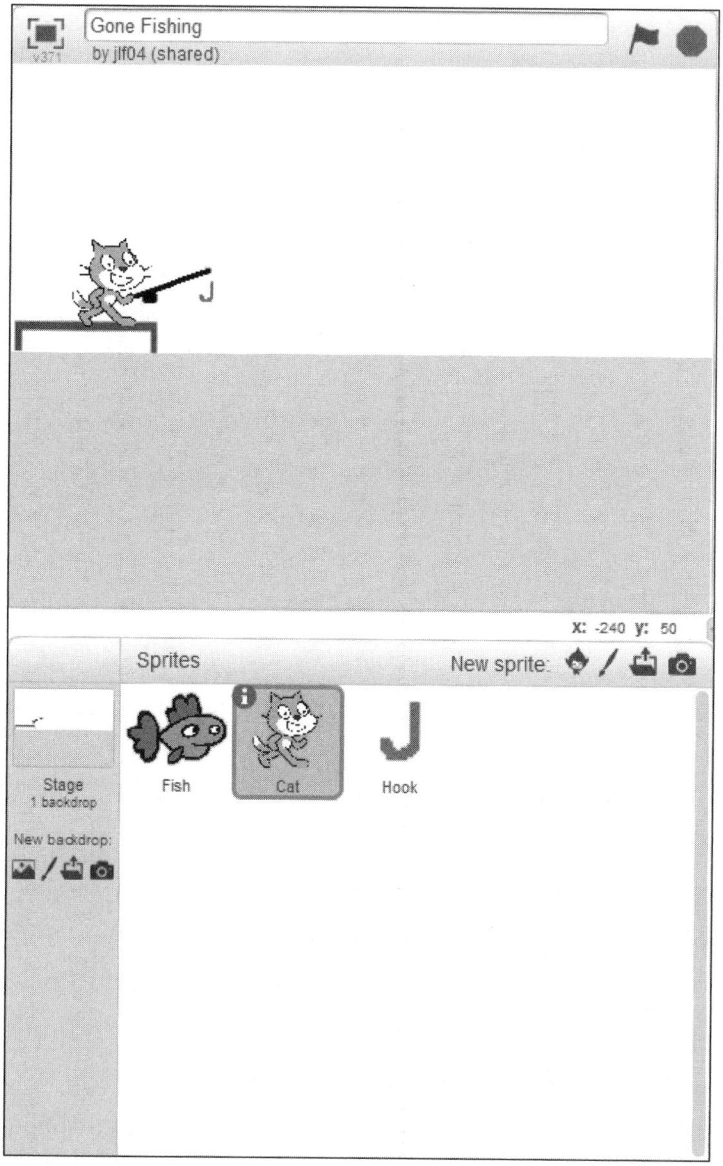

Figure 13.9

The Gone Fishing project consists of three sprites.

© 2014 Lifelong Kindergarten Group

This application uses the default sprite: Cat. Its default size is too large, but you can reduce it by clicking on the Shrink icon located in the Program Editor menu and then clicking on the image of the sprite on the stage five times. Next, click on the Choose Sprite from Library icon located in the sprite's area, select the Animals category, and then select the Fish1 sprite and click on OK. Rename this sprite Fish. This sprite should not be visible when the application is initially displayed. So clear the sprite's Show option after you rename it.

Lastly, use the Paint Editor to create a sprite that looks like a fish hook. To do so, all you have to do is click on the Paint Editor's Text button and then click the mouse pointer on the middle of the drawing area to open a text field. Type the capital letter J. This letter is the perfect size and shape for the application's fish hook. Next, click on the Set Costume Center button located in the upper-right corner of the Paint Editor and then position the mouse pointer over the letter and click, as demonstrated in Figure 13.10. Lastly, now that the fishing hook sprite has been added, rename it Hook.

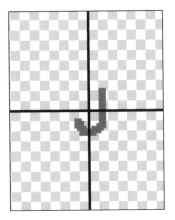

Figure 13.10
Setting the costume center for the Hook sprite.
© 2014 Lifelong Kindergarten Group

Step 4: Defining an Application Variable

The Gone Fishing application needs a variable to keep track of the number of fish that are caught. This variable is initially set to zero at the beginning of game play and then increments by one every time a fish is caught. The end of game play is triggered when the value of this variable is set to six, indicating that all fish have been caught.

To add this variable to the application, click on the Data category in the blocks palette and then click on the Make a Variable button and create a global variable named NoOfFishCaught. By default, Scratch 2.0 displays a monitor on the stage for this variable. The game does not require the monitor. Therefore, you should clear the monitor check boxes for the NoOfFishCaught variables.

Step 5: Creating Scripts Used to Control the Application

At this point, your backdrop and sprites have been added to your application. All that remains is to develop the scripts needed to bring the application to life. Begin by clicking on the stage's thumbnail, and then add the script shown below to it. Also, take the time to add the comment that is shown.

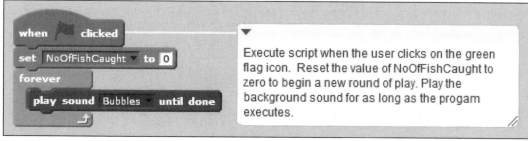

Execute script when the user clicks on the green flag icon. Reset the value of NoOfFishCaught to zero to begin a new round of play. Play the background sound for as long as the progam executes.

When executed, this script initializes game play, setting the value of NoOfFishCaught to zero. In addition, this script is responsible for playing the Bubbles sound repeatedly for as long as the application is executing. The project's next three scripts, shown here, belong to the Fish sprite.

▶ Controlling Program Logic Section

```
when [flag] clicked
repeat 6
    create clone of [myself ▾]   ── ▶ Create six clones of the Fish sprite

when I start as a clone   ── ▶ This script runs once each time the Fish sprite is cloned
if  pick random 1 to 2 = 1  then   ── ▶ Pick a random number between one and two
    point in direction 90▾   ── ▶ If a random number of 1 is picked point the clone to the right
    go to x: pick random -200 to 200  y: pick random -150 to -40   ── ▶ Randomly place the clone on the bottom portion of the stage
    Swim   ── ▶ Execute the Swim procedure
else
    point in direction -90▾   ── ▶ If a random number of 2 is picked point the clone to the left
    go to x: pick random -200 to 200  y: pick random -150 to -40   ── ▶ Randomly place the clone on the bottom portion of the stage
    Swim   ── ▶ Execute the Swim procedure
```

▶ Procedure Section

```
define Swim
show   ── ▶ Display the fish on the stage.
forever
    if on edge, bounce   ── ▶ Switch direction when fish reaches the edge of the stage
    move 1 steps   ── ▶ Move the fish 1 step each time the loop repeats
    if  touching Hook ?  then                ▾
        hide                          Check to see if the fish has collided
        change NoOfFishCaught ▾ by 1  with the hook. If a collision has
        stop this script ▾            occurred hide the fish. Update the value
                                      of NoOfFishCaught by 1. Since the fish
                                      has been caught this script's execution
                                      is then stopped.
```

© 2014 Cengage Learning®

These scripts have been carefully documented using comments. Add all these scripts to your project, being sure to add the comments as well. These scripts populate the stage with clones, place them in random locations, and determine when fish are caught. Since the comments included with the script carefully document each script's programming logic, a detailed review is not required. However, it should be noted that the scripts belonging to the Fish sprite further demonstrate each of the three major topics covered in this chapter: the use of procedures, comments, and cloning.

The next script to be added to the project, shown here, belongs to the Cat sprite.

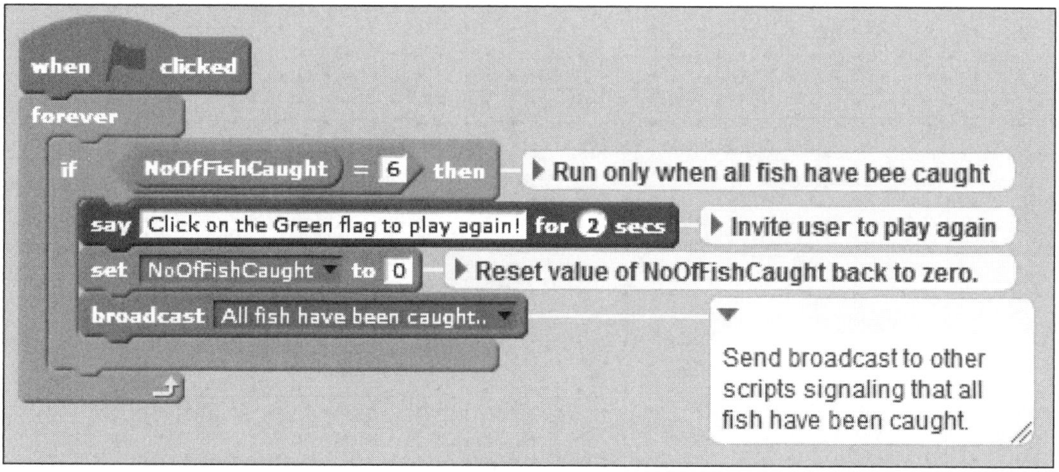

© 2014 Cengage Learning®

This script is responsible for determining when game play ends, which it signals to other scripts in the application by sending out a broadcast message. Again, since ample comments are included within the script explaining the script's programming logic, a detailed review of its construction is not required.

The rest of the project's scripts, shown next, belong to the Hook sprite. These scripts are organized into two groupings. The first grouping consists of four scripts located at the top of the scripts area. Comments are used to document the roles that each script performs.

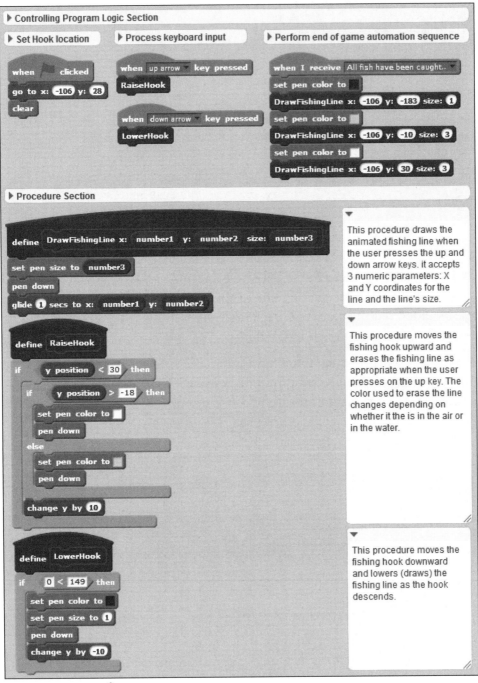

The remaining three scripts in the scripts area are three procedure scripts that execute only when called upon to do so by the scripts located at the top of the scripts area. The first of these procedures is named DrawFishingLine and is responsible for drawing the animated fishing line when the player presses the Up and Down keyboard arrow keys. This procedure processes three numeric arguments representing the X and Y position where the Hook sprite is to be moved and the size of the pen to be used when drawing the fishing line.

The second procedure is named RaiseHook. Its job is to raise the Hook sprite whenever the player presses the keyboard's Up arrow key. Conditional checks are made to determine when the Hook sprite is in the air versus in the water so that the fishing line is erased with the appropriate color as the hook to which it is connected is raised. The third and final procedure is named LowerHook. Its job is to lower the Hook sprite when the player presses on the keyboard's Down arrow key.

Step 6: Testing Your Scratch 2.0 Project

That's it! You now have everything you need to create and execute the Gone Fishing application. Assuming that you did not skip steps and that you followed along closely with all the instructions that were provided, you should be ready to give your new application a whirl. If you have not done so yet, assign a name of Gone Fishing to your new project, and then switch to Full Screen mode and test its execution. Game play continues until all the fish have been caught, at which time you are prompted to play again.

CHAPTER 14

GAME DEVELOPMENT USING COLLISION DETECTION

At this point in the book, you have learned how to work with the Scratch 2.0 development environment and the fundamentals of application development using Scratch 2.0. This chapter focuses on computer game development, specifically good, old-fashioned, arcade-style games. You learn a number of fundamental game development techniques, and then everything you have learned is tied together through the development of a computer game: Scratch Pong.

The major topics covered in this chapter include

- Learning about key features found in most computer games
- Learning how to manage game state
- Controlling sprite movement and determining when collisions occur
- Reviewing the fundamentals of capturing and processing player input

KEY FEATURES FOUND IN MOST COMPUTER GAMES

At this point, you should have a good understanding of how to display text, draw, and specify the placement of graphics on the stage as well as how to integrate sound effects into your Scratch 2.0 projects. These are all important elements of game development. However, before you can start creating your own arcade-styled games, you need to learn a few more things, including

- Managing game state
- Controlling game play with loops

- Managing screen refresh rates

- Controlling the movement of sprites around the stage

- Controlling sprite visibility

- Using sounds for special effects and background music

- Detecting collisions between sprites

- Processing player input captured via the keyboard and mouse

- Controlling mouse pointer location

Each of these topics is explored throughout this chapter, and many are demonstrated further through the development of this chapter's game project: Scratch Pong.

Managing Game State

Many computer games have different states. They may begin by displaying a welcome screen that provides instruction for game play or a series of menu options. A game may switch between states when the player clicks on a keyboard key or clicks on a sprite on the stage. Some games support a paused state, allowing players to temporarily halt game execution and resume play later. These represent just a few of the different types of states that a computer game may support.

You can use variables as a way of controlling game state. For example, you can add a variable like the one shown here to track the player's score and then to change the game state based on its assigned value.

© 2014 Cengage Learning®

Using this variable, you can, for example, terminate game execution, as demonstrated in this example.

© 2014 Cengage Learning®

Here, a broadcast message of Game Over is sent when the value assigned to PlayerScore becomes 10. The broadcast message waits until all receiving scripts have completed their execution, helping to ensure an orderly end of game play, and then halts the execution of any other active scripts, changing the game state.

Another way to change a game's state is to pause it when a key event occurs. You can do this using the following code block.

© 2014 Cengage Learning®

Here, the game status pauses for 1 second. You can use this time, for example, to provide the player with time to get ready for a new round of play.

Another way to change the game state is to use either of the two combinations of code block shown here.

© 2014 Cengage Learning®

The first combination of code blocks pauses script execution until the player presses the keyboard Space key. The second combination of code blocks pauses script execution until the player presses the mouse button. Placing either of these two combinations of code blocks in the main game loop, discussed a little later in this chapter, effectively suspends game play until the player decides to take action.

Controlling Game Play with Loops

Games are interactive computer applications. This means they must have a controlled means of collecting and processing player input. For example, in a game in which players battle against one another using robots, the game needs to be able to collect and process a constant flow of player input that directs the game where to move the player robots. In addition, the game must capture and process player instructions to shoot. Once received, the game must integrate both players' input and use it to keep the game continually updated and display any changes on the stage. The key to making everything work in a controlled and synchronized efficient manner is the game's main game loop.

Most of the time, game loops are set up to run forever. They terminate only when the player wins or loses or when the player has signaled a decision to quit playing. Although you can use any of the control block loops that Scratch 2.0 provides, the forever block is most often used in setting up game loops, as demonstrated in the following example.

This loop contains the code blocks responsible for controlling the overall execution of the game to which it belongs. It runs forever. Under its direction, sprites are moved around the stage, and multiple procedures are executed that perform tasks like tallying the player score, determining when the game is over, and managing collision detection (discussed later in this chapter).

Managing Screen Refresh Rates

By default, Scratch 2.0 executes your projects at a smooth and efficient pace, adequate to ensure smooth operation of sprite movement and animation. However, some games require a bit of tuning to allow them to proceed at a smooth pace. This is especially true of complex games with lots of sprites moving around the screen and lots of other activity going on.

In Scratch 2.0, there is a small pause that occurs by default between the execution of code blocks. Scratch 2.0 does its best to keep the game updated (refreshed) as game play occurs. It automatically manages your game's synchronization rate or frame rate. If you take advantage of Scratch 2.0's ability to use procedures, you can configure procedures to run without screen refresh. This causes any procedures to execute without delay between procedure code blocks, allowing them to run a little faster, which can be helpful in resource-intensive games.

To eliminate screen refresh in a procedure, you must enable the Run Without Screen Refresh option when defining a procedure, as demonstrated here.

Tip

Scripts that run a little sluggishly can be sped up a bit by executing them in Turbo mode. To enable turbo mode for your project, click on Edit, Turbo mode.

Moving Things Around the Stage

Arcade-style computer games depend on the movement and interaction of sprites on the stage. For example, in a game like *Pong*, three sprites are used to display paddles and a ball. When started, the ball starts moving and must be made to bounce around the stage, bouncing off the top and the bottom of the stage when it comes into contact with them. In addition, the ball must bounce off player paddles.

In Scratch 2.0, sprite movement is controlled using motion blocks, which you learned about in Chapter 5, "Moving Things Around." As a refresher, consider the following example, which was previously developed and explained in Chapter 13, "Improving Code Organization."

© 2014 Cengage Learning®

Here, motion blocks position a cloned instance of a soccer ball sprite on the stage, configure its rotation style, and set its direction, after which it is repeatedly moved 10 steps at a time, bouncing off the edges of the stage when reached. An adaptation of this programming logic is used later in this chapter in the development of the Scratch Pong game.

Making Sprites Visible and Invisible

Another key aspect of computer games is the ability to make sprites appear and disappear. For example, in robot-versus-robot games, robots should disappear from the stage when they are shot. In similar fashion, when a new round of play is initiated on a new battlefield, it might be useful to be able to make the robots invisible for a few moments and then after a short pause display them so game play can resume.

By default, sprites appear on the stage when you add them to your Scratch 2.0 projects. You can hide a sprite in the Program Editor by selecting a sprite's thumbnail in the sprite's list, clicking on the blue *i* icon located in its upper-left corner, and then clearing the Show option.

You can programmatically control the display of sprites using the Show and Hide look blocks, as demonstrated here.

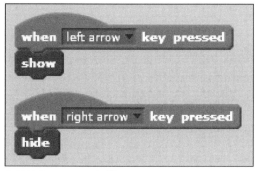

If you are working with clones in place of multiple instances of the same sprite in your scripts, you can add a new clone at any time. Clones, like sprites, are automatically displayed on the stage. The following example can populate the stage with 10 instances of a sprite.

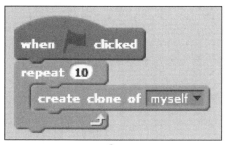

When a clone is no longer needed, all you have to do to remove it from the stage is delete it, as demonstrated here.

In this example, the clone is placed at a random location on the stage. The clone then says Hello! for two seconds and is deleted, making it disappear.

Making Some Noise

As you learned in Chapter 11, "Spicing Things Up with Sound," you use sound blocks to add sounds and play musical notes from various instruments in your projects. You can also use sound blocks to control the volume and change the tempo. In the case of computer games, the two code blocks that you will use the majority of the time are shown here.

© 2014 Cengage Learning®

The first code block is all you need to add background music or sounds to your games. Typically, background sounds are played throughout game play. If this is the case, the stage is usually the best place to store the sound, which can then be played over and over using a loop like the one shown here.

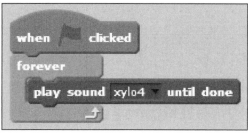

© 2014 Cengage Learning®

The second code block is often best used to add sound effects to your game, such as explosions, beeps, and other quickly played sounds that are played one time when a specific effect occurs, such as when a player scores a point or an object explodes. For example, the following procedure is part of the Scratch Pong game that you learn how to create later in this chapter.

© 2014 Cengage Learning®

The project's main game loop continuously calls this procedure. When called, it determines if the ball sprite has come into contact with either player's paddle. If it has, the pop sound is played.

DETECTING COLLISIONS

In addition to knowing how to do things like manage game state, set up a game loop, override screen refresh, control sprite movement and visibility, and establish realism using sounds, another essential programming technique required by many computer arcade games is collision detection. Collisions occur whenever two objects (sprites or clones) run into one another on the stage. For example, they occur in the classic *Asteroids* arcade game whenever an asteroid hits the space ship.

Being able to detect sprite collisions is a key aspect of many computer games. Scratch 2.0 supports a number of different ways of implementing collision detection. For starters, Scratch 2.0 automatically detects when a sprite reaches the edge of the stage. Scratch 2.0 prevents sprites from disappearing entirely off the stage, ensuring that at least a portion of sprites always remain visible. Using the motion block shown here, you can instruct Scratch 2.0 to bounce a sprite whenever it reaches the edge of the stage. The motion block is embedded within a loop, facilitating the constant check for a collision with the edge of the stage.

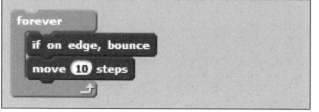

© 2014 Cengage Learning®

In this example, the sprite is bounced and then moved 10 steps in the other direction. The exact direction of the sprite after being bounced varies depending on its prior trajectory, as demonstrated in Figure 14.1, where four different collision paths are depicted. In example A in Figure 14.1, a sprite's path is depicted. In this example, the sprite approaches the top of the stage at an upward angle of approximately 20 degrees and bounces off the top of the stage at a downward angle of approximately 20 degrees. Example B shows that when the approach of the sprite is straight on 90 degrees perpendicular to the site of the stage, it bounces back in the reverse direction along the same line. Examples C and D provide examples of sprites moving at various other angles and depict their trajectory after they are bounced off the side of the stage.

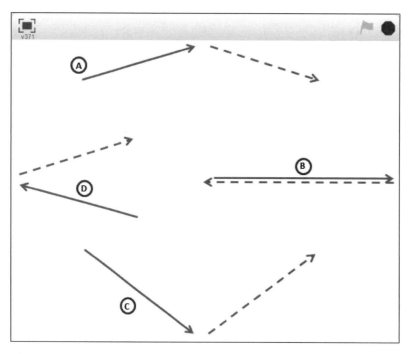

Figure 14.1
A demonstration of how sprite direction is affected after a bounce.
© 2014 Lifelong Kindergarten Group

Another way of determining collisions with the edge of the stage is to use the sensing block shown in the following example. Here, a sensing block is embedded within a control block, which itself is embedded within a loop. Each time the loop iterates, a check is made to see if the sprite in which the script is embedded has made contact with the edge of the stage. The difference between this collision detection example and the previous example is that here you are responsible for the redirecting of the sprite. In the case of this example, redirection is done using another motion block, which rotates the sprite to the right by 90 degrees, allowing it to continue moving in a new direction.

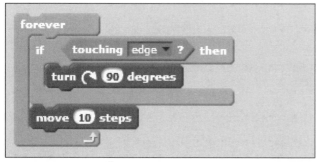

© 2014 Cengage Learning®

In addition to using the sensor block to detect collisions with the edge of the stage, you can use it to detect collisions with sprites, as demonstrated here.

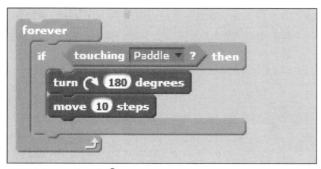

© 2014 Cengage Learning®

In this example, a check is performed to see if the sprite that the script belongs to has collided with another sprite named Paddle. If this is the case, the sprite is turned around 180 degrees and moved 10 steps in its new direction.

Figure 14.2 shows an example of two sprites that have collided with one another.

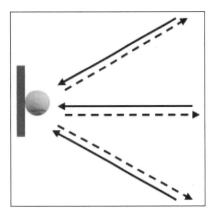

Figure 14.2
Several examples of a ball colliding with a paddle in the Scratch Pong game.
© 2014 Lifelong Kindergarten Group

In the case of the last script example, the sprite that the script is assigned to is the `Ball` sprite, and the `Ball` sprite would be redirected back along the same line of approach that brought it into contact with the `Paddle` sprite (because it was rotated 180 degrees). Figure 14.2 shows examples of how the script affects the `Ball` sprite's movement upon collision with the `Paddle` sprite.

The previous collision example executes any time one sprite comes into contact with any portion of a second, specified sprite. Using the example that follows, you can further refine and limit collisions such that they only occur when the sprite that contains the script comes into contact with a second specified sprite *and* the sprite comes into contact with a specific color on the second sprite, as specified by the color specified in the sensing code block color swatch.

```
forever
    if   touching color ■ ?  then
        turn ↻ 180 degrees
        move 10 steps
```

© 2014 Cengage Learning®

You can further refine and limit collisions using the sensing block shown here. In this example, for a collision to occur, a specified colored portion of the sprite where the scripts reside must come into direct contact with a specified colored portion of a second sprite. Otherwise, even though the two sprites may have come into contact with one another, the script does not process the collision.

To clarify this example, take a look at Figure 14.3, which provides two examples. A collision does not occur in the first example, but it does occur in the second example. In the first example, even though the frog sprite and the butterfly sprite have already come into contact with one another, a collision is not processed. In the second example, a collision occurs when the red colored portion of the frog sprite (its tongue) comes into contact with the yellow portion of the butterfly sprite.

Figure 14.3

An example that demonstrates how collisions based on color provide for greater precision.

There may be times when you want a sprite to act as if a collision has occurred when, in fact, it simply comes near to another sprite. As an example, consider the situation depicted in Figure 14.4. Here a fish in a fish tank is moving toward the right edge of its tank. Rather than wait until the fish runs into the side of the fish tank and then bounce it back in the opposite direction, it would be kinder to the fish to turn it around before the actual collision occurs.

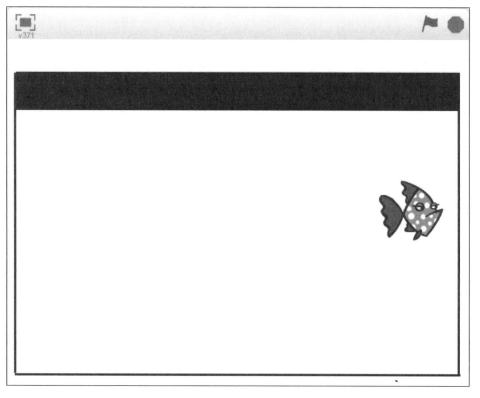

Figure 14.4

By substituting distance in place of actual contact, you can generate less precise collisions.

You can use the following script to turn the fish sprite around before it collides head on with the right and left sides of the fish tank, providing greater realism than simply bouncing it off the side of the tank's walls.

© 2014 Cengage Learning®

As you can see, two sensing blocks are used to determine when the sprite comes within a distance that is less than 50 pixels from the left or right wall of the tank. When either of these situations occurs, the sprite is rotated 180 degrees, and the fish proceeds to swim to the other side of the tank.

COLLECTING PLAYER INPUT

To play any type of game, players need a way of providing input. The type of input varies based on the nature of the game. For example, keyboard input is probably best used in a word game, whereas a strategy game may require that players use a mouse to select objects to be controlled or targeted. Computer arcade games, on the other hand, may work with either the keyboard or a mouse. Scratch 2.0 supports the collection of both keyboard and mouse input via a number of different code blocks.

Capturing Keyboard Input

Most computer keyboards have at least 104 keys, although many have even more. Regardless of the keyboard type, make, or model, Scratch 2.0 lets your applications monitor and respond whenever the following keys are pressed:

- Up, Down, Left, and Right arrow keys
- Space key
- A–Z keys
- 0–9 keys

When it comes to computer games, besides the Space key and the arrow keys, the four most commonly used keyboard keys are the Up, Down, Left, and Right arrow keys. These keys often control movement and direction games. However, in some games, like first-person shooters, the W, A, S, and D keys are used in place of the arrow keys so that the player's right hand is freed up to work with the mouse.

Scratch 2.0 provides two ways of capturing keyboard input. The first way is through the use of the event block, shown in the following example.

© 2014 Cengage Learning®

Here, a script has been added to a sprite that executes every time the Q key is pressed. When this occurs, a broadcast message is sent to all other scripts in the application to instruct them to terminate execution. Once the application has completely processed the broadcast message, the last code block in the script halts any remaining script that may be executing.

The other way of capturing keyboard input is through the use of the sensing block shown in the following example.

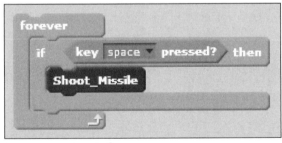

© 2014 Cengage Learning®

Here, a loop is set up that continually checks for and responds to the Space key being pressed. When this happens, a procedure named Shoot_Missile is executed. This script might be assigned to a tank sprite in a tank-versus-computer tank game so the player can fire missiles at his computer opponent.

Capturing Mouse Input

Just like keyboards, there are many different types of mouse devices. A typical mouse has two buttons. Newer mice may also have a wheel or more than two buttons. Touch pad and track ball devices represent variations of mice and perform the same way, producing identical output to a mouse. All these mice variations provide input that specifies X- and Y-coordinate information. In addition, these devices provide input indicating when their buttons are clicked. In computer games, mouse button input can be used to control the firing of a laser cannon, the display of an inventory of items collected during play, or any number of other purposes.

Tracking Mouse Movement and Location

A primary use of the mouse is to control the movement of the pointer around the stage. Scratch 2.0 makes it easy to track mouse movement. You can use the mouse x block to retrieve the location of the pointer on the X-axis and the mouse y block to retrieve the location of the pointer on the Y-axis. As an example of how to work with these two sensing blocks, let's look at an example.

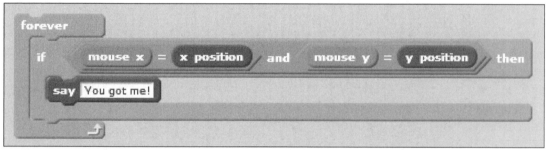

© 2014 Cengage Learning®

Here, the mouse x and mouse y sensing blocks are used to retrieve the X- and Y-coordinates of the mouse pointer and compare them to the X- and Y- coordinates of the sprite containing the script (retrieved using the x position and y position motion blocks. When you move the mouse pointer over the sprite's costume center, the text You got me! is displayed in a speech bubble. Using this example as a starting point, you can develop a script that displays clues on the stage in a treasure hunt game as the player moves the mouse pointer around the stage looking for clues and hidden objects.

Detecting Mouse Button Clicks

Besides keeping track of the mouse pointer's location, it is often important to be able to determine when the player clicks on the mouse's left button. This allows your game to use left mouse button clicks as a means of controlling when sprites jump, shoot, and so on. There are two ways of determining when the left mouse button has been clicked. For starters, you can use the events blocks shown in the following script to capture and respond whenever the player positions the mouse pointer of a sprite and then clicks on the left mouse button.

© 2014 Cengage Learning®

The second way of capturing mouse clicks is to use the sensing blocks shown in this next example.

© 2014 Cengage Learning®

Here, a loop has been set up within which a control block is embedded. Within the control block is the sensing block. Because the loop iterates forever, the loop enables the player to continuously execute the Shoot_Missile procedure by clicking with the left mouse button. You can use these code blocks as the basis for creating a script that controls when a sprite such as a jet plane or tank fires a missile at an enemy combatant.

CREATING SCRATCH PONG

This chapter has provided you with a review of fundamental game development programming techniques and explained and demonstrated how to implement them using Scratch 2.0. This has included learning how to manage game state, control game play with loops, detect collisions between sprites, process player input, and so on. The rest of this chapter ties many of these new programming techniques together through the creation of a new Scratch 2.0 project called Scratch Pong, shown in Figure 14.5.

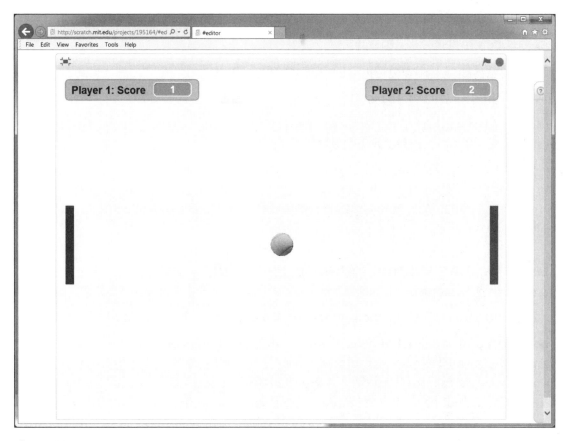

Figure 14.5
The Scratch Pong game.
© 2014 Lifelong Kindergarten Group

Scratch Pong is a two-player game. Players score points by deflecting the game ball past each other's paddles. Player 1 controls his paddle movement by pressing the A key to move it up and pressing Z to move it down. Player 2 controls his paddle movement by pressing the Up key to move it up and pressing the Down key to move it down. The game is started when one of the players clicks on the green Flag icon. Game play begins, as does each subsequent point by placing player paddles in the center of the stage on the far left and far right sides. The game ball is placed in the center of the stage. To initiate the playing of a point, one of the players must press the Space key. Game play ends as soon as one of the players scores 10 points.

You can create this application project by following a series of steps, as outlined here:

1. Create a new Scratch 2.0 project.
2. Set up the backdrop and add and remove sprites.

3. Add sound effects.

4. Define variables.

5. Create scripts that control the Scratch Pong game.

6. Test your Scratch 2.0 project.

Step 1: Creating a New Scratch 2.0 Project

To begin work on the Scratch Pong project, you need to create a new Scratch 2.0 project. Do so by either opening the Scratch 2.0 Project Editor, thereby automatically creating a new Scratch 2.0 application project, or clicking on the File menu and then selecting New.

Step 2: Setting Up the Backdrop and Adding and Removing Sprites

In total, the Scratch Pong game is made up of a backdrop, 3 sprites, and 12 scripts.

The first step in the development of the Scratch Pong game is to add a suitable backdrop to the stage. The application has a simple blank backdrop that is painted yellow. You can easily create this backdrop using the Paint Editor. To do so, all you have to do is select the default backdrop thumbnail and then click on the Backdrops tab to display the backdrop in the Paint Editor. To paint the backdrop yellow, click on the Fill with Color button, displaying the color gradient at the bottom of the Paint Editor. Click on one of the yellow color swatches, and then click on the stage to fill it with that color.

Now that you have painted the backdrop, it is time to add the application's three sprites. To add the first sprite, click on the Choose Sprite from Library icon located at the top of the sprite area to display the Sprite Library window. Next, click on the Things category, scroll down and select the tennis ball sprite, and click on OK. Resize the sprite by clicking on the Shrink button located on the Program Editor menu bar and then clicking on the sprite three times. Rename the sprite Ball. Using drag and drop, reposition the sprite in the center of the stage.

To add the project's second sprite, click on the Paint New Sprite icon at the top of the sprite area to add a new sprite to the application. To create the paddle, click on the Rectangle button, and then click on one of the dark blue color swatches displayed at the bottom of the Paint Editor. Draw a vertical rectangle in the center of the paint window that is .25 inches wide by 2.25 inches tall. Click on the Set Costume Center button located at the top-right side of the program menu bar, and then click the mouse pointer in the center position of the rectangle. Rename the sprite Paddle1, and then, using drag and drop, reposition the sprite in a center position on the left side of the stage, as shown in Figure 14.5.

You can use the Paddle1 sprite as the basis for creating the application's third sprite by clicking on the Duplicate button located on the Project Editor's menu bar and then clicking on Paddle1. This adds a new sprite to the project that is automatically assigned the name Paddle2.

Step 3: Adding Sound Effects

The Scratch Pong game uses the default pop sound that is automatically added to every backdrop and sprite to play a sound every time the ball collides with the top and bottom of the stage or with one of the player's paddles. In addition, the Ball sprite requires a new sound to be played whenever one of the players scores a point. To add this sound, select the Ball thumbnail and then click on the Sounds tab located at the top of the scripts area. Next, click on the Choose Sound from Library icon to open the Sound Library window, locate and click on the AlienCrack2 sound, and then click on OK.

Step 4: Defining Variables

The Scratch Pong game requires several variables to keep track of players' scores and to keep track of and control the speed at which the ball moves during game play. To add these variables to your project, click on the Scripts tab and then click on the Data category in the blocks palette.

To add the game's first variable, click on the Make a Variable button and create a global variable named Player 1: Score. By default, Scratch 2.0 displays a monitor on the stage for this variable. The game uses this monitor to display the player's score during game play. Using drag and drop, reposition the monitor to the upper-left corner of the stage, as shown in Figure 14.5.

Using the steps just outlined, add the game's remaining two variables, naming them Player 2: Score and Steps. Using drag and drop, reposition the monitor for the Player 2: Score variable in the upper-right corner of the stage, as shown in Figure 14.5. The game does not use the steps monitor, so you should clear its display, as shown in Figure 14.6.

Figure 14.6

Defining variables of the Scratch Pong project.

Step 5: Creating Scripts Used to Control the Scratch Pong Game

At this point, your backdrop, sprites, and sounds have all been added to your application. All that remains is to develop the scripts needed to bring the application to life. Begin by clicking on the Paddle1 sprite thumbnail, and then add the following scripts to it, making sure to take the time to include the comments that are shown here.

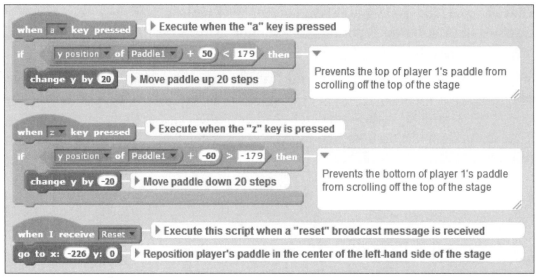

The first two of these scripts is responsible for controlling the movement of Player 1's paddle whenever the player presses the A or the Z key. Both scripts include programming logic that prevents the top and bottom of Player 1's paddle from being able to partially disappear at the top and bottom of the stage.

The last of these three scripts executes whenever a broadcast message of Reset is received (sent by a script belonging to the Ball sprite). The Reset broadcast message is a signal to this script to reposition the player's paddle back in the center position on the right side of the stage, readying the player's paddle to play a new round.

In similar fashion, you should add the following scripts to the Paddle2 sprite. They are mirror images of the same three scripts that were assigned to Player 1's paddle.

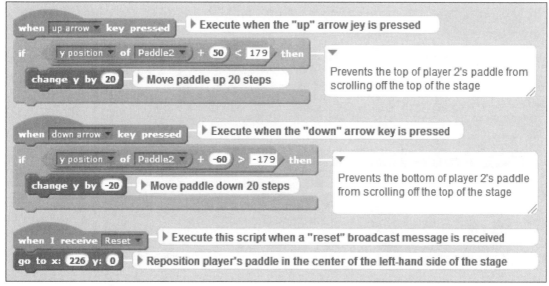

© 2014 Cengage Learning®

Now that you have programmed both of the players' paddles, all that remains is to provide the programming logic required to control the actions of the Ball sprite. In total, you will add six scripts to the Ball sprite, four of which are procedures. Each procedure is designed to perform a specific task.

The first of these scripts is shown here. This script executes when one of the players uses the mouse to click on the green Flag icon. When this occurs, all the application's variables are set to their default starting values. This includes setting both the Player 1: Score variable and the Player 2: Score variable to zero and the Steps variable to 5. The purpose of the first two variables is to maintain a running total of each player's score. The Steps variable is used by motion blocks within other scripts to specify how many steps the Ball sprite is moved each time the main game loop iterates. By gradually increasing the value assigned to Steps, you can increase the speed at which the Ball sprite moves around the stage during game play, making the game grow more challenging as points last longer.

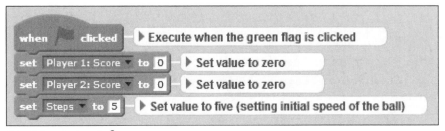

© 2014 Cengage Learning®

The second of the Ball sprite's scripts, which contains the game's main game loop, is shown here.

when space ▾ key pressed — ▶ Execute when the space key is pressed
forever — ▶ Establish the main game loop
  repeat 300 — ▶ Repeat loop 300 times
    move Steps steps — ▶ Move the ball
    BounceOffEdgeOfScreen — ▶ See if edge of stage has been reached.
    if   x position ▾ of Ball ▾ > 220 then — ▶ Player 1 scores if the ball passes this point
      PlayerHasScored Player: ❶ — ▶ Process player score
      DetermineIfGameOver — ▶ See if the game has ended
      stop this script ▾ — ▶ Halt all script execution
    if   x position ▾ of Ball ▾ < -220 then — ▶ Player 2 scores if the ball passes this point
      PlayerHasScored Player: ❷ — ▶ Process player score
      DetermineIfGameOver — ▶ See if the game has ended
      stop this script ▾ — ▶ Halt all script execution
    ProcessPaddleHits — ▶ Check for collisions with player paddles
  change Steps ▾ by ❶ — ▶ Increase ball speed

© 2014 Cengage Learning®

As you can see, this script is started whenever one of the players presses the Space key. Once it's started, it is responsible for coordinating the game's activities and for managing overall game play for each point that is played in the game. Once the Space key is pressed, a `forever` block controls the game loop. Within this loop is a second loop. This second loop is configured to repeat 300 times. Each time the loop iterates, it performs a series of tasks. Those include moving the `Ball` sprite around the stage, handling collisions between the `Ball` sprite and the edge of the stage, determining when points are scored, updating player scores, checking to see if the game is over, and ensuring that the ball is deflected anytime it collides with a player paddle. By the time the inner loop has iterated 300 times, a considerable amount of game play will have occurred, with the `Ball` sprite having been bounced back and forth repeatedly around the stage. After the inner loop completes its 300th iteration, the value of `Steps` is incremented by 1. The result is that the ball begins to move a little faster around the stage. At this point, the inner loop once again executes another 300 iterations. This cycle continues until one of the players scores a point or the game ends.

The main game loop is an especially important piece of code in any computer game. It has to manage and coordinate a lengthy and complicated collection of programming logic. Rather than creating one extremely large and complicated script that would be challenging to update and maintain over time, four procedures have been defined, each of which is designed to perform a specific set of tasks.

The first of the `Ball` sprite's procedures, shown here, is named `BounceOffEdgeOfScreen`.

```
define  BounceOffEdgeOfScreen       ▶ This procedure determines when the game is over

if     touching  edge ▼  ?    then   ▶ Check for collision with edge of stage

    if on edge, bounce    ──   ▶ Bounce the ball

    play sound  pop ▼            ▶ Play pop sound
```

The main game loop calls on this procedure to execute every time the `Ball` sprite is moved to determine if the sprite has collided with the edge of the stage. If this is the case, the sprite is bounced and the `pop` sound is played. If this is not the case, the procedure does not take an action. Either way, once the procedure has finished executing, control is returned to the main game loop.

The second of the `Ball` sprite's procedures, shown here, is named `PlayerHasScored`.

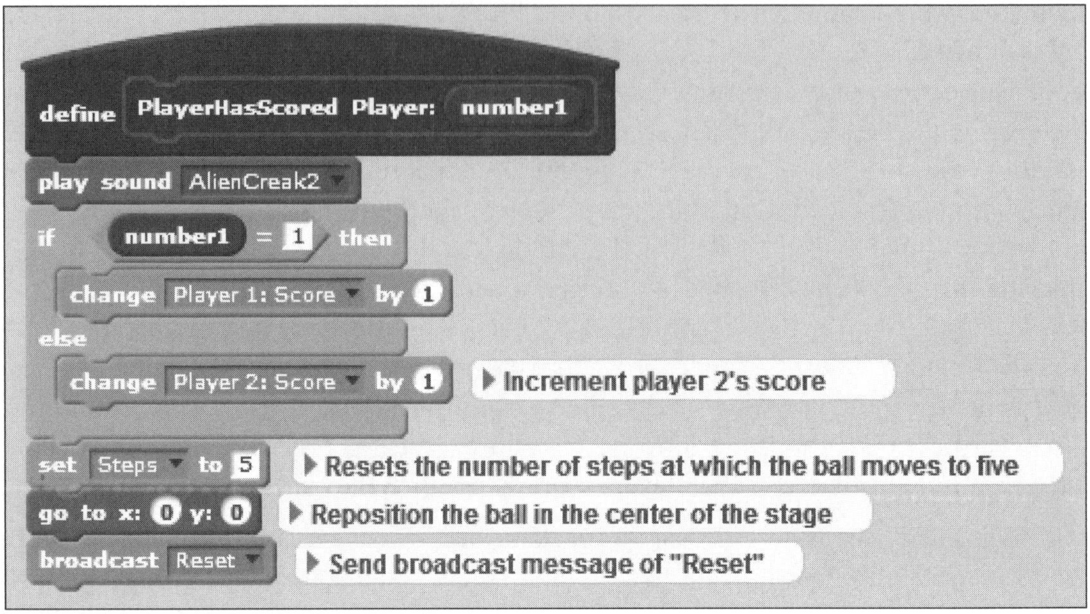

© 2014 Cengage Learning®

The main game loop calls on this procedure to execute whenever it determines that the Ball sprite has moved beyond one of the player's paddles. This procedure has been defined to accept a single numeric argument, representing the number (1 or 2) of the player who just scored the point. The first thing the procedure does when executed is play a sound indicating that a point has been scored. Next, it examines the numeric value that has been passed to it (stored in number1) and then updates the appropriate player's score. It then resets the value of Steps to its starting value of 5, repositions the Ball sprite to the center of the stage, and sends out a broadcast message of Reset.

The third of the Ball sprite's procedures, shown here, is named DetermineIfGameOver.

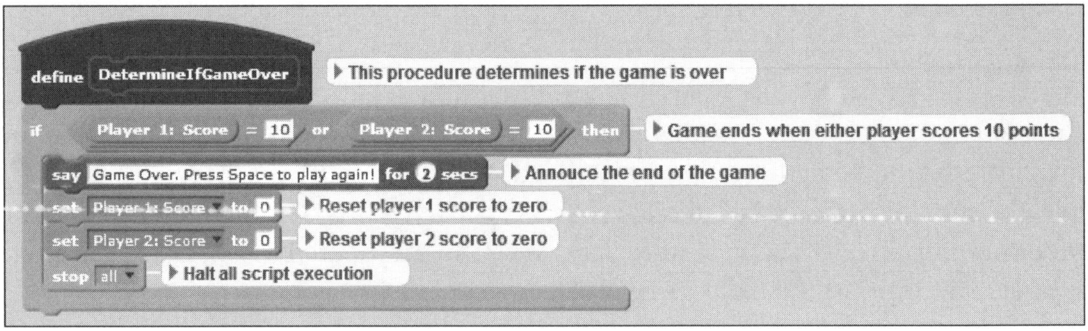

© 2014 Cengage Learning®

The main game loop calls on this procedure to execute immediately after it executes the PlayerHasScored procedure. The first thing this procedure does is examine the value of both Player 1: Score and Player 2: Score to see if either player has accumulated a total of 10 points. If this is not the case, the procedure does not take action and control is returned to the main game loop. If one of the players has scored 10 points, the game has been won and should be ended. The procedure displays a text message informing the player that the game is over. It then sets the value of both variables back to 0 and halts the executions of all scripts.

The fourth and final of the Ball sprite's procedures, shown here, is named ProcessPaddleHits.

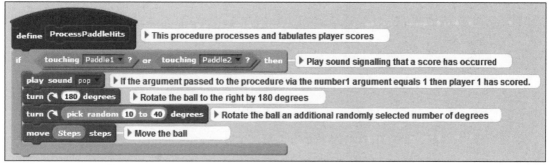

© 2014 Cengage Learning®

The main game loop calls on it as the last code block in its inner loop. Each time it executes, this procedure checks to see if the Ball sprite has collided with either the Paddle1 or the Paddle2 sprite. If this is not the case, the procedure does not take action, and control is returned to the main game loop. If this is the case, the pop sound is played, and the Ball sprite is turned 180 degrees and then randomly turned an additional 10–40 selected degrees. The call sprite is then moved 10 more steps, and control is returned to the main game loop.

Step 6: Testing Your Scratch 2.0 Project

At this point, you have everything you need to create and execute the Scratch Pong game. Assuming that you did not skip any of the steps that have been outlined, you should be ready to test your new game. If you have not done so yet, assign a name of Scratch Pong to your new project, switch to Full Screen mode, and test its execution. As you play the game, make sure that ball and paddle movement works as expected. In addition, keep an eye on the score to ensure that it is being correctly tallied. Once you are confident everything is working like it should be, go find a friend to play with you.

INDEX